Mass. Committee on Water Supply

Evidence and Arguments

on petition of the City of Boston for leave to take water from Shawsheen River

Mass. Committee on Water Supply

Evidence and Arguments
on petition of the City of Boston for leave to take water from Shawsheen River

ISBN/EAN: 9783337302313

Printed in Europe, USA, Canada, Australia, Japan

Cover: Foto ©Suzi / pixelio.de

More available books at **www.hansebooks.com**

EVIDENCE AND ARGUMENTS

ON

PETITION OF THE CITY OF BOSTON,

FOR

LEAVE TO TAKE WATER FROM SHAWSHEEN RIVER,

BEFORE

COMMITTEE ON WATER SUPPLY OF THE MASSACHUSETTS LEGISLATURE,

OF

1886

BOSTON:

PRESS OF ROCKWELL AND CHURCHILL, 39 ARCH STREET.

1886.

EVIDENCE AND ARGUMENTS

ON

PETITION OF THE CITY OF BOSTON,

FOR

LEAVE TO TAKE WATER FROM SHAWSHEEN RIVER.

FIRST HEARING.

MONDAY, March 29, 1886.

The committee met at 10.45 A.M., Senator SCOTT presiding. The chairman announced that the committee was ready to take up the petition of the City of Boston, and invited Mr. Bailey to proceed.

OPENING STATEMENT FOR THE PETITIONERS BY CITY SOLICITOR BAILEY.

Mr Chairman, the following petition has been presented to the Legislature : —

CITY OF BOSTON, EXECUTIVE DEPARTMENT, Dec. 5, 1885.

To the Honorable Senate and House of Representatives in General Cour
assembled : —

In conformity with an order passed by the City Council of Boston, Dec. 3, 1885, and approved this date, I have the honor to hereby petition the General Court for the right to take the waters of the Shawsheen river for an additional water-supply for said city.

HUGH O'BRIEN,
Mayor.

That petition was advertised to the satisfaction of the Secretary of State, and we are now here upon it. The petition was presented in obedience to the following order of the City Council : —

CITY OF BOSTON, BOARD OF ALDERMEN, Nov. 30, 1885.

Ordered, That His Honor the Mayor be authorized to petition the General Court for the right to take the waters of Shawsheen river for an additional water-supply for the city of Boston.

Passed in Board of Aldermen. Sent down for concurrence.

December 3 came up concurred.

December 5 approved by the Mayor.

A true copy.

Attest :

AUGUSTUS N. SAMPSON,
Clerk.

So you see, Mr. Chairman and gentlemen, this is a petition presented to the Legislature after careful consideration by the City Council of the city of Boston. It is to be presumed, at the outset, that the City Council of no city would ask for authority to take the waters of any stream or pond in the Commonwealth which would involve an expenditure of something like $2,000,000 or $3,000,000, unless there was a pressing necessity in the opinion of the City Council for it. And I should ask that the committee regard, as a part of the evidence in 'this case, the fact that the City Council, after mature consideration, has asked the Legislature to authorize it to go to the expenditure of this large sum of money in order to obtain an additional water supply for the city.

In 1861 the city of Charlestown obtained authority from the Legislature to furnish the people of Charlestown with the waters of the Abbajona river, having collected them into what was called the Mystic upper pond, using that as a storage-basin, and from thence distributing the water in pipes to the city of Charlestown ; and, subsequently, under contracts authorized by this Legislature, distributing it also to the people of Somerville, Chelsea, and Everett. Between the years 1861 and 1863 the authority was obtained, and the water-works were established.

At that time the population of the district was in the neighborhood of 50,000, in round numbers. In 1885 we find the population of the district has increased so that it numbers now 98,700; or, putting it in round numbers for convenience of reference, 100,000. Within the last twenty-five years, therefore, the population has doubled. The average daily supply from the Mystic, upon which this population relies, is about 7,000,000 gallons. Now, it has been found by actual experience in the city of Boston, and in other large cities, especially in cities bordering upon the seaboard, that between sixty-five and seventy gallons per day per individual is the lowest amount to which the consumption can be reduced. So you see, with 100,000 inhabitants for this district, at seventy gallons a day for each inhabitant, the supply is now just about equal to the demand; and such has been our experience for the last two or three years; and in some years, notably in 1880 and 1883, the supply was far short of the demand, so that we were in danger for two or three months in each of those years of a water-famine. The waters of the lake were drawn down, by means of pumps put in for temporary service, below what was a safe point in view of the large section of territory that was dependent upon it.

Therefore, if there was no other reason why the city should be granted the waters of the Shawsheen river, it should have them to eke out the supply from the Mystic; because it is patent to everybody — it needs no very astute arithmetician to figure it — that if the population has increased and doubled in the years from 1860 to 1885, and is now drawing upon this supply to the full extent that the supply is capable of furnishing, in the course of three or four years there certainly will not be water enough.

But there is a stronger reason. The time has been fast approaching, and has now arrived, when the city of Boston must look squarely in the face the fact that the Mystic water-shed has become unfit to draw a water supply from for any community. I shall show you what the character of that territory is. There are some eighty large manufacturing establishments on it, and the business carried on is tanning and currying. Moreover, all the towns are without any system of sewerage, and, therefore, whatever water is used in those towns must go into the ground and ultimately must find its way into those reservoirs where the water is collected for distribution. The water-shed of the Mystic valley is about twenty-six square miles in extent, and on that territory are now settled 22,000 people ; about 900 to the square mile. The towns of Winchester, Woburn, and Stoneham, each of which, as this committee knows, is rapidly growing, are situated on this territory ; and during the past twenty years the population and the number and size of the manufactories have nearly doubled.

So we say, and we hope to show you by experts we shal put upon the stand, that while the water of the Mystic supply at present is a good, fair, drinking-water, yet it has become, in the opinion of sanitarians, unfit to be relied upon, for the reason that, while it may be pure at the present time, the dangers of pollution, the prospects of pollution, and the immediate liability of pollution from such an extensively populated area are too great to warrant the city in expecting people to be content with such a supply. If this Legislature should to-day grant authority to take the water of the Shawsheen river, it will be three or four years before we can avail ourselves of it.

Therefore, taking into consideration the growth of the population of the district that is to be supplied, and that we are at the present time up to the limit of that supply, also that the source of supply is becoming so dangerous to use that, in the opinion of those versed in the subject, it ought to be given up, — taking all these things into consideration, and then the further fact that if you grant the authority this year it will be three or four years before we can avail ourselves of the water, — I think if we shall prove these things to you you will say the city of Boston should be given the authority to take this source of supply so that it can avail itself of the water as soon as possible. Such, gentlemen, is what we propose to show to you. I shall put upon the stand a few witnesses to substantiate the statements I have made, and with that shall rest our case. I will now call Col. Horace T. Rockwell, the chairman of the Water Board of the city of Boston.

Testimony of Horace T. Rockwell.

Q. (By Mr. Bailey.) You are chairman of the Boston Water Board?

A. I am.

Q. And you have been a member of the Boston Water Board for how long?

A. About six months or a little over.

Q. You have been intimately connected with city affairs for quite a number of years?

A. Yes, sir.

Q. For how many?

A. Well, in one way or another, for twenty-five or thirty years.

Q. Now will you state to the committee the position of the Boston Water Board, and, as you understand it, the position of the city of Boston, in regard to this request for the waters of the Shawsheen?

A. Our position, Mr. Chairman, is substantially as stated by Mr. Bailey, and I do not know that, without going into matters of detail, which should be given by engineers and other experts, I can add very much to what he has said. The present Mystic supply, in round numbers, what we call the safe supply, is 7,000,000 gallons per day, and the average consumption is very nearly that amount. During the year 1885 the average consumption was 6,300,000 gallons. To be sure, we had more water during the year 1885, but, with the later experience in regard to water-supplies, we consider that the concurrence of two dry years would reduce our supply to about that amount, so that we are now practically working upon the extreme limit of our supply. It therefore becomes necessary for us to provide for the increase of population which is certain to come, more water. And the possibilities of the development of the Mystic supply, even if it were desirable water, are such as to make it undesirable to spend money in that direction. And being also confronted with the fact, as stated by Mr. Bailey, that the water-shed is deteriorating all the time, and must continue to deteriorate, as we believe, in spite of all precautions, it seems to be necessary for us to abandon this supply for a better, if it can be obtained.

I would say in regard to the report of the present Water Board made in the autumn of 1885, which gave a qualified opinion in a somewhat different direction, that the Board as at present organized had then been in office but a month or two, and had not had opportunity to consider the matter fully. We have, however, become satisfied since, upon close investigation, of what previous Water Boards have been satisfied of, viz., that the time must come when the Mystic water-supply must be abandoned, for the protection of the health of the people who use it.

Surveys were made of this territory where we now propose to go in 1873 and 1874, with reference to obtaining a supply for the city of Boston, just previous to the time the Sudbury was taken. At that time the Shawsheen water was highly commended as coming from a district very little contaminated, with a very small population, and very few manufacturing establishments upon it, and as likely always to be exceptionally pure and good water. We have made new investigations in that line, and we find that the rate of increase of the population in that territory is no greater than before, and that there is now on the territory from which we ask to take the water only a population of about 4,200 people, or about one-tenth the number to a square mile that there is on the Mystic water-shed, and that the territory lies in such a position, with respect to railroads and other things which affect population, that it probably always will remain a comparatively secluded country.

We have also caused tests to be made of the water, and we find that the conclusions reached by the medical commission in 1874 were correct, and that the water is exceptionally good.

It therefore seems to us that as this water-shed lies within a few miles of the city of Boston, is absolutely the nearest supply that can possibly be obtained, it is the best we can get; and we desire to remove the dangers which the Mystic threatens us with, by substituting for the Mystic supply at as early a day as possible the Shawsheen water. As I have said, I do not care to make statements as to the details of cost, and so on, which matters can be testified to by the engineers and experts we shall put on.

Q. There have been several examinations made of the different sources from which a supply can be obtained, since 1872, have there not?

A. Yes, sir.

Q. Is there any other place to which the city of Boston can go, which you are aware of from the records, except the Shawsheen?

A. Not on that side of the Mystic river.

Cross-Examination.

Q. (By Mr. MORSE.) I understand, Mr. Rockwell, that you prefer that questions in regard to the cost of this improvement and the reasons for it should be asked of the engineers and not of yourself?

A. While I can state generally what the cost will be as we derive it from them, I should not be prepared to be cross-examined with regard to details.

Q. On the general proposition of taking a supply from the Shawsheen, you are rather accepting the advice of the engineers than stating the result of any independent inquiry of your own, I suppose?

A. No, sir. We have made an independent inquiry by personal examination of the territory, by observing the quality of the water, and by getting the statistics of the population; and we have also made a careful study of the previous investigations. I have here a volume published in 1874 which relates entirely to the subject of an additional water-supply, and contains the results of the investigations made at that time by the engineers and a medical commission. Our opinion is largely based upon the records, as to which we have obtained by our personal investigations no facts contravening.

Q. Have you stated the present supply of the Mystic system?

A. Yes.

Q. What is it?

A. Seven million gallons a day.

Q. Is that the entire amount that you can get from it?

A. We are getting more than that, but that is the amount which we must base our calculations upon as the amount to be obtained in time of drought. That is the minimum supply.

Q. Have you built all the basins that can be built there?

A. No, sir.

Q. Have you built all the basins that were contemplated by Mr. Wightman?

A. Several basins have been projected, but most of them, those that would furnish any considerable amount of water, have been condemned as impracticable. For instance, the building of a basin on the lower Mystic pond is considered an almost impracticable thing; and the basins that might be built on the upper waters of the Abbajona would not afford a very large quantity of water, would not give us, perhaps, more than 2,000,000 or 3,000,000 gallons in addition to what we have now, and the cost would be very large in proportion to the amount of water we would get.

Q. Was not the statement made by Mr. Wightman, or by some of the city engineers in previous hearings, that it was practicable to get 20,000,000 a day from the Mystic?

A. Yes, sir, I think so.

Q. Do you consider that that opinion is still a good one?

A. I do not, now, because, in the first place, the previous calculations as to that supply have been based upon a saving of twelve inches of rainfall in a year, and the experience of the last five years has been that we do not collect so much water as that; that ten inches is all that can be safely relied upon in times of drought. Therefore any calculations made in previous years as to the quantity of water would have to be reduced, supposing the capacity of the basins were the same, by that difference in the calculations of the quantity of water that can be saved.

Q. Then you think the opinions expressed by experts here in previous hearings as to the amount of the supply should be modified in view of the experience of the last five years?

A. Yes, sir.

Q. How much water, in your judgment, leaving out the question of quality, could you get from the Mystic if you construct as many basins there as are practicable?

A. Including the lower Mystic pond, which was included, I believe, when the calculations were made?

Q. Exclude that, if you please, in the first place.

A. I do not carry the figures in my mind exactly so I could divide them, but I should say, subject to correction, that, excluding the lower Mystic pond, 12,000,000 would be as much as we could get under any circumstances.

Q. Including that, how much could you get?

A. Sixteen millions.

Q. How long would that supply be sufficient?

A. About fifteen years.

Q. In regard to the quality of the water, the plan proposed has been to build a sewer there, has it not?

A. There is a sewer project before the Legislature this winter.

Q. If that project should be adopted, would not that meet the difficulties with regard to the quality of the water?

A. I do not think it would, sir.

Q. Is not that one of the main points urged in support of the project, that it is to keep that water pure?

A. I do not think it is. I think the report of the drainage commission is based entirely on the question of drainage, and not on the question of water-supply.

Q. You do not think any system of drainage there would prevent the pollution of the water?

A. No, sir, it would not prevent it; it would undoubtedly ameliorate it.

Q. I wish you would state to the committee, for probably some of the members are not familiar with it, what has been done with regard to protecting the purity of the Mystic water-supply.

A. The city of Boston has built a sewer running up to Woburn, which takes the drainage of all the tanneries which can enter into it by gravitation, and of some which can enter into it by pumping, and it is discharging about 500,000 gallons of tannery drainage every day.

The CHAIRMAN. — Does not the sewer take any sewage from Winchester?

A. It takes tannery drainage from Winchester as it passes through there.

Mr. MORSE. — What has been the effect upon the water of building this sewer?

A. Well, it has kept out of the water, of course, for the time being, this tan-vat drainage, which would have affected the color and the taste of the water very much if it had gone into it.

Q. Is there any serious difficulty with the quality of the Mystic water now?

A. It is very much inferior to the water which we have on this side.

Q. Is it unhealthy?

A. Well, I do not know that it is to-day ; but it does not improve at all. We are doing what we can to keep pollution out of it, by coaxing, and threatening injunctions, etc.

Q. That you have to do to protect any water system ; you have had to do that on the other side, with the Sudbury, certainly, haven't you?

A. Yes, sir.

Q. Wherever you go for a water-supply, if it comes from a river, you would expect to be engaged all the time in either coaxing or threatening, in order to keep your water pure?

A. Yes, sir.

Q. If I understand you, then, so far as the Mystic supply is concerned, you have the means of getting there a supply which would be sufficient for the next fifteen years, in quantity?

A. In quantity, yes, sir.

Q. And so far as quality is concerned, you have undertaken to guard it by the sewer which has been already built ; and you would expect, I suppose, to take additional precautions in the event of building more basins, would you not? You have taken sufficient precaution, so far, so that the water, you say, is not unhealthy, and you have protected the supply to a considerable extent?

A. Well, of course it has been protected by building the sewer, to the extent to which the sewer relieves the water of the drainage of these factories ; but there still remains a very large number of factories which cannot be drained into it, and a very large population, so that house drainage gets into it ; and the lay of the land is such that it seems to us impracticable to adopt any scheme which will keep the water pure.

Q. You recognize the fact, Mr. Rockwell, do you not, that if you go anywhere within fifty miles of Boston to take a river water-supply you are going to get a certain amount of pollution from manufacturing establishments, and from houses, and other places along the borders of the river?

A. I should say that might be true of almost any river except the Shawsheen.

Q. My attention is called to the following statement made by Mr. Greenough, when he was chairman, I believe, of the water committee in 1880: "I believe I am justified in saying that nothing goes into the Mystic that will compare with the filth now going into the Cochituate. The Mystic is at present the cleaner system. There is nothing in the Mystic supply as bad as there is in the Sudbury river."

Mr. BAILEY. — That is three years ago, brother Morse; that has been remedied since.

Q. Which is the better now?

A. By Mr. ROCKWELL. — The Cochituate water, by analysis, is very much better water than the other water.

Q. Have you not had more difficulty in protecting the purity of that supply than of the other?

A. Yes, sir, because it covers four or five times as much territory. And, in fact, I would say that the efforts to remove the pollutions on the Mystic have not been so vigorous as they have been on this side, because, as it appears to me, the former Water Boards have thought it was a hopeless task; it looks that way to me.

Q. What is your estimate of the supply that can be obtained fiom the Shawsheen?

A. The estimate of the supply is about 20,000,000 gallons.

Q. How many basins does that call for?

A. Three.

Q. Does that allow any water to run over the dam for the benefit of the manufacturers, or make any provision for the manufacturers.

A. That is simply the result of the storage capacity; we did not make any calculation as to waste.

Q. Do I understand you to mean that, taking all you can get from the Shawsheen,.you would get 20,000,000 gallons a day?

A. Well, that, of course, is the bottom line, the same as it is when we speak of the present supply; it is the starvation line.

Q. It is the capacity of the river which you feel you could rely upon in the dryest times, is it?

A. It is the storage capacity.

Q. How long would that supply be sufficient for the district you are now supplying with the Mystic water?

A. Well, I should say for from twenty to twenty-five years.

Q. Then the plan proposed to the committee is, to take a supply which at the end of twenty or twenty-five years confessedly would be insufficient, is it?

A. That may be true. On the other hand, we are supplying other municipalities besides Boston, — Somerville, Chelsea and Everett; and whenever the supply is exhausted, or seems likely to be exhausted, we have a perfect right to say to them, " We cannot supply you with any more water; you will have to get it somewhere else."

Q. Why do you not cut them off now, then, and use your Mystic supply for Boston?

A. Because it is a matter of equity all around; the works are built in their neighborhood, and there is no reason why they should not have the benefit of them.

Q. What is the limit of the contracts with these other places?

A. There is no limit; new contracts are about to be made with them this year.

Q. Will you give us, if you please, the proportionate number of water-takers in the different parts of the district that is supplied by the Mystic system?

A. In Charlestown, 6,336; in Somerville, 5,718; in Chelsea, 5,227; in Everett, 1,216; a little over 18,000 altogether.

Q. Everett, Somerville, and Chelsea are supplied by contract?

A. Yes, sir.

Q. And you say the contract provides in effect that whenever the supply is insufficient the city of Boston can cut them off?

A. That is so as to Somerville and Everett. I think it is so with regard to Chelsea.

Q. You mentioned, as a course which the city of Boston could take in the event of its getting the Shawsheen supply, that at the end of the twenty years or so, if the supply then proved insufficient, the city of Boston could cut off Everett, Somerville, and Chelsea, either or all of them, from a supply of water; is that so?

A. It might, as an extreme measure.

Q. Well, it would have to do it at that time, would it not?

A. There might be some more water obtained somewhere else, possibly, then.

Q. Where do you expect to get water from at the end of the twenty years?

A. I think the present problem is sufficient for us to-day.

Q. It is going to take you five years to finish the construction of the Shawsheen system, is it not?

A. I do not think it would take so long as that, sir; but, as I am advised by the engineers, I think it would take three years to build the necessary constructions, and it would probably take another year from that time to fill the basins so that we could begin to use the water. It would probably take four years from the time of obtaining the authority.

Q. Well, if you estimate it at four years now, it would be fair to assume it would take at least five years, would it not?

A. No, sir, I do not think so. I think, with energy, it might be cut down a year. We were estimating upon taking it easy.

Q. There would be an interval of say four years, during which time the pollution of the present supply is steadily to increase?

A. Yes, sir.

Q. You spoke of the Shawsheen supply being, perhaps, sufficient for twenty or twenty-five years. You mean twenty or twenty-five years from now, of course?

A. Well, we speak in a general way, because that is a matter which can be estimated upon a probable increase of population a good deal closer that I can state it.

Q. But, speaking roundly, it would be safe to say, would it not, that at the end of fifteen years from the time when your construction of the Shawsheen system was finished, it would be insufficient to supply the district now supplied by the Mystic?

A. In a time of drought it might possibly reach that point.

Q. Well, you always speak of the time of drought as a fact to be recognized?

A. Exactly.

Q. And you are figuring now upon the supply with reference to a time of drought?

A. Yes; but still it would not follow absolutely that these other towns would have to be cut off in a year of drought. If the average supply exceeded that amount of 20,000,000 by two or three or five millions of gallons, that would carry us three or four years longer, and if we did have a time of drought, there might be temporary expedients which would furnish a few gallons, more or less, to help them out for the time being. We would not, perhaps, be brought absolutely to the point of cutting off any of these towns when we reached a period of drought.

Q. But even on the basis on which you yourself put it now, do you think it is good policy for the city of Boston to abandon this Mystic supply without looking ahead and planning on a larger scale than merely to get this little supply from the Shawsheen?

A. Well, it seems to me good policy to take a good water supply of the size of this Shawsheen, and to make use of it as far as it will go.

Q. Without looking ahead at all as to what you will do at the end of that period?

A. We are looking ahead a quarter of a century. Our children must take care of themselves at that time, if we do not do something else in the meantime.

Q. Have you considered at all what your children would do at the end of that time, — where they would go for water?

A. Yes.

Q. Where do you think they would go?

A. Well, I think there are possibilities, for instance, of connecting the Shawsheen supply with a feeder from some other stream.

Q. What other stream?

A. I speak of it as a possibility; it is not a plan, of course; it is only a guess; there is a possibility of connecting the Shawsheen with the Concord; there are lots of possibilities.

Q. What is the supply from the Concord?

A. It depends upon where it is taken; it might run anywhere from 30,000,000 to 50,000,000.

Q. Then the supply from the Concord is much larger than the supply from the Shawsheen?

A. Yes, sir; but it is not desirable to take it unless in case of extremity.

Q. What is your estimate of the cost of the Shawsheen, the cost of damages for taking property, and then the cost of construction?

A. The cost of damages has not been considered, because that is a matter we could not estimate on. The amount of land damages we do not think could be very large, because the land there is not particularly valuable. The question of other damages is a problematical one.

Q. You say you have not considered it at all?

A. We have considered it in its general relations; we have considered how many manufactories there are, and other things about them, but we have not made any estimates as to the damages.

Q. You have not made any estimate?

A. No, sir.

Q. Do you think it would be prudent for the city to undertake this business without making an estimate?

A. Yes, sir. Our ground is that the present supply is so poor that in a few years it will not be fit for consumption. We must obtain water, whether it costs us $100,000 or $200,000, more or less.

Q. You have no judgment, yourself, to express to the committee, even in round numbers, as to the probable cost of taking the Shawsheen?

A. Yes, sir, I have. Our estimates of constructing dams and basins and conduits will not —

Q. Excuse me, I did not mean the cost of construction, but I meant to ask you whether you had any judgment to express as to the cost of taking, — the damages?

A. No, sir, except in a very general way. I do not think I ought to mention any figures at all with regard to that; that is a thing we must take our chances about.

Q. Two or three millions of dollars?

A. Land damages and mill damages?

Q. Yes, damages.

A. Hardly.

Q. You do not care to express any judgment yourself, however?

A. Well, I do not know how I can. I know how many manufactories there are; I know how many acres of land we want; but the question of damages is one that must be settled with the individual parties, and it is impossible for me, or anybody else, to estimate that.

Q. Well, leaving out for a moment all those points, what do you say with regard to the cost of construction?

A. The complete scheme would probably cost about $3,000,000; possibly it might run over that.

Q. Do you mean by the complete scheme the construction of the three basins?

A. Yes, sir.

Q. And the conduits?

A. And the conduits, pumps, and everything of that sort.

Q. At least $3,000,000, you think?

A. Yes, sir.

Q. Possibly it might run over that?

A. Yes, sir.

Q. Perhaps it might run up to $4,000,000?

A. Well, our estimates are $3,500,000, in round numbers.

Q. Then you might have added on the $500,000, I suppose, when you gave me the statement before?

A. I might. I might have added another million, and called it $4,000,000.

Q. No; but you say your estimates are $3,500,000. What is the present condition of the city in regard to spending that money? You are familiar, I suppose, and I am not, with all the laws that affect the incurring of a water debt.

A. The water debt is not included in the law relating to taxation. We can create as much water debt as necessary.

Q. There is no limit to that?

A. No, sir.

Q. It would be necessary for the city to provide for $3,500,000, you think, at least, for construction?

A. Undoubtedly.

Q. You would want to add on $1,500,000, at least, for damages, would you not?

A. No, sir.

Mr. Morse. — You are very non-committal about that.

The WITNESS. — Possibly you' could give us a better estimate than I could.

Q. How much has the Mystic system cost the city of Boston?

A. I cannot tell you exactly, sir, but I can tell you what the present debt is. I do not know whether any of the debt has been paid off; but I think it must have been.

Mr. BRUCE. — If you will look at your last report you will find it is stated as $1,650,805.32 on the first day of January.

Q. How much of that cost would be lost in case this system is abandoned?

A. Well, if the present Mystic dam should be taken away and the water run down there, of course that part of it would be lost ; but our conduits and pumping-works, and our reservoir in Somerville, would all remain, and remain in use. I cannot say what proportion, but I should imagine half of it, at least, speaking in a general way.

Q. The city has paid a considerable amount for damages on the Mystic system, has it not?

A. I am not familiar with the history of that: that was a Charlestown matter, before it came into Boston.

Q. It has paid a large sum for the construction of this sewer?

A. Yes, I think it cost about $200,000. I have not those figures here, but they are all in our reports.

Q. I understand that the recommendation of the Water Board is, that in case the Shawsheen should be taken and adopted as a source of supply the Mystic should be abandoned altogether, is it not?

A. We believe, from present appearances, it ought to be abandoned soon, unless something can be done which we do not foresee.

Q. You do not propose to get the Shawsheen and to use the Mystic also, do you?

A. No, sir ; that is not the present plan. We do not believe it is possible to do it. We think that the Mystic supply must be abandoned soon.

Q. Then there would be a certain amount of debt lost on the Mystic system, would there not?

A. Undoubtedly.

Mr. BRUCE. — That portion of the city of Boston that used to be the city of Charlestown does not increase much in population from year to year, does it?

A. Less rapidly than other sections of the city.

Q. Isn't its whole territory built over?

A. It is pretty much; there is not much opportunity for increase.

Q. For a series of years there has practically been no increase in the amount of water consumed in Charlestown?

A. There has been an increase in the amount of water used in Charlestown.

Q. It is very slight, is it not?

A. Yes; it is not large.

Q. Has there not been a decrease in the last few years?

A. I think not, sir; I have not looked it up to see exactly, but I am very certain the revenue from Charlestown last year was larger than the year before.

Q. That might be, and still no increase in the quantity of water used?

A. The rates are the same as they were year before last.

Q. As matter of fact, Charlestown uses about 2,500,000 gallons a day?

A. It must use more than that, I think.

Q. Tell us how much.

A. I do not find here at hand the statement of the amount of consumption, but I see the revenue from Charlestown last year was about $110,000, which I find was a slight falling off from the year before, but it is about the average of the last ten years. The amount received from the other three places was about $140,000.

Q. Was not the population of Charlestown in 1873, 33,556, and in 1880, 33,734?

A. I cannot tell you about that, sir.

Mr. BRUCE. — Those figures are from the statistics, and they show that Charlestown, certainly, is not a growing territory.

The WITNESS. — I suppose that, independent of the influence of the Navy-Yard, the population of Charlestown might be considered as practically stationary; and the mere fact of a few more or less people being employed there makes a difference of a thousand or two thousand people in the population for the time being.

Q. And the tendency in the future would be, would it not, to the occupation of the territory for purposes of manufacturing, so that, as matter of fact, the population, instead of increasing in the future, would probably be less?

A. I do not think so, sir. It does not lie in such a position that any considerable amount of it, more than is now so used, can be used for manufacturing.

Q. Do you remember what the current expenses of the Mystic Water Board were in 1885?

A. As I carry them in my head they were about $135,000.

Mr. BRUCE. — As I have it, it is $122,000, independent of the interest on the debt.

The WITNESS. — I had the estimate for this year in my mind; it is going to cost a little more this year than last.

Q. I understood you to say the estimate of the Shawsheen river was 20,000,000 gallons daily; that was the report made by Mr. Davis, the former engineer of the Water Board.

A. Yes, sir.

Q. Now was not that estimate based upon the saving of a rainfall of twelve inches instead of ten?

A. Yes, sir.

Q. So that really you have to take off one-sixth of that, in order to get at the actual capacity?

A. No, sir.

Q. Why not?

A. Because we propose to build our basins deeper and save more water.

Q. You still think you could get what would be equivalent to twelve inches of rainfall and save it?

A. No, sir; we think we shall get ten inches of rainfall, and out of the ten inches have 20,000,000 gallons of water.

Q. Mr. Davis estimated 20,000,000 on a rainfall of twelve inches, did he not?

A. Yes; but the basins were to be built with what is called shallow flowage; that is, simply the dams were to be built. But since that time it has been decided that no basins should be built with a flow of water of less than seven or eight feet; and our estimates are based on a very much greater excavation than the estimates made in 1874.

Q. You do not understand that the city of Boston is under the least obligation to supply the city of Somerville, or Chelsea, or Everett, except under its contracts with them, from the Mystic water-supply, do you?

A. If there is an obligation, I do not know what the character of it is. I have never been advised.

Q. You do not understand that there is?

A. I have never been advised that there is.

Q. And the moment the Mystic water-supply is abandoned, then you are under no obligation whatever to supply these places with water?

A. That is a matter, I think, you had better ask Mr. Bailey about and not me : it is a matter of law.

Q. You do not understand it to be so, do you, — that you are under any obligation to supply these places?

A. I understand that if our supply is not sufficient for our own people — the people of Charlestown — the other places can be cut off.

Q. Have you a copy of the contract here?

A. No, sir.

Q. Will you furnish it?

A. Yes, sir.

Q. What revenue do you get from these three places, from the sale of water?

A. The present contract varies according to the quantities they use. The cities of Chelsea and Somerville have been receiving, of late years, something over twenty-five per cent. of the amount of rates collected, and the town of Everett has been receiving fifteen per cent.

Q. That is, it is arranged on a sliding scale : for the first 20,000 it is 15 per cent. ; on the next 10,000, 20 per cent. ; on the next, 25 per cent. ; and then 30 and 40, which is the maximum : whether or not that has been and still is, a very profitable contract to the City of Boston?

Mr. BAILEY. — There ought to be some limit to this, and it ought not to be gone into unless there is some real necessity for it.

If you are going into the question of the contracts, I shall want to put in something more, and the hearings will be extended beyond the limit of the sitting of the Legislature, if we are not careful. What is the object of this?

Mr. BRUCE. — I think this committee ought to know whether or not the city of Boston is seeking for this water for its own use, or whether it is for somebody's else use, or whether it is for public reasons, or for the sake of profit.

The WITNESS. — I think my answer will be a sufficient explanation.

Mr. BAILEY. — I do not see how what my brother Bruce wants can be settled by these contracts. We will admit we have contracts with these towns; we will admit we are seeking water for the inhabitants of these towns; and we will admit, furthermore, that if the Legislature will say to us, " You can cut off those towns," we should be very glad to do it. But as long as we have made an arrangement with them, we propose to act in good faith, and to get water for them.

Mr. BRUCE. — But you do not understand you are under any obligation to furnish water for these other places, except from the Mystic supply, and that conditionally?

Mr. BAILEY. — I do as long as we have water from that source; just as long as we get water from the Mystic side of the river we are obliged to supply these places, provided we have more than water enough to supply the inhabitants of Charlestown.

Q. Whether or not they are profitable contracts?

A. No, sir, there is no profit in the contracts. The only persons who got any profit were the people who bought the bonds and got a rate of six per cent. interest on them, on a short loan. The city of Boston gets no benefit from it. And, to go further, the people of Chelsea, Somerville and Everett have appealed to us to give them a larger percentage of these rates, and in order to do it, the city of Boston has voted to extend the loans formerly made by the city of Charlestown, for periods of ten, twenty, or thirty years, or whatever the law gives us a right to, at a lower rate of interest in order that they can, out of these water-rates, pay the interest and meet the requirements of the sinking-fund, and give hese people fifty per cent. of the water-rates; and that matter is now in the process of arrangement. It is not a matter of profit to the city of Boston.

Q. Do you really mean to say this contract with Somerville and Chelsea has not been a profitable contract to the city of Boston?

A. It is not of the least interest to the city of Boston, one way or the other. Every dollar goes to the bondholders' interest and interest account; it is not credited to anything else.

Q. Wait one moment. Supposing, however, that the profit to the city of Boston had been sufficient so that from it you had been able to pay and wipe out the whole debt for the construction of the Mystic works, would you not then say it was a profitable contract to the city of Boston?

A. All the money would have gone into the interest account and to pay the bonds; and when the bonds had been paid, these people would be entitled to a new contract at any time.

Q. Supposing they were, still it would be a profitable contract, would it not, if, by the means of this contract, without any tax on the city of Boston, the city of Charlestown had been able to pay for the construction of the Mystic works?

A. Our people in Boston are paying just the same for their water as those people over there. It is a question of water-rates, and not a question of profit to anybody.

Mr. POOR. — Does your plan contemplate an entire diversion of the waters of the Shawsheen above this dam?

A. It of course contemplates it at some time, not immediately, necessarily.

Q. Would the city be willing to enter into an agreement, or take a bill, which would let a certain amount of water per day go by?

A. I should say they would, so long as there was more than was required. If a period of time could be fixed, supposing there could be some provision of that kind, it would be entirely acceptable.

Mr. POOR. — It would not do anybody any good, as you put it.

Mr. BAILEY. — You are acquainted with the main features of the sewer system proposed by the State Commission, aren't you?

A. I have read the report.

Q. Would the building of that sewer, unless it was accompanied by a complete system of sewers in every one of the towns on this water-shed, do any good, so far as the purity of the Mystic water-supply is concerned?

A. I should say it would leave a great many, or several, portions of the water-shed entirely unprotected.

Q. Would not all the water used by the inhabitants of these towns, if it did not go into the sewer, go into the ground, and then soak through the ground into the water-supply?

A. Undoubtedly.

Q. And would not a complete system of sewers, in protecting the purity, also take away a very large part of the supply?

A. Undoubtedly.

Q. Whether or not you are acquainted with this fact, that the sewer on Russell brook was built to take the discharge and refuse from some eight or ten tanneries which were situated immediately on the banks of that brook, and that there was but one of two things for the city to do, either to build a sewer to take their refuse, or else to take the tanneries themselves?

A. I understand that was the fact.

Q. And in order to avoid the expense to the city, and the destruction of the business of these tanneries, the city preferred to build the sewer?

A. Yes, sir.

Mr. Loomis. — Is there any connection between the Mystic and Sudbury systems, so one can reënforce the other?

A. There is no connection now; that is, no active connection. The pipes are so laid that water can be run into Charlestown if necessary.

Q. The pipes are already laid so water can be run in without additional expense?

A. Not at all; in order to supply Charlestown it would be necessary to put in an entirely new system of pipes.

Q. Why so?

A. Because the present pipes are merely emergency pipes for a small district, and they would not be sufficient to supply one-quarter of the people.

Q. You could, however, reënforce the present supply from the Sudbury system; that is, you could supply a portion of the district?

A. We could run in a short supply there, of course.

Q. Do you save all the water in the Sudbury system now which it is possible for you to save?

A. No, sir.

Q. Do you not lose large quantities over the dams every year?

A. Oh, yes, sir.

Q. Have you built all the storage-basins on the Sudbury system that are projected?

A. No; there were more basins projected which are not yet built, but none of any large capacity.

Mr. SMITH. — I do not know as I understood you with regard to the projected drainage system. Did I understand you to say that if that were built and in operation it would not practically protect the Mystic system from impurities?

A. It would undoubtedly remove a great many impurities, but, in my judgment, the topography of that district is such that no sewerage system will ever leave the Mystic water in the future in a good drinkable condition, as compared with other waters that we consider good waters.

Q. Do you mean to imply that if that drainage system should be put into operation, it would not protect it more than it now is, so that the water would be practically purer than it is to-day?

A. I have said I believe it undoubtedly would carry a great deal of impurity away from that region.

Q. So that the water would be better than it is to-day?

A. It might be, for the time being; but if the population and manufactories on that territory should increase, so that by-and-by the mere surface drainage alone might bring the impurities up to the very point where they are now, then we should be as badly off as we are to-day.

Q. What is the object of this projected system of drainage?

A. I suppose it is intended for drainage, for the health of the people of that district.

Q. And is not one of the great objects of that whole system to protect the water-supply of Boston?

A. I have never heard so. I have understood that the city of Malden and other places in that district have very much fear for their health, as they ought to have, and they want these sewers built entirely independent of any water supply.

Q. Now take it on the other side : is it not contemplated that this drainage system shall protect the Sudbury system of water-supply?

A. The project in Natick and Framingham, if you allude to that.

Q. Well, is not this one grand system designed not only for the protection of the individual towns and cities but also to furnish a means of taking off the sewage, so that it will not pollute the water-supplies?

A. The plan with reference to the drainage of Natick and Framingham is undoubtedly designed with a double purpose of drainage and a protection of the water. There is no question about that. But the case on the other side is different, as I look at it.

Mr. BAILEY, of Everett. — Are not these proposed new contracts with Somerville, Chelsea, and Everett dependent upon the three places agreeing?

A. No, sir; we can contract with any one of them, and if the other two do not choose to accept these terms they must fall back on their present contract, or go to the Supreme Court.

Q. Boston will contract with either one of them, if they agree to the terms?

A. Oh, yes; we are not bound to make the three contracts, we are only bound to make them all alike. If they decline to accept such terms as are offered, they must either go on under the present contract at a lower rebate, or go to the Supreme Court and have commissioners appointed.

Mr. MORSE. — Before the next witness is called I would like to make a suggestion which, it seems to me, should be considered, in order that we may know exactly what the issue is before the committee. I do not understand that any bill has been drawn and presented to the committee, and perhaps that is not necessary at this stage ; but there is one point which, in the previous hearings, has always been discussed *pro* and *con* by counsel and parties, and which is very material. I understand from private conversation what the position of the city of Boston is upon that point, but I would like to have it distinctly stated before the committee. In the hearings of 1881 and 1882, where bills were presented in behalf of the city of Boston and the city of Cambridge, which then petitioned for the right to take the Shawsheen, sections were inserted in the bill for the protection not only of the towns but of the mill-owners. I would like to read a section which was then offered by me, and was substantially agreed to by Mr. Hammond, City Solicitor of Cambridge, who, at that time, was quite active in conducting these hearings. It is as follows : —

" Said city shall permit the inhabitants of the towns of Billerica, Wilmington, Burlington, Bedford, and Lexington to take from the Shawsheen river so much of the water hereby granted as shall be necessary for extinguishing fires, for ordinary domestic household purposes, and for the generation of steam. It shall also cause a running stream of at least 10,000,000 gallons per day, for each and every day in the year, to flow in said river at the lowest dam which it may construct and maintain in pursuance of this act. The Supreme Judicial Court, sitting in equity for either of the counties of Suffolk or Middlesex, shall have jurisdiction, on complaint of any person aggrieved by the failure of said city to observe the regulations of this section, to compel such observance, by injunction or otherwise, and to give any other suitable relief; or such aggrieved person may maintain an action of tort against said city for the recovery of his damages."

The whole of that section was adopted by Mr. Hammond, with the exception of the last clause, giving the right of action, and was incorporated in the bill that was submitted to the committee, and was discussed before them. I understand from Mr. Bailey that the city of Boston does not propose in the grant which it now asks from the committee to incorporate this provision in regard to an allowance for the mill-owners, and I simply would like to have it stated, in order that we may know at the outset where we are.

Mr. BAILEY. — The city of Boston has asked here for authority to take the waters of the river. Of course we do not say a quarter of the water of that river, nor a third of it. At the time this section which has been read was put into the bill the city of Cambridge was asking for authority to take 8,000,000 gallons of the water of the Shawsheen river, and it was willing to put in a proviso that 10,000,000 should be allowed to run down the river, because more than 8,000,000 would still be left after the 10,000,000 gallons had been let go. Of course, if this committee think the necessities of Boston at the present time are not such as to warrant them in giving the city the whole of the river, they can specify that for a certain number of years a certain amount of water shall be allowed to run down the river. That is in the discretion of the committee always in drawing up their bill as they may think proper.

The CHAIRMAN. — It is understood, then, that you ask for the whole?

Mr. BAILEY. — We ask for the whole of the river.

The CHAIRMAN. — Regardless of the towns or of the manufacturers?

Mr. BAILEY. — Regardless of anybody. If there are any rights to be preserved, of course those rights are preserved and guarded in the bill. So far as the first part of that section is concerned, about the inhabitants having a right to take the water, we should not object to it, because that goes into every water bill.

TESTIMONY OF DEXTER BRACKETT.

Mr. BAILEY. — Your position is what?

A. Assistant engineer in the office of the engineer of the city of Boston.

Q. Whether surveys and examinations of the Mystic and Shawsheen water-sheds have been made under your supervision?

A. No, sir.

Q. Have you made examination yourself about certain matters with regard to those rivers?

A. Yes, sir.

Q. Will you state what the full supply of the Mystic water-shed is at the present time?

A. Seven million gallons per day.

Q. What is the population that is using that 7,000,000 gallons?

A. About 100,000 people.

Q. What has experience taught to be a safe supply to allow for each inhabitant using water in large cities?

A. I should not consider it was safe to estimate upon less than 70 gallons, — between 60 and 70 gallons.

Q. What has been the average daily amount consumed during the last year by the 100,000 people who use the Mystic water?

A. About 6,730,000 gallons.

Q. So that practically the whole supply has been used during the last year?

A. No; the whole supply has not been used during the past year, but an amount equivalent to the supply in a year of drought.

Q. The safe supply, you mean?

A. Yes, sir.

Q. You are acquainted with the character of the territory of the Mystic water-shed?

A. Yes, sir, to some extent.

Q. And to what extent is that populated?

A. It has a population of nearly 900 people per square mile.

Q. About 22,000 or 23,000 on the whole territory?

A. Yes, sir, I think about that.

Q. And about how many manufacturing establishments are there there? Do you know about that?

A. No, sir.

Q. Are there very many?

A. Yes, sir, there are very many.

Q. What is the character of those manufacturing establishments?

A. Well, they are of a character which would tend to pollute the water-supply, that is, the tanning industry, which is carried on to a large extent.

Q. That is, they are tanneries?

A. Yes, sir.

Q. And besides them, there is a factory which takes the products of the tanneries?

A. Yes, sir, a glue factory.

Q. How large an establishment is that?

A. I do not know the number of employés; I could not give you that.

Q. Do you know the number of gallons of water that come out of that establishment?

A. No, sir, I do not.

Q. Is it a very large establishment?

A. Yes, sir.

Q. Do you know how much ground it covers?

A. No, I should not want to state the acreage, as far as the buildings are concerned.

Q. Do you know how many acres the establishment occupies?

A. No, sir, I do not.

Q. Do you know the processes they pursue there?

A. No, sir.

Q. Now, sir, how are these tannery industries situated, so far as the streams are concerned? Are they in the immediate vicinity of the streams, or some distance away?

A. Generally in the immediate vicinity of the streams, — almost invariably, I should say.

Q. Take Russell brook, for instance : are not many of them imdiately on the brook?

A. Yes, sir, follow directly along on the borders of the brook.

Q. Now, is it possible to take care of the drainage from them so that it will not pollute the water?

A. Not entirely ; it is done to a certain extent at present.

Q. But could all the sewers that could be put in there take away all the discharge of the products and refuse of the tanneries, so that nothing would soak through the soil into the water?

A. Not without taking away the entire water-supply, or the greater portion of it.

Q. Would anything but a complete system of sewers in every one of these towns upon this water-shed be effectual to prevent the pollution of the water by the inhabitants and by the industries which are carried on there?

A. I should not say that even that would.

Q. Why not?

A. Because there would still remain, in a thickly settled territory, a large amount of surface drainage which would not be removed by the sewerage system as contempleted.

Q. Whether or not the time has come, in your judgment, when the condition of that territory is such that it is becoming dangerous to use that water-shed for a water-supply?

A. I should say that it had.

Q. Now, sir, have you examined the Shawsheen water-shed and made an examination as to the amount of water which can be depended upon from that source?

A. Yes, sir; I have made calculations as to the amount of water.

Q. What is the supply of the Shawsheen valley, taking it above the railroad, as it is usually termed?

A. Between 19,000,000 and 20,000,000 gallons per day.

Q. How many basins would it be necessary to construct?

A. Three.

Q. Supposing only the lower basin were constructed, what would be the supply derived from that source?

A. I have not made any calculation upon that; I made it in a round sum; still, I know it would be the greater portion.

Q. About 17,000,000 gallons, wouldn't it, or don't you know?

A. I do not know.

Mr. BAILEY. —That is the fact, that with one basin there would be 17,000,000 gallons.

Q. How long, if the city had authority to take the water this year, and should begin with the immediate construction of that basin, before it would be available?

A. I could not answer; I have not made any figures on that.

Cross-Examination.

Mr. MORSE. — Will you state to the committee the entire consumption of water in Boston, including the amount furnished to Everett, Somerville, Charlestown, and Chelsea, from all sources?

A. For the last year it was 32,344,000 gallons.

Q. A day?

A. Yes, sir.

Q. Do you know how that compares with the amount supplied five years ago?

A. It is very much less.

Q. In 1881, the amount of water consumed in the same district was 36,000,000, was it not?

A. I think likely.

Q. Then the condition of Boston, so far as its supply of water is concerned, is better than it was five years ago, is it not?

A. As to the actual quantity they are now using.

Q. How do you account for that difference in the quantity?

A. It is owing to the saving of waste.

Q. The population has increased considerably during that period, has it not?

A. Yes, sir.

Q. Do you know what the ratio of increase is?

A. I do not exactly.

Q. Can you state it approximately?

A. For the last five years?

Q. Yes.

A. I do not know what it is.

Q. What is the total population now supplied by the 32,344,000 gallons?

A. About 456,000.

Q. Of that how much do you allow for the population of Boston?

A. For the population supplied by the Cochituate works?

Q. No, I mean the whole population of Boston.

A. The whole population of Boston is about 390,000.

Q. Then the population outside of Boston, which is supplied with water by Boston, is about 66,000, is it?

A. Yes, sir.

Q. The entire population supplied by both the Sudbury and the Mystic systems is 456,000?

A. Yes, sir.

Q. And of that 456,000, 390,000 are the population of Boston, and 66,000 the population of Everett, Somerville, and Chelsea?

A. Yes, sir.

Q. And that population to-day uses 32,344,000 gallons of water, against 36,000,000 five years ago?

A. Yes, sir ; that is, the 36,000,000 is your statement.

Q. That is the statement of Mr. Wightman made five years ago, and I presume it is correct. How much of that 32,244,000 gallons comes from the Sudbury?

A. Twenty-five million six hundred thousand.

Q. How many basins have you now on the Sudbury?

A. Four. When you speak of the Sudbury, that includes the Sudbury and the Cochituate supplies?

Mr. Morse. — I meant to include both.

The Witness. — Then there are five. The fifth basin is just

completed; it has not been in use up to the present time, and does not appear in any of the figures which you have used.

Q. Then we will leave that out for the moment. How many basins have you had in use from which you have obtained this supply of 25,000,000 a day?

A. Four basins.

Q. How much additional supply will you get from the basin just completed?

A. About four millions and a half.

Q. So you will get a supply of about 30,000,000 from your five basins?

A. You are figuring on what we did get in the last year, not on what we might get in a minimum year.

Q. I am taking the figures just as they are. You say that during the last year you had four basins in use, and you got 25,-600,000 gallons a day from them?

A. Yes, sir.

Q. And an addittional basin will give you 4,500,000 more?

A. Yes, sir.

Q. That would make 30,000,000 from the five basins, would it not?

A. Yes, sir.

Q. How many more basins are projected on that system?

A. There have been three, I think.

Q. Supposing those are built, how much additional supply will you get?

A. As you have figured it now, you have started out with what we had during the present year; if you will tell me what you have got down already, I will tell you how much more we will have.

Mr. MORSE. — We have already got up to 30,000,000, — 25,600,000 you had last year, and 4,500,000 you are going to get from the new basin.

The WITNESS. — We will get about 12,000,000 more.

Q. That would bring it up to 42,000,000 gallons a day?

A. Yes, sir.

Q. Now, supposing you leave out the Mystic system altogether —

The WITNESS. — The Mystic system is not included in that figure.

Q. I understand. Supposing you take the 42,000,000 gallons that can be obtained from the Sudbury system, and abandon the Mystic altogether, for how long a period would the 42,000,000 gallons be a sufficient supply for the population now supplied, — Boston and the three other places?

A. I do not have the figures in my head.

Q. I do not expect you to give exact figures, but give your best judgment to the committee as to how long that would last. You are allowing 70 gallons a day for each individual, are you?

A. Yes, sir.

Q. Which is a very high estimate, is it not?

A. No, sir, I do not think it is; it is very nearly the present consumption, with the measures which have been adopted to prevent waste.

Q. We will not discuss that, but allowing 70 gallons a day to every inhabitant in the district, 42,000,000 gallons would supply a population of 600,000?

A. Yes, sir.

Q. How long, in your judgment, will it be before this territory will have a population of 600,000? During the last five years you have reduced the amount supplied about 3,500,000 gallons, and if you continue in that direction, you can go on a good many years with a supply of 42,000,000 gallons, can you not?

A. Somewhere in the vicinity of twenty years.

Q. Now, Mr. Brackett, was it not contemplated, at the time when the Sudbury system was projected, to depend upon that as the sole supply for all this territory?

A. I think not.

Q. Do you not know that the reports of the Water Board recommending that supply contained a statement that if it were adopted it would be sufficient for the needs of the city for the next fifty years?

A. I was not aware that it included the district now supplied by the Mystic.

Mr. MORSE. — Let me call your attention to a statement of Mr. Cutter, who was chairman of the Water Board in 1879, that the supply from the Sudbury would be, beyond all question, an adequate supply of pure water for the city of Boston for the next fifty years.

The WITNESS. — Perhaps that did not include these three other places, but only the city of Boston.

Mr. BAILEY. — That did not include Charlestown.

Mr. MORSE. — My attention is called to a statement made by Alderman Stebbins, in discussing this matter in 1879, that, "In the opinion of the City Engineer there is abundance of water in Chestnut-hill reservoir for Boston and all the existing region supplied by the Mystic service, and the city of Cambridge, also, if they want it."

Mr. BAILEY. — Chestnut-hill reservoir is not our water-supply; it is only a storage-basin.

Q. Now, coming back to these figures, is there anything to prevent the use of the Sudbury water in supplying the Mystic district?

A. The present works could not supply it without an additional cost.

Q. How much additional cost?

A. Well, at least $500,000.

Q. Is it not a fact, that by spending $500,000, the city of Boston could ensure a sufficient supply for the next twenty years from the Sudbury system, abandoning the Mystic system altogether?

A. No, sir.

Q. What?

A. No, sir.

Mr. MORSE. — Then I misunderstood your figures.

The WITNESS. — We based our figures of 600,000 on the present population supplied from the Cochituate works, not including the Mystic.

Mr. MORSE. — I understood you to say that, in your judgment, there would be a sufficient supply for twenty years for the whole of the district now supplied by the Sudbury and the Mystic.

The WITNESS. — Oh, no.

Q. Not if you increase the supply from the Sudbury to the extent of the storage capacity there?

A. No, sir.

Q. How long would it last?

A. It would only last for about ten years.

Q. It would be getting a supply, then, for ten years in that way, as against a supply that is good for fifteen years from the time when the works on the Shawsheen are finished?

A. I do not accept that statement of fifteen years.

Q. What is your reckoning?

A. My reckoning would be nearer thirty-five than fifteen.

Q. Do you mean to say there is a discrepancy of twenty years between you and the chairman of the Water Board?

A. Yes, sir.

Mr. BAILEY. — The chairman of the Water Board stated particularly that on these matters he did not pretend to be an expert.

Mr. MORSE. — If we have got to undo the figures given by the Water Board, we shall have to begin at the beginning again.

Mr. BAILEY. — The chairman gave you fair warning of it, Mr. Morse.

Q. What is your estimate of the amount of the supply from the Shawsheen?

A. I have stated that; about 20,000,000.

Q. How long do you think that 20,000,000 gallons would supply the district now supplied by the Mystic?

A. About thirty-five years.

Q. What do you estimate the population of that district will be at the end of thirty-five years?

A. I should have to stop to figure that up; I do not pretend to carry all those things in my head always.

Mr. MORSE. — I supposed, if the city of Boston was coming here to present some plan to the committee, it had a lot of tables and figures all prepared.

Mr. BAILEY. — So we have, if you will just indicate what you want.

Mr. MORSE. — I want anything you have.

Mr. BAILEY. — Oh, no, we do not prepare our case in that way; we are putting in what we think is necessary to prove our case.

The WITNESS. — Perhaps I can answer your question now, if you will repeat it.

Mr. Morse. — My question was as to what you estimate the population of that district will be at the end of thirty-five years?

The Witness. — About 250,000.

Q. And you allow them how much a day?

A. Seventy gallons; it is on that basis.

Q. At the end of that time what should you propose to do for the people in that district?

A. That I have not considered.

Q. Don't you think that the city, in going into an enterprise of this kind, should look ahead for a longer period than thirty-five years?

A. It has not been the custom in the past.

Q. And do you not think the trouble with the water-supply of Boston has been that the city has not looked ahead far enough in making provision?

A. I do not know that I do.

Q. When the Cochituate was taken it was assumed that would be sufficient for the needs of the city for a very long period, was it not?

A. Yes, sir.

Q. And when the Sudbury was taken was not that urged upon the ground that that it would be sufficient?

A. The Sudbury, if not used for any other supply, will be sufficient for some length of time.

Q. Why should you not use the entire supply from the Sudbury, and exhaust that, before seeking a supply like the Shawsheen?

A. Because, in the course of ten years we should exhaust the supply, and it would be a very few years before we should have to begin to get a supply somewhere else.

Q. Is the quality of the water of the Shawsheen any better than that of the Sudbury?

A. It is full as good.

Q. Is it any better?

A. I do not know that it is any better.

Q. You have, then, today, within reach, a supply that you say yourself would be sufficient for ten or twelve years?

A. For ten years.

Q. For the whole population of Boston and the district including these three other places?

A. Yes, sir.

Q. How much can you get from the Mystic?

A. I do not know as I understand what you mean by that question.

Q. I will put it this way, how much do you get from the present basins on the Mystic?

A. Seven millions of gallons per day is the safe supply.

Q. How much can you get if you build all the basins that have been projected?

A. I should say about 16,000,000 gallons.

Q. It has been given as 17,000,000 gallons, has it not, in some of the estimates?

A. It has been given up as high 20,000,000.

Q. But you would put it at 16,000,000?

A. Yes, sir.

Q. Add the 16,000,000 to the 42,000,000, and you have 58,-000,000 a day, have you not?

A. Yes, sir.

Q. And that is a supply at 70 gallons per inhabitant for a population of over 800,000?

A. Yes, sir.

Q. Which would be almost double the population of the district now supplied?

A. Yes, sir.

Q. How long do you think it will take to double the present population?

A. Perhaps 25 or 30 years.

Q. Then if you had both the Sudbury and the Mystic systems, you would have, so far as quantity goes, an amount sufficient for at least the next generation?

A. Yes, sir, for 25 or 30 years.

Q. And I suppose the only objection you would urge against that is the quality of the Mystic, is it not?

A. Yes, sir.

Q. And in regard to the quality, that has been improved by the sewer that was built by the city?

A. It is a question whether it has been improved. Perhaps it is better to-day, I might say, than it would have been if the sewer had not been built.

Q. Do you not recommend it in your reports as good drinking-water?

A. Yes, sir.

Q. Well, of course, you believe it to be, do you not?

A. Yes, sir.

Q. If the Mystic water can be kept as good as it is to-day, is there any reason why it should not be a proper water to drink for the next 25, 30, or 35 years?

A. Well, I do not know that I consider myself as an expert on the quality of water.

Q. The consumers in the district are satisfied with the present condition of the water, are they not?

A. No, sir.

Mr. MORSE. — Let me call your attention to the report made on the first of January, 1886, of the Mystic department, and to this sentence on page 95 of that report : —

"During the past year the water has been good and abundant."

Mr. BAILEY. — That is so ; there is no question about it.

Mr. MORSE. — You say there is no question about it, but I understood Mr. Brackett to question the quality of the water.

Mr. BAILEY. — We claim that the dangers of pollution are so great it must be given up ; not that the water is so bad to-day it must be given up.

Mr. MORSE. — My question was, supposing you could keep the quality of the water as good as it is now, would it not be satisfactory?

A. I do not think I am competent to answer that question.

Q. Do you understand that this system of drainage, which is contemplated for that region, will tend to protect the purity of the water?

A. To a certain extent.

Q. You would say, would you not, as Colonel Rockwell did, that wherever the city goes for a supply of water you will have to fight to protect the supply from pollution?

A. Probably.

Q. So you are no better off in that respect if you go to one river than if you go to another?

A. Well, yes; because if one river has a thousand sources of pollution, and another only one, there will be a thousand times more fighting to do to protect the former.

Q. What is to prevent the establishment, from time to time, of objectionable places on the banks of this stream?

A. I think there are laws to prevent that.

Q. If there are such laws, why do you not prevent the establishment of objectionable places on these other streams?

A. They are already established.

Q. You can buy them, or take them, can you not?

A. Certainly.

Q. It is simply a question of cost, is it not, to remove them?

A. You would have to buy up the whole town.

Mr. MORSE. — Brother Bailey announced a pretty liberal policy in saying they proposed to take the whole of the Shawsheen.

Mr. BAILEY. — I say so, and we are willing to take every foot of the land if they will sell it, so we can have a water-supply that we can protect.

Mr. MORSE. — If you are dealing on such a large scale as that, why do you not buy up the manufacturing places on the Mystic?

Mr. BAILEY. — Because it would destroy the industries and ruin towns which have a population of more than 20,000.

Mr. BAILEY. — Do you know the number of the inhabitants in the Shawsheen valley, on this territory from which it is proposed to take the water-supply?

A. I have made up the figures, but I do not carry them in my mind.

Q. Only about 90 persons to the square mile?

A. Yes, sir; 88.

Q. And on the Mystic territory there are nearly 900?

A. Yes, sir.

Q. Do you know how many manufactories there are in the Shawsheen valley?

A. I do not.

Q. Are there more than three or four?

A. There are very few. I know that.

Q. And are they small mills?

A. Yes, sir.

The CHAIRMAN. — You mean that part of the valley above your dam?

A. Yes, sir.

Mr. BRUCE. — What is the capacity of the conduits that bring the water from the Cochituate supply?

A. Well, they are good for about 17,000,000 or 18,000,000. The conduits from the Cochituate and the Sudbury have a capacity of about 100,000,000.

Q. And those were built with the expectation that a supply could be got from that direction which would furnish that amount?

A. Yes, sir.

Q. And from what sources was it contemplated that an additional supply should be taken?

A. It could be obtained from the Charles river.

Q. And the Assabet?

A. Yes, sir; I think that was considered.

Q. And a supply sufficient to come up to the maximum of about 100,000,000 a day?

A. Yes, sir; that is what the conduit was built to carry.

Q. That was in contemplation by the city when they went out in that direction for that supply, that ultimately they would be able from that side of the city to get a supply equal to 100,000,000 gallons per day, was it not?

A. I should assume so.

Q. And there is no reason to suppose they cannot get it, is there?

A. That I could not say.

Q. Have you never estimated or examined to find out whether or not upon that side of the city you could get that amount of water?

A. No, sir.

Q. You have not studied that problem at all?

A. No, sir, I have not.

Q. You have only studied one problem. When first did you

begin to investigate the question of obtaining a supply from the Shawsheen river?

A. My investigations have been generally calculations as to the yield, and have been made in the office. I have had a general knowledge of the subject for the last ten or fifteen years.

Q. Then really all you have done has been to figure out in the office what would be the cost of it, and what would be the amount of the supply?

A. I have never made estimates of the cost.

Q. Have you ever heard of any complaints as to the quality of the Mystic water being made by the consumers?

A. Yes, sir.

Q. Did you hear of any complaints last year?

A. No, sir; I do not think there were any made during the last year.

Q. The year before?

A. No, I do not know.

Q. The year before that?

A. Some three or four years ago there were complaints.

Q. Before the construction of that sewer there were complaints; but since that sewer was built has there been any complaint made as to the quality of the Mystic water by any of the persons who are supplied from that source?

A. I could not say.

Q. You do not know of any?

A. Well, there have been complaints when we have been troubled with a vegetable growth in the water.

Q. That was years ago, was it not?

A. It is a question in my mind whether it was since the construction of the sewer or not.

Q. No, it was before. You know where the supply of the city of Cambridge is, Fresh pond?

A. Yes, sir.

Q. That is right on the borders of their city, is it not?

A. Yes, sir.

Q. And so far as liability to contamination from a thickly populated territory, it would be very much more exposed to it than the Mystic supply, would it not?

A. Well, I am not sufficiently acquainted with the drainage area of the Cambridge supply to answer that question, but I should say, from the character of the population, that the Mystic would be fully as bad as Cambridge.

Mr. MORSE. — Is there any one here from the Engineer's department, or the Water Board, who is able to state the history of the checking of waste in the consumption of water in Boston, or can you state it?

A. I suppose I can as well as any one.

Q. I want to call your attention to the statement you made a few minutes ago with regard to the allowance of 70 gallons per inhabitant per day : do you know what was the amount consumed five years ago?

A. It was aobut 90 gallons.

Q. Do you know what are the figures in other cities?

A. They are all the way from 40 gallons to 130 gallons.

Q. Isn't 40 gallons the average quantity consumed in a great many cities?

A. No, sir ; not in cities of any magnitude. In fact, I do not think you will find any city of anywhere near the size of Boston which consumes less than 59.

Q. What is the consumption in Providence?

A. I think it is between 40 and 50.

Q. How is it in New York?

A. In New York it is about 90, or 100, I think.

Q. Haven't you the figures?

A. I know it has been as high as that, and I think at present it is somewhere in the vicinity of 90 gallons.

Q. What is it in Baltimore?

A. I could not say.

Q. In Philadelphia?

A. In Philadelphia it is about 60, I think. These figures change from year to year, and I have not examined into them very lately.

Q. Is it not entirely practicable, in your judgment, to reduce the consumption in Boston to 50 gallons per inhabitant?

A. No, sir.

Q. Do you know the results of some experiments that were tried in Charlestown five years ago?

A. I made them; I made all the experiments, and have had charge of work that has been done with regard to preventing waste.

Q. What was the consumption shown at that time after the use of the meters?

A. I think it was some 37 or 38 gallons, if I remember right.

Q. It was reduced, was it not, from 58.5 to 37.7?

A. Yes, sir.

Q. To what did you attribute that reduction?

A. Simply to the efforts which were made to stop the waste in the sections in which the meters were applied. I might say that those sections did not include the manufacturing portons of Charlestown, they were simply residential parts of the district.

Q. Assuming that to be so, it was a reduction of more than one third of the entire consumption, was it not?

A. Yes, sir.

Q. And to what was that waste due?

A. It was due generally to leaky house-fixtures, — plumbing; and some of it was due to wilful waste.

Q. Is it not the fact that at the hearing five years ago a great deal of attention was given to that subject, and that, as the result, partly, of that hearing, the Water Board has been giving a great deal of attention to the matter of the reduction of consumption?

A. I do not know whether it is the result of that hearing, but it is the result of efforts that have been made for a number of years.

Q. And perhaps, also, to a change in the Water Board itself?

A. I could not say.

Q. It is a fact, is it not, that within the last year or two there has been a very great improvement in the matter of the consumption of water?

A. Yes, sir.

Q. It has come down from about 90 gallons to about 70?

A. Yes, sir.

Q. Do you think you have reached the lowest limit?

A. I think it may be reduced, possibly, to a certain extent.

Q. To what extent?

A. Well, perhaps, 5 or 10 gallons.

Q. Why should we not come down to as low a rate as Providence?

A. Because the class of the population is different. We have a large floating population in the city of Boston, which they do not have in Providence; and I think the city of Providence, when their works are as old as those in the city of Boston, will show nearly as much water used as we do here. They are gaining every year.

Q. The floating population is not responsible for this waste of water, is it?

A. It is responsible for the use of it.

Q. Isn't the great use due to the manufacturing establishments?

A. No, sir; you say, " The great use,"— a certain portion of the use is.

Q. You think for every man, woman and child in Boston, without regard to age, a supply of 70 gallons per day is pretty near the minimum supply, do you?

A. I think, if you base your calculation upon the population, you will need 70 gallons. At least, I do not consider it safe to use less than 70 gallons in making an estimate of the probable needs of the city.

Q. Are you not aware of the fact that a great many very experienced and skilful engineers have given their opinion that an allowance of 40 or 50 gallons is ample?

A. Yes, sir; and they have had to build new works as the result of their calculations. I do not think you will find any such estimates in late years.

Q. Five years ago the Water Board did not think they could reduce from 90 gallons, did they?

A. I cannot say what the Water Board thought.

Q. It was stated here at these hearings, was it not, that they were very economical of water in the city of Boston?

A. I was not here: I do not know.

Q. How long have you been connected with the Engineer's department?

A. Seventeen years.

Q. And how long have you given attention to these water questions?

A. Ever since I have been there.

Q. And during that time you have not heard that the Water Board had taken the ground that the consumption of five years ago was a reasonable and economical one?

A. I did not take that ground.

Mr. BAILEY. — I do not think the Board took that ground. I think you will find Mr. Wightman testified that at one time the consumption was reduced to 60 or 70 gallons, and he thought, by proper means, it could be done again.

Mr. MORSE. — Do you know what the daily consumption is in Worcester?

A. No, sir.

Q. About 42 gallons, is it not?

A. I do not know.

Mr. MORSE. — Haven't you any table or schedule you can put in here before the committee showing the daily consumption of water in the various cities?

Mr. BAILEY. — You can show it. You can make it up from your engineers as well as we can.

Mr. MORSE. — You say you have been an engineer connected with the Water Department for seventeen years : I ask you if you can state to the committee, or if you have any figures at hand which will give it, the comparative consumption in the different cities?

Mr. BAILEY. — You have it right in your own possession now, and why not put it in? Mr. Crafts made it up last year, and you can put it in.

Mr. MORSE. — Why not let Mr. Brackett answer the question?

Mr. BAILEY. — Because he has told you repeatedly he has not made it up ; he can simply state it to you from memory.

The WITNESS. — I can give it to you for some years back, but I haven't it for the last year.

Mr. MORSE. — Did you know that in 1881 the city of Philadelphia used only 58 gallons per inhabitant?

A. I did not.

Q. Did you know the city of Providence at that time used only 35 gallons?

A. I did not.

Q. And the city of Lowell 33?

A. I do not carry those figures in my mind.

Q. And the city of Fall River 36, and the city of Lawrence 44?

A. No, sir.

Adjourned to March 30, at 10.30 A.M.

SECOND HEARING.

TUESDAY, March 30, 1886.

The committee met at 10.30, Senator Scott in the chair.

Cross-Examination of MR. DEXTER BRACKETT. — *Resumed.*

Mr. MORSE. — Have you obtained any more information upon the matter that I was inquiring about, as to the consumption of water in different cities?

A. I have looked up the subject to a certain extent, as far as the consumption of cities of the size of Boston is concerned, and I might say that I find that the consumption at present in all cities of the size of Boston, and even some smaller cities, like Baltimore, with a population of 380,000, is in the vicinity of 70 gallons per head.

Mr. BAILEY. — Suppose you give them.

A. In regard to New York, I was not able to find the information. In Philadelphia, for the year 1884, the consumption was 73 gallons per head. In Brooklyn, 67, for the year 1885. In Chicago, 114, for the year 1884. Boston was 71 for the year 1885. St. Louis, 61, for the year 1884; and Baltimore, 70, for the year 1885.

Mr. MORSE. — The cities on the lakes draw their water from the lake and discharge it into the lake, do they not?

A. Generally, yes, sir.

Q. So that you would not regard Chicago, or cities similarly situated, as any standard of comparison, would you?

A. Certainly I would.

Q. Is not the tendency of any such system as that to very great wastefulness?

A. I should say, on the other hand, that in a city like Chicago, where they are obliged to pump all their water, and where pumping means dollars and cents, they would be more likely to save it than they would in a city provided with a gravity supply, where, after the works are once built, there is no expense in that direction.

Q. The cost is simply for the pumping, and there is no expense for the water?

A. No; but there is great cost in pumping.

Q. But there is no waste of water, because it runs back into the lake?

A. As far as the quantity of water is concerned, there is not.

Q. The water is cheaper there than it is in Boston, is it not?

A. I am, not acquainted with the rates.

Q. Have you the rate of consumption in Cincinnati?

A. No, sir.

Q. Or of Columbus?

A. No, sir. I stated that I simply took the cities running down as low as Boston, and one or two cities below, in population.

Q. How much of this consumption of 70 gallons a day in Boston is, in your judgment, legitimate consumption and how much is waste?

A. I should. say that the legitimate consumption would be probably between 40 and 50 gallons per head.

Q. Then you would say that at least 20 gallons run to waste per inhabitant?

A. Yes, sir.

Q. Is that waste due to imperfect pipes mainly?

A. It is due to that to a certain extent. I do not know that it is possible to say to just what it is due or in what proportion it is due to one cause and another.

Q. I understood you to say yesterday that the principal cause was the improper pipes in buildings?

A. I said that was found to be so in Charlestown.

Q. Well, is not that true of the whole city?

A. No, sir, I don't think that it is. Yes, I will say that the main cause is imperfect fixtures.

Q. Has there not been some legislation giving authority to control the matter of plumbing in houses?

A. Yes, sir.

Q. What is the nature of that?

A. The nature of it is to control the class of fixtures which are used.

Q. And that is under the charge of the Board, is it not?

A. Well, under the charge of the Inspector of Buildings, I think, to the greatest extent.

Q. Does the Water Board have any control over any officers whose duty it is to look after the plumbing?

A. Yes, sir.

Q. What are they called?

A. They have inspectors who look after the plumbing of new buildings.

Q. How is it about old buildings?

A. There is a department of inspectors whose duty it is to look after leaky fixtures in old buildings.

Q. What I want to get at is whether there is a department whose duty it is to inspect the plumbing in the old buildings in Boston?

A. There is.

Q. And if that department was increased in efficiency by more men or a better system, would it, in your judgment, be practicable to reduce the waste that now exists?

A. I think it is possible that the waste may be reduced to a certain extent.

Q. If the entire consumption is 70 gallons per head and 20 gallons of that run to waste, you have not any doubt, have you, that it is entirely practicable in some way to reduce the waste?

A. To a certain extent. I do not consider that it is practicable or possible to stop it entirely in a large city. The larger the city the more difficult it would be, and the larger and older the system the more difficult it would be to reduce the waste.

Q. But a reduction of ten gallons per head on the present population included in this district would be a reduction of four or five millions of gallons per day, would it not?

Q. Yes, sir, using the term " district" as covering Boston and the three other cities or towns.

Mr. Gamwell. — I understood it in that way ; that the question included the whole city.

Mr. Bruce. — Are you aware that the city of Cincinnati, in a period of two years, has been able to reduce the consumption of water by a system of inspection over 20 gallons per individual?

A. I know that they have made a great reduction; I don't remember the exact figures. I know that we have reduced the consumption in Boston more than that.

Q. It was reduced there from the year 1881 to the year 1883 from 87 gallons per individual to 55?

A. That is your statement.

Q. That would be 32 gallons per individual. Did you understand what system of inspection was introduced into Cincinnati?

A. Yes, sir.

Q. And how it was carried out?

A. Yes, sir.

Q. And you knew the results of it, didn't you?

A. Well, I knew in a general way that they had made a large reduction in their consumption.

Q. Do you say that Boston has made as large a reduction?

A. Yes, sir.

Q. From what figures?

A. Reduced from 92 gallons, I think, to about 70.

Q. That would be only 22, and in Cincinnati it was 32.

A. Your first statement was that they had reduced it 20 gallons.

Q. Now, in estimating the supply from the Shawsheen, don't you think there is rather a natural tendency in your mind to overestimate what you can get from a river you want to take and a little tendency to underestimate the quantity which can come from that which you have?

A. No, sir.

Q. Not the least?

A. I don't think that there is.

Q. What was the maximum flow in the Sudbury river this year?

A. What do you mean? This present year, 1886?

Q. Yes, per day.

A. Per day it was about two billion gallons.

Q. If you could store the water of Sudbury river it would be sufficient for the whole of Boston, wouldn't it?

A. If you could store the entire yield of the water-shed, which is not a practicable thing to do.

Q. Did you state yesterday when it was that you commenced

making your estimates of the Shawsheen river at the request of the Water Board? What was the date of it?

A. My estimates were simply as to the yield, the quantity.

Q. I say, when did you commence making them?

A. During the present year.

Q. Well, this year?

A. Yes, sir.

Mr. Poor. — Would it not be practicable to supply the Mystic district from the Sudbury or Cochituate side of the city?

A. It would for a very few years.

Q. Would it not be entirely practicable to increase the supply on the Cochituate side very largely by taking in other streams and ponds which you have not now in your system?

A. Of course such a thing is possible.

Q. Do you know whether you have secured all the ponds which might be made to feed that system in connection with the Sudbury or Cochituate system?

A. We have not entirely.

Q. What ones, for instance, have you not secured?

A. Whitehall pond, for instance.

Q. Where is that?

A. It is in Hopkinton.

Q. How large is it?

A. It is about 576 acres.

Q. Is there any storage basin there from which you have water now?

A. There is a reservoir there from which we receive such water as the proprietors allow to run down the river or stream.

Q. If you were to take or buy that pond you could make a very large storage basin, couldn't you?

A. Yes; we could make a large storage basin there.

Q. Why would it not be cheaper to do that than to go out on the other side and take the Shawsheen?

A. Because the Whitehall pond would simply increase our supply four millions and a half, and it would be but a few years before we should have to go somewhere else.

Q. That is only one pond; are there not others?

A. There is one on the other side that was contemplated as a reservoir. That is the only one there of any magnitude which was considered.

Q. What one was that?

A. That was what was termed Reservoir No. 7.

Q. What would be the capacity of that, if it were built?

A. That would be about 600,000,000 gallons, or it would give two millions and a half, or thereabouts, per day.

Q. So there would be six and a half millions from those two sources?

A. Yes, sir; seven millions.

Q. That is as much as you get from the Mystic supply now?

A. Yes, sir. In other words, if we abandon the Mystic system, we should be just where we are to-day.

Q. Would it be as expensive to conduct the water across to the Mystic system from the Sudbury or Cochituate as it would to take the Shawsheen?

A. The simple expense of conducting the water across would not be ; but the expense of building storage basins and paying the mill damages is something which I cannot judge of.

Q. Do you know the estimated expense of building storage basin No. 7? You must have some figures on that.

A. No, sir, I have not.

Mr. BRUCE.— You remember that two years ago, when the city of Cambridge was here asking to be supplied with water, the city of Boston was then quite ready to take the responsibility of furnishing them with a daily supply, were they not?

Mr. BAILEY. — I beg pardon ; there was nothing of the kind.

Mr. BRUCE. — I ask him.

A. I was not here.

Mr. SMITH. — I understand you to say that you have made an estimate of the volume of water to be obtained from the Shawsheen yourself personally?

A. Yes, sir.

Q. Within a short time?

A. Yes, sir.

Q. On what basis did you make your estimate?

A. It was made on the basis of the yield of the Sudbury supply in the dryest seasons of which we have any record.

Q. Did you make it upon an estimated rainfall of 10 or 12 inches?

A. Well, it was made perhaps not quite as low as 10. The records of Sudbury river give us the rainfall, and the minimum is 11 inches. I used those figures for a basis, and I got a yield of something more than twenty million gallons — I think about twenty-one million gallons — per day.

Q. Why should you estimate that at 11 and the Mystic water-shed at 10?

A. Because the records of the Mystic water-shed show that we have had years when we have not been able to collect more than 10 inches of rainfall.

Q. What evidence have you that the Shawsheen water-shed would afford any more than the Mystic?

A. One reason of that diminution in the Mystic supply is that we now take from the Mystic supply a certain portion of the water and divert it to the sewer. That, of course, diminishes our available yield from the Mystic water-shed, and I considered that the records of Sudbury river were more applicable to the Shawsheen.

Q. You would not feel that it was safe to estimate it above that point?

A. I should prefer to estimate it at ten, in order to be perfectly safe.

Q. Was not the original estimate of the water-shed of the Shawsheen, made years ago, that it would yield twenty millions?

A. Yes, sir.

Q. It is found practically that the rain-fall does not average that?

A. That the minimum certainly is not that.

Q. Well, that estimate of twenty millions was based upon a certain storage capacity. If you increase the storage capacity you can increase your average daily supply without any increase in the rain-fall. What are the data upon which you estimate the volume of water to be obtained in a given district?

A. It would be the rain-fall which can be collected and the size of the storage basins which you can construct.

Q. Does the size of the storage basin make any difference in the quantity of water that is to be had?

A. Certainly.

Q. Does that make any difference in the quantity of rain-fall?

A. It does not make any difference in the quantity of rain-fall, but it makes a great difference in the available yield of the water-shed. Of course you cannot get anything into Boston unless you make a basin.

Q. But is not the amount or volume of water to be obtained within a certain circuit determined by two data, — the water-shed and the rain? Have you anything else?

A. That simply gives the amount of water which will flow down the stream past the point at which you make your observations.

Q. Certainly; but when you get your basins you take it all, don't you?

A. No, sir.

Q. Why not?

A. Because, except on a very few water-sheds, it is impossible to store the entire water-supply.

Q. Very well; then you do not get twenty millions anyway?

A. Yes, you do; you get your twenty millions.

Q. I do not see it, if twenty millions is all that that water-shed will yield.

A. I did not say that twenty millions was all the water-shed would yield.

Q. What will it yield? You have two data upon which to estimate the yield, — the extent of water-shed and the amount of rain?

A. Yes, sir; but the building of storage basins allows you to store water from one year to another, so that although you may not have but ten inches of rain-fall which you can collect this year, if the storage basin is of sufficient size, you may be using water which you stored the year before.

Q. That is simply carrying it over from one year to another, like anything else; but what I want to know is, whether you get there anything more than what falls down?

A. You have in your storage basin whatever you carried there and stored the year before; perhaps more than fell the next year.

Q. I know you might carry the whole of it over, and not use any of it; then you would have twice as much; but that does not come into the twenty millions a year; that is all that the clouds afford in a given year. The two data for the estimate are, the water-shed and the rain-fall. Put those two things together, and you have the whole amount of water that you can get.

Mr. GAMWELL. — The witness says, as I understand him, that the whole rain-fall is more than twenty millions, but he estimates that he can store twenty millions only.

Mr. SMITH. — I did not understand him to say that there was more than that fell.

Mr. BRUCE. — I want to ask you one more question. What is the capacity of the basins upon which your estimate is made?

A. It is four thousand million gallons.

Q. The estimate of Mr. Davis was three thousand one hundred and seven million gallons?

A. Yes, sir.

Q. And you have enlarged the basins?

A. Yes, sir.

Q. And in order to get the supply that you refer to, you have got to enlarge your basins, haven't you?

A. Yes, sir.

Q. On Mr. Davis' estimate, you could get how much?

A. I have not made the calculation on that basis, but it would be two or three millions less.

Mr. LOOMIS. — How do you increase the storage capacity of the basins? By excavation?

A. Yes, by excavation; and the later surveys have shown that the basins would be of somewhat larger capacity than the first surveys showed to be the case.

Q. When were those surveys made?

A. During the present season.

Q. What is the excavation that it is proposed to make? Is it proposed to remove the whole of the surface soil?

A. That question I cannot answer.

Q. What depth of water have you estimated in that basin?

A. I have not made those calculations.

Q. Is there any other plan in contemplation in this city for taking a supply from the other side, namely, from the Assabet side of the city? That is, from the Concord river below the point where the Sudbury river enters? I understand the Sudbury and the Assabet unite and make the Concord river. Now, is it in contemplaion to take the Assabet river, or any portion of it?

A. Not to my knowledge.

Q. Has it been found, as a matter of experience, that it is cheaper to use, where it is possible, natural basins, such as ponds, than it is to use those excavated basins such as you have made upon the Sudbury river?

A. If you could find a natural storage-basin with a sufficient area of water-shed, it would be advisable, — that is, other things being equal, cost and everything else, — it would be advisable to use it.

Q. Has the area been considered which embraces Nagog pond, Fort pond, Long pond, and Spectacle pond, all of which are tributary to the Assabet river?

A. Not to my knowledge.

Mr. BAILEY. — Where are they?

Mr. LOOMIS. — The Assabet river, where it enters the Concord river, is about the same distance from Boston as the Shawsheen. These ponds all flow out through the Assabet river.

Q. What is the length of this conduit which you propose to make to the Shawsheen?

A. That I cannot tell you. I have not made those estimates.

Q. Do you propose to make an artificial conduit the whole distance from the dam you propose to construct to the city of Boston, or do you propose to use natural channels or streams?

A. I understand it is proposed to build a covered conduit the entire distance.

Mr. MORSE. — Can you give any judgment to the committee how long that conduit would be?

A. I cannot, because I have not made any calculation.

Q. Do you know how it would compare in length with a conduit from the ponds that Mr. Loomis has asked you about?

A. No, sir, I do not.

Mr. SMITH. — I would like to ask you how large a proportion of the water that is now consumed by Boston is used for manufacturing purposes?

A. That is rather a difficult question to answer. There is no way of deciding that question.

Q. I don't expect that it will be perfectly accurate, but, in your judgment, about how large a proportion of it?

A. For manufacturing and business purposes, probably 20 gallons per head.

Q. That is, two-sevenths of it is used for manufacturing purposes?

A. Of course that is a rough estimate. It might vary from fifteen to thirty, or from fifteen to twenty-five.

Q. So that if that part used for manufacturing purposes was taken off and the water was used only for domestic purposes, strictly speaking, the consumption would be reduced very much, would it not?

A. I included in that not only manufacturing but business purposes.

Q. I mean the manufacturing purposes, from which you draw your largest profit from the sale of water?

A. Well, I don't know that we draw our largest profit from that source. The entire metered consumption of the city, taking both supplies, I think is somewhere about 15 gallons per head, but that includes not only manufacturing and business purposes, but also includes the large consumption of hotels, large boarding-houses, and family hotels.

Q. So that you think the consumption for manufacturing purposes would not amount to quite 15 gallons per head?

A. Oh, no. The consumption for manufacturing purposes alone I don't think would amount to ten.

Q. Half as much as the Shawshsen river would afford you?

A. Well, ten gallons per head per day. I am not speaking of millions.

Mr. LOOMIS.— I want to ask you one more question. You state that the storage capacity of those reservoirs which you have calculated for is to be four billions?

A. Yes, sir.

Q. Now, I want to get at the factors which go to make up that result. How did you estimate that four billions? If you take the Shawsheen you will store perhaps four billion gallons of water?

A. Yes, sir, in three storage-basins.

Q. Now, how did you get the answer, four billions? By doing what sum?

A. I took those figures from an estimate of Mr. Jackson.

Q. What calculation have you made in order to get at that four billions?

A. In order to get at the four billions I assume that four billions is the storage capacity of the basins which we propose to build.

Q. How do you know your basins will hold four billions?

A. As I said, that is from surveys which have been made under Mr. Jackson's direction, and also from the statements which were made in previous reports.

Q. So that you are not able to tell the dimensions, the depth, or any facts about the basins?

A. No, sir, I am not.

Mr. SMITH. — How many years will it take to fill those basins?

A. They would be generally filled every year.

Q. If you were drawing from them?

A. Yes, sir.

Mr. BAILEY. — These results that you have given here are the results of examinations, surveys, and estimates that have been made by various engineers during the last five or six years, are they not?

A. Yes, sir.

Q. And which you and other engineers, both Mr. Wightman and the present City Engineer, Mr. Jackson, were satisfied were correct?

A. Yes, sir.

Q. You said, as I understood you, that 20 gallons of the 70 consumed per day per head is waste. Do you mean that that is water running to waste from the leakage of pipes, or do you mean that it is waste in the sense that it results from the way of using the water? Which do you mean?

A. Well, I mean that it is waste. I mean that it is waste from leaky fixtures, and also from leaks that may occur in the street pipes.

Q. Now let me ask if it is practicable to prevent that?

A. No, sir; neither practicable nor possible.

Q. It is the same waste that takes place in every city that has a water supply of the kind that Boston has?

A. Yes, sir.

Q. And necessarily results from the use of water through pipes?

A. Yes, sir.

Q. Whether or not you regard it to be the minimum when you have cut down the consumption to 70 gallons?

A. No, I will not say that. I think that it may be possible to reduce it somewhat below that, but I do not feel certain of the fact. I should not consider it proper to make any estimate on which to base a supply of any less than 70 gallons per head.

Q. Now, about Basin 7, the construction of which you have been asked about. Is that what is called the Marlboro' basin?

A. Yes, sir.

Q. What would be the character of that basin if it was constructed?

A. It would be a shallow basin, which all late experience has shown not to be desirable.

Q. Whether or not it has always been contemplated in the Engineer's department, and is now contemplated, only to build that basin in case of the greatest emergency?

A. Yes, sir.

Q. Both on account of the character of the basin and on account also of the unsettled question of the disposal of the Marlboro' sewage? Am I right?

A. That has been the fact.

Q. You have been asked whether, by the construction of the sewer on the Mystic water-shed that is contemplated by the commissioners, the purity of that water would not be protected. Would anything but a complete system of sewerage in all those towns be effectual to protect the purity of that water?

A. I do not think, as I stated yesterday, that laying a complete system of sewerage in all those towns would render the Mystic a suitable supply, or that it would be a suitable supply in the course of a few years.

Q. If that system of sewers was constructed, what would be its effect upon the Mystic supply?

A. Of course, if that system was adopted, the effect would be to diminish the water supply.

Q. That is, every ten gallons, or every thousand gallons, which you put in the sewer would be so much taken out of the supply from the Mystic water-shed?

A. Certainly.

Q. Does the estimate that you made of sixteen millions for the Mystic include the use of Mystic lower pond for one of the basins?

A. Yes, sir.

Q. And whether or not the Harbor Commissioners have strenuously objected in very elaborate report which they made, to the use of that pond in any manner?

A. Let me correct that last statement about the sixteen millions. I should say eighteen millions with the lower Mystic and fifteen without.

Q. Whether or not, as I say, the use of that lower pond has not been objected to in the strongest manner by the Harbor Commissioners, and by all parties who have been concerned with the preservation of Boston Harbor?

A. It has; and not only that, but it would be a very doubtful question whether that basin could ever be made suitable for use.

Q. Do you regard it practicable in any manner to use that pond as a storage basin?

A. No, sir.

Mr. MORSE. — I want to read you one question and answer from the examination of Mr. Wightman at the hearing in 1881 : —

" *Question.* How much of that daily supply of thirty-seven millions do you estimate runs to waste?

" *Answer.* Well, they use on an average eighty-seven gallons per head in that entire district. That is, counting the population 412,000, on the basis of last year, they use, an average of eighty-seven gallons."

Q. Now, you notice that at that time the consumption was 87 gallons per head. That was in 1881, and in four years the Water Board have succeeded in reducing the rate to 70 gallons?

A. Yes, sir.

Q. Do you see any reason to doubt that in the next five years or so the same authority will be able to reduce the rate to 60 gallons?

A. I doubt it very much, from the fact that in the last —

Q. They have succeeded in reducing the rate in East Boston considerably below that, have they not?

A. They did in certain sections of East Boston.

Q. To what rate? Do you remember?

A. I don't remember the rate.

Q. It was somewhere about 50, wasn't it?

A. I should think probable.

Q. How near 60 gallons per head do you think it would be practicable to reduce the consumption?

A. It may not be possible to reduce it any lower than it is to-day. We have used every exertion for the last year, and the consumption for the year 1885 was as large as it was for the year 1884. The reduction in the consumption was accomplished between '82 and '84, and during the past year the consumption has not been reduced; it has been held where it was. If it can be reduced it will be; that is all.

Mr. BRUCE. — Did you not make a report which showed that the *per capita* rate for the whole of East Boston, including shipping and manufacturing and business purposes, was 48 gallons per day?

A. On a certain day.

Q. At a certain time?

A. Yes, sir.

Q. And that is what you yourself accomplished?

A. That was simply an observation taken on one day, which would not follow as a yearly record.

Mr. BAILEY. — That was not an average?

A. No.

Q. You say all this reduction was made between the years '82 and '84; what was done to reduce the consumption down to that point? What were the means adopted, I mean?

A. It was house-to-house inspection and the use of waste detectors.

Q. The city purchased the best approved means for detecting the waste of water, and they put on a large force of inspectors, did they not?

A. Yes, sir.

Q. And whether or not they have kept that force and those same means to the present day?

A. They have.

Q. I understand you it was reduced in '84 to the present point, and has not gone below during the last year?

A. It has not.

Q. And you have used just as careful, if not more careful, means to do it?

A. Yes, sir.

Testimony of William Jackson.

Mr. Bailey. — You are the City Engineer of Boston?

A. Yes, sir.

Q. Have you made an estimate of the cost of the city's availing itself of the Shawsheen river as a source of water supply?

A. Yes, sir, I have.

Q. Will you give the committee what, in your judgment, will be the cost of procuring a supply of 17,000,000 gallons of water per day from the Shawsheen river?

A. It will cost about $2,500,000. It may be reduced a little below that for a few years.

Q. And to avail yourselves of a supply of 20,000,000 what would it cost?

A. It would cost about $3,000,000; that is, in the course of thirty years.

Q. Whether or not, in your judgment, if the city procures that supply from the Shawsheen river it should discontinue, when the time comes that that supply can be used, the Mystic system?

A. Yes, sir, I think it should.

Q. From the present indications do you think it imperative for the city soon to discontinue the Mystic?

A. I think it is.

Cross-Examination.

Mr. Morse. — What elements does your estimate of cost include?

A. It includes the cost of building a dam and storage-basin, cleaning the mud and muck out of the basin, and of making the shores of the basin of such character that the depth and flow will be about eight feet at high water.

Q. It does not include any allowance for damages?

A. No, sir.

Q. Have you made any estimate of that?

A. No, sir.

Q. Have you any judgment about it?

A. Not reliable. I don't know enough about what the damages would be to form any judgment.

Q. Are you sufficiently informed about that to be willing to recommend the city to go into the expense of the scheme?

A. I am ; and for this reason, that I do not know of any other stream where the damage would be any less.

Q. But you have not examined into this matter of damage at all, have you?

A. Not enough to form any correct idea what the damage would be.

Q. Did you compare the Shawsheen with other streams?

A. Except incidentally. No, not with all the other streams.

Q. Supposing that we had a law to-day which authorized the city of Boston to take the Shawsheen, are you so clear in your own mind that the city of Boston ought to go into it that you would recommend the city to take it?

A. From all I know now I should, unless I learn something which I do not know to-day.

Q. You would consider, however, that the amount of damages to be paid was a very important element in determining as to the advisability of taking the Shawsheen, would you not?

A. Certainly.

Q. What is the length of your conduit?

A. The pipe-line would be about 14 miles.

Q. At what point do you take the water?

A. Take the water to the present Mystic pumping-station for the present.

Q. I mean out farther. At what point on the Shawsheen would you take it?

A. Where the Middlesex canal crosses the Shawsheen.

Q. In what town is that?

A. It is in the town of Billerica, I think. The map will show that.

Q. What is your estimate of the possible yield from the Mystic?

A. My estimate is gathered from the records of the office, and without the lower Mystic pond it would be, as Mr. Brackett stated, about fifteen millions as the possible supply which might be obtained by building storage-basins.

Q. That is, fifteen millions against the present supply of seven millions?

A. Yes, sir.

Q. How much would it cost to build the necessary basins to get the additional eight millions?

A. I have not made any estimate of that, because the character of the basins is such that I do not consider them practicable basins to build.

Q. Have not your predecessors recommended them as practicable basins?

A. Well, Mr. Wightman did not. In one of his reports he stated that the character of the basins was such that it would not be advisable to build them, if I remember rightly.

Q. At all events, you are not prepared to express to the committee any opinion as to how much it would cost to build them?

A. No, sir, I am not.

Q. Do you think that it would cost half as much as it would to build the basins on the Shawsheen necessary to get seventeen millions?

A. I think it would cost more than half as much.

Q. What is your estimate of the additional supply that it is practicable to get from the Sudbury system?

A. The Sudbury and the Cochituate together will give about forty-two millions as a safe supply.

Q. As against how much at present?

A. As against thirty-five millions.

Q. How much are you going to get by the new basin which has just been constructed?

A. About four and a half millions.

Q. Is that four and a half millions included in the thirty-five?

A. Yes, sir. Call it five millions.

Q. How much are you getting now independently of that basin?

A. About thirty millions.

Q. And the additional five millions would be available how soon?

A. Available now.

Q. How long would it take to construct the additional basins and get seven millions more?

A. About two or three years.

Q. What would be the cost of those basins?

A. I have not made any estimate of the cost of them. The cost of the Marlboro' basin will be large, on account of the character of the country in which the basin is to be built, and the cost of constructing Whitehall-pond basin will also be quite large. The question what the cost will be is to be determined by investigation. That is something I could not tell you without investigation.

Q. What do you regard as the proper allowance of water *per capita?*

A. Well, in Boston we have got down to the amount that it has been found necessary to have, and that is 70 gallons *per capita.*

Q. Why do you say it is necessary to have that amount?

A. Because we have not been able to get along with less.

Q. Five years ago, when they consumed 87 gallons per day, it would seem that it was necessary for them to have that amount, would it not?

A. It was, under the system that then prevailed, but since then the use of water has been curtailed, and been reduced to 70 gallons.

Q. Do you think that no improvement is possible in the system?

A. No, sir; I do not. I think it can be reduced a little more, but I should not want to recommend the construction of works on any less basis.

Q. Have you examined the estimates made by different engineers on this subject?

A. I have partly and incidentally. I have not examined all the engineers' reports.

Q. You are aware, I take it, that Mr. Wightman stated 60 gallons per head as sufficient?

A. Yes, sir; if the consumption could by any means be reduced to that.

Q. Did he not say that, in his opinion, that was the proper standard for a city of the size of Boston?

A. I think very likely. I never heard him say so.

Q. Perhaps you may know that at the same time the Chairman of the Water Board, Mr. Cutter, thought that 87 gallons per head was the proper quantity?

A. I don't know that he did.

Q. There is considerable difference of opinion among engineers and persons of experience on that point, is there not?

A. I don't know about that.

Q. What I want to get at is, whether the present rate of consumption, 70 gallons per head per day, is to be accepted as any more determinate limit or necessarily any better limit than the rate of consumption five years ago?

A. I think it is. It is certainly lower. The only question is what the use of water is going to be in the future. For water, like everything else, new uses are constantly being found.

Q. Do you agree with Mr. Brackett, that of that 70 gallons 20 gallons are probably waste?

A. That is a matter that Mr. Brackett knows more about than I do, because he has had to do with it more or less in the city of Boston for the last fifteen years.

Q. You would not differ from him in that opinion?

A. His opinion is more reliable than mine.

Q. You would rely upon it, wouldn't you?

A. I should rely upon it, certainly.

Q. Taking, then, his basis, would you say that it is practicable to save some of that waste water?

A. Well, I don't know about that. There is a certain element that enters into the waste, and that is leakage in pipes, which cannot be reduced beyond a certain limit, because the leaks can only be repaired as found, and wherever the pipe system prevails such leaks are likely to occur; and there is also a certain element of leakage on account of faulty fixtures, which is a constant quantity. The fixtures are constantly wearing out and being constantly replaced by new. That is a constant quantity which cannot be reduced, practically.

Q. Is there any doubt, Mr. Jackson, that the wisest expenditure that this city, or that any city, can make in reference to its water-supply is in reducing waste?

A. I don't think there is any doubt of it.

Q. Would it not be better for the city of Boston to-day to increase 'its force, even at considerable expense, and try to reduce the consumption down to the standard fixed by Mr. Wightman, — 60 gallons per head, — than to get some new source of water-supply.

A. Well, that depends on a great many things.

Q. Do you know how many inspectors are employed now to do this work?

A. No, I don't. I think about thirty.

Q. For this whole district?

A. I think so. I am not sure about it.

Q. Does that include the whole 456,000 people?

A. I think so; but that is a matter which does not come under my observation. I don't know much about it.

Q. Do you know whether there is any system of inspection in Chelsea, Everett, and Somerville?

A. I know there is, but to what extent I don't know.

Q. Do you know whether that is under the control of the Board?

A. I do not. I presume it is.

Q. You do not know whether the thirty inspectors include what are needed in those places as well as in Boston?

A. No, sir, I don't. That is a matter which has not been under my direction at all.

Q. Don't you think if there were three hundred instead of thirty, that more could be done?

A. In what way?

Q. In the way of keeping down waste?

A. I don't know about that.

Q. Have you not any opinion about it?

A. It would depend upon what kind of men you have.

Q. Supposing you had as good men as you have now? Do you think that thirty inspectors to look after the plumbing in the houses of 456,000 people is a sufficient supply?

A. I cannot answer that question intelligently, because I have not investigated the matter and really do not know much about what they do.

Q. Who does know about that?

A. Mr. Cashman, I believe, is the name of the inspector in charge.

Q. Is he here?

A. No, sir. Mr. Brackett knows all about it. I will state one thing, Mr. Morse, that I have only had a connection with the Water Department for about a year. Before that time I was employed on other parts of city work.

Q. That leads me to ask you how long you have been City Engineer?

A. About a year.

Q. Before that time what were your duties?

A. Before that time I was employed on the Boston Drainage Works.

Q. You had nothing to do with the Water-Works?

A. Not for a few years previously. In 1868 I was connected with the Water-Works, and in 1872 and 1873; since 1875 I have not been until this last year.

Q. Since '75 until this last year your attention has not been given to that part at all?

A. No, sir.

Mr. Loomis. — Have you had any experience in connection with the surveys which have been made?

A. Yes, sir.

Q. Can you state the acreage in the different towns which you propose to take for your different basins?

A. I cannot, off-hand, now. The maps which you have give it very nearly. They are not absolutely correct, but they are near enough for all practical purposes.

Q. They do not state the relative amounts in the different towns from which land is taken?

A. No, sir, they do not.

Q. Will you state how those surveys were made on which these areas were based? Do you reckon for one uniform depth all over the reservoir?

A. No, we couldn't do that. We take the ground as it is found, run a contour line around the basin, and then take cross-sections of the sides of the basin. From that we can determine the best flow-line to adopt.

Q. What has been your estimate as regards excavations?

A. They have been determined by surveys made on the ground.

Q. Are you able to state the amount of excavation, the price per cubic foot, and the estimated cost of it?

A. I would not undertake to, off-hand. The cost of preparing the basins would be about $870,000.

Q. What is the estimated storage capacity of those basins?

A. I have estimated the storage capacity which can be made by building the basins to store water at a greater or less level. There is the minimum storage capacity on that plan, and by raising or lowering the pond we can make it practically anything that it is desirable to get.

Q. Do you propose to construct three dams or one?

A. We propose to construct three, unless we find we can get the storage capacity in one, which we shall endeavor to do.

Q. You do not know whether you can get sufficient storage capacity in one or three?

A. I think very likely in two.

Dexter Brackett. — *Recalled.*

Mr. Morse. — Will you state what is the system of inspection in Boston?

A. The system of inspection as at present carried on in the city is in the hands of the Inspection and Waste Division. That is, there is a force of inspectors, I think about thirty, who visit the houses to inspect for waste and also for revenue ; and in addition to this force we have in operation a system of waste detectors or waste-water meters, and in the operation of these there are employed about fifteen men. The waste in particular streets is detected by this force, who have charge of the waste detectors, If waste is discovered in any street the houses on that street are visited by inspectors connected with the Inspection and Waste Division, who find in what houses the waste is, so that the total force employed is about forty-five or fifty men. And it is not necessary in order to discover the waste, or to prevent the waste, under the present system, to visit every house in the city of Boston, but simply those on the street, or, in a great many cases, simply those where the waste is shown by the waste-detector to exist before the premises are visited.

Q. What are those waste detectors? Where are they applied?

A. They are applied to the street mains, and detect not only the waste in the street mains, but also the waste in the houses, in certain sections.

Q. How many of those are in use?

A. Sixty-nine.

Q. In other words, there are sixty-nine sub-divisions of the territory supplied by water, are there?

A. These sections are again sub-divided. There are about 127 sub-divisions, I think, in the city.

Q. The object of the waste detector is to show that somewhere within the limits of a district there is waste?

A. We are not only able to determine within the limits of a district, but within the limits of a particular section or street, and about 5,000, or one-tenth of our services, are now supplied with a waste-detecting stopcock, by means of which we can detect the amount of waste in individual houses.

Q. Does this system extend to Chelsea, Somerville, and Everett?

A. It does not.

Q. Is there any system there?

A. The house-to-house inspection system, which is done by these thirty-five inspectors.

Q. But there are no waste detectors there?

A. There are not.

Q. Is that because the law does not now authorize the Water Board to put them on, or why is it?

A. That I could not say. Of course the distribution systems of those cities and towns are controlled by their own municipalities, and it is not as convenient for us to operate them, or has not been, up to the present time.

Q. Has the Water Board ever proposed to put them there?

A. The matter has been talked of.

Q. How recently?

A. Well, I have heard it spoken of within a few weeks.

Q. But it has never been adopted?

A. No, sir.

Q. Is it your judgment that the adoption of the waste-detector system in those three cities would tend to the reduction of waste?

A. It would.

Q. Then there is one method which has not been tried in three cities?

A. Yes, sir. The method which has been adopted in Cincinnati has been spoken of. In Cincinnati they have one method of detecting waste, in Boston we have another, and in Cambridge, for instance, they use simply house-to-house inspection alone. I might say that any one of them, if properly carried out, will accomplish the result; but it is simply a question which is the cheaper and which will do it the best. Although we have not had the Deacon system in these cities of Somerville, Chelsea, and Everett, still the waste has been reduced there.

Q. It is entirely evident to you, however, is it not, that a perfect system has not yet been adopted of detecting waste and preventing it?

A. In those districts?

Q. In the whole district, including Boston?

A. Well, " perfect system "? I don't know. I won't say that the system is perfect.

Q. If, under the present management, twenty gallons out of seventy run to waste every day, it is apparent to anybody, is it not, that there is some defect in the system of detecting waste?

A. No, sir, I don't think that that follows. I would like to re-state a statement which I made in regard to twenty gallons being the amount which is wasted by defective fixtures. I did not mean to state that that was simply waste due to defective fixtures; but I should also include a large amount of local waste through fixtures which would occur if they were in perfect order, and which is quite a large proportion of the amount of waste.

A. To go back for a moment to your statement with regard to inspection, you say you have from thirty to thirty-five men whose duty it is to make house-to-house inspection all over the district, including three places besides Boston?

A. Yes, sir.

Q. If that force could be increased, would it not be more efficient?

A. I don't think that it would.

Q. You think that thirty-five persons could go into 90,000 buildings, more or less?

A. As I stated before, it is not necessary for them to go into 90,000 houses.

Q. There are three places where you do not have any waste-detectors at all?

A. Well, we have not at present.

Q. How many persons are employed as inspectors within the limits of the Mystic department?

A. That I cannot say. I think that a number of the men are employed there, but they are not employed in any department continuously.

Q. Can you tell how many of those 30 or 35 men, on the average, are within the limits of the Sudbury system, and how many within the other?

A. I cannot. Those men are not under my control.

Mr. BAILEY. — The consumption in the district supplied by the Mystic system, where you say the Deacon system has not been used, has been reduced to 68 gallons per head, has it not?

A. Yes, sir.

TESTIMONY OF DR. GEORGE B. SHATTUCK.

Mr. BAILEY. — Are you acquainted with the territory that forms the Mystic water-shed?

A. I have been over a certain part of it, yes.

Q. And you know the character of the manufactures and industries carried on there?

A. Yes, sir.

Q. And the density of the population?

A. Yes, sir.

Q. Whether or not, in your judgment, that is a fit water-shed to be used by the city of Boston?

A. I do not think that it is a safe water-shed to-day, and I think it is liable to be less safe in the future.

Q. You think there is great danger from pollution of that water-shed?

A. Yes, sir.

Q. And if the city of Boston could find a substitute for that water-shed, whether or not you would think it was incumbent upon this city to get it?

A. I think it would be. If my opinion were asked whether it was advisable for the city of Boston to abandon the Mystic as a source of water supply, I should say that I thought it was.

Cross-Examination.

Mr. BRUCE. — When were you first asked to examine the character of the Mystic valley?

A. I was appointed on a committee of two medical societies, as chairman of the committee, to go out there and examine that supply and the other water supplies of Boston.

Q. When?

A. That was last summer, in July.

Q. By whom were you appointed?

A. By the presiding officers of those medical societies.

Q. Where did your society meet?

A. Met at its usual place of meeting, at the rooms of the Medical Library Association, in Boylston place. It was the Suffolk District Medical Society.

Q. Do you remember at whose suggestion that committee was appointed?

A. I don't know. I was not present at the meeting at which the committee was appointed.

Q. Don't you know how it came about?

A. I was merely notified by the secretary that I had been appointed on this committee.

Q. Had you ever heard of the appointment of a similar committee before?

A. Yes; there have been committees appointed for various sanitary purposes by the society.

Q. I know, but for the purpose of examining this valley or any other where Boston gets its water supply?

A. That I cannot say.

Q. You never heard of one before?

A. I do not remember of any committee appointed by this medical society to examine water supplies, but we have had —

Q. Never mind about that; I was simply inquiring about the water supply. Who were the other medical gentlemen who were appointed with you?

A. There were three or four gentlemen belonging to the Suffolk District Medical Society, and a certain number belonging to the Norfolk District Medical Society.

Q. Do you remember who they were?

A. I think Dr. Folsom was appointed on the committee; I think Dr. A. L. Mason was appointed on the committee; I think Dr. V. Y. Bowditch was appointed on the committee. That is, from the Suffolk District Medical Society.

Q. Who went with you when you visited the supplies?

A. Dr. A. H. Nichols, Dr. H. J. Barnes, Dr. C. F. Withington, Dr. E. P. Gerry.

Q. When did you go?

A. It was in July of last summer.

Q. How long did you stop there?

A. We spent the afternoon.

Q. Go out by carriages or by rail?

A. We went out by rail and drove to the different points.

Q. You got out at Winchester Village, did you?

A. Yes, sir.

Q. Where did you go?

A. We went first to Waldemeyer's tannery.

Q Then where did you go?

A. Then, as I remember, we drove to Maxwell's tannery.

Q. Then where did you go?

A. Then we went to Dow's.

Q. Anywhere else?

A. Yes, sir; we went eventually to the brook below Cumming's tannery. We visited one or two other tanneries, but I can't remember at the present moment the names.

Q. Do you remember what time you came back?

A. I think it was half-past five or six.

Q. Did you ever visit that valley before or since?

A. No, I have not.

Q. Then you were out there, I suppose, about two hours and a half, or so?

A. No; we were there longer than that; something like three or four hours, I should say.

Q. That is, from the time you got out to Winchester until the time you took the train to come back?

A. Yes.

Q. Did you visit Mystic pond?

A. We did not visit Mystic pond.

Q. Have you ever visited it?

A. I have not visited the pond.

Q. Did you visit the Abbajona river?

A. Yes.

Q. Where did you go to that?

A. We went to that at Waldemeyer's tannery, and went to it at Maxwell's tannery.

Q. But your chief inspection of the valley was confined to the tanneries, was it not?

A. It was confined to the tanneries and to the streams flowing from the tanneries into the pond.

Q. You did not go to the mouth of the streams where they empty into the pond to see what was the character of the water there, did you?

A. We went to the mouth of Town Meadow brook, where it empties into Horn pond.

Q. But you did not go down to Mystic lake, where we get our water, did you?

A. I did not go down to the lake itself.

Q. Did you examine the water of Mystic lake?

A. No.

Q. Not at all?

A. No.

Q. And from that casual inspection you come here and say you think that the city of Boston ought to abandon that water supply, do you, and express that opinion?

A. From that casual inspection, and what I have known of the character of the country and the nature of the supply.

Q. Well, what is the other knowledge that you possess from which you have drawn this conclusion of yours?

A. The reports on the subject.

Q. Of whom?

A. Of commissions.

Q. Appointed by whom?

A. Appointed by the State.

Q. Well, tell us what the reports are.

A. There was a report in '75, a report in '82, and a report in '85.

Q, Well, by whom signed?

A. The report in '75 is signed by Messrs. Chesborough, Folsom, and Lane.

Q. What was the object of that investigation?

A. With reference to suitable sewerage for the district north of Charles river.

Q. That was the sole object, was it not, of the report?

A. Yes.

Q. And they made a report stating what would be a perfect system for that valley, didn't they?

A. No; not what would be a perfect system, but what would be the best system which they could recommend.

Q. Did you examine into the character of that report?

A. I have read it on several occasions.

Q. What was your opinion in regard to the character of the system recommended for the sewerage of that valley?

A. I think the expense is one objection; the danger of contaminating the shores where it is proposed to empty it into the ocean is another objection; and a third objection —

Q. I don't care about its effect down here, but so far as it affects the valley of the Mystic?

A. The objection there is the expense.

Q. That is all?

A. No, it is not all, sir; the fact that the surface-drainage is only partly provided for is another objection.

Q. Have you examined or studied the recent report which has been made upon a system of drainage for that valley?

A. Yes, sir.

Q. Does it meet with your approval?

A. It does not, for the reason that it does not undertake to provide for the surface-drainage at all.

Q. But the adoption of either system, or any system, would tend to improve the character of that valley, would it not?

A. The adoption of either system, or of any similar system, would work for good in one way, and for harm in another. It would work for good in so far as it removes a certain amount of contaminated water from that water-shed; it would work for harm in so far as it removes water from that water-shed; it diminishes the supply which remains, and makes it a less desirable supply on that account, and also concentrates more such impurities as are left, the supply being smaller.

Q. Now, what is your opinion, on the whole? Is it good or bad?

A. The water?

Q. Oh, no. On the whole, would this system of drainage, or either system of drainage, be an advantage to the water-shed, or would it be a disadvantage?

A. From the point of view of the inhabitants it would be an advantage, for, sooner or later, it is a necessity.

Q. Wait a moment. From the point of view of its effect on this source of water supply for the city of Boston, would it be good or bad, on the whole?

A. I should find it a little difficult to determine on which side to put the balance, whether on the side of advantage or disadvantage.

Q. Do you really want to leave it as your opinion that either of the systems of sewerage which have been recommended to be adopted would, on the whole, be practically of no advantage to the Mystic valley as affecting it as a source of supply of water?

A. I don't think my statement indicated that I think it would be of no advantage to the supply of water.

Q. You have said there were certain advantages and certain disadvantages. Now, I want to know what, on the whole, is your opinion: whether it would tend to improve the water of Mystic Lake, as a source of supply, or injure it?

A. I think that is something the answer to which could only be given by experience. After you have built your sewers in such a country as that, you have got to increase your connections with your sewers, and you have got to see that the sewers are always in good condition.

Q. Wait a moment. You have an opinion that you can express on that question, haven't you?

A. I don't think a positive opinion can be given on that question without a practical test, and that is one reason why I gave the opinion that I think it better for the city to abandon the water supply, because it seems to me impossible to be sure, or to be approximately sure, that, after you have gone into all this expense, you are going to have a result which will pay you for it. That would be my answer; and to make so costly an experiment as that, it seems to me, is not advisable for the city.

Q. What do you mean? A costly experiment for whom? Do you assume that the expense of this thing is to be borne by the city of Boston?

A. No.

Q. By whom?

A. Of course, in so far as the system applies to the towns, the experiment is to be made by the towns. The proposition in the first report is to assess the towns.

Q. Then it is to be no expense to the city of Boston to try the experiment?

A. That would not be, — no.

Q. You say it is a necessity for the people dwelling in the valley to have it, don't you?

A. I think it is.

Q. Then it is going to be done?

A. No; I think that is just the difficulty, that we don't know how soon it may be done.

Q. Well, assume that it is done early, as a necessity, to accommodate the people of the valley, and that it is done properly, then what would be its effect upon the water supply of Mystic lake, — good or bad?

A. Well, whether the towns pay for it, or the city of Boston pays for it, it is not an easy thing to answer as to what its effect will be. Of course, if the towns can be induced to pay for it, the city of Boston is to have no charge in the matter, and the city of

Boston can continue to use its Mystic supply, and abandon it afterwards if the result of the system is not favorable.

Q. Yes; but, on the whole, don't you think that the system is worth trying?

A. Well, that is a question in regard to which I should be in doubt. My own idea is that in any case, in a water-shed of that character, with so concentrated a population, and so many manufacturing establishments, the difficulties of keeping the refuse of the manufactories out of the stream, which is not provided for at all by the scheme of 1885, and of keeping the sewage, even after you get your system, out of the stream (which is · amply proved elsewhere), and the difficulty of enforcing connections with the system, — I think these would prove so great that the city would eventually have to give up its supply.

Q. You say "eventually." What does that mean? How long hence?

A. I mean that if these towns could be persuaded to bear their proportion of the expense, and this thing could be carried through (I don't know how long that would take), the city might wait a certain number of years, and they would still have the supply as an unsafe supply all the time. Whether it is worth their while to do that or not, I think is scarcely an open question.

Q. Supposing the water to-day is perfectly good, as good as any water that is brought into the city of Boston, assuming that eight or ten years ago it was poor water, if that change has been brought about by the system of drainage that has been adopted, don't you think that an improved system, such as has been recommended, would tend to keep that water reasonably pure for a great many years?

A. I don't know what the latest analyses of the water show.

Q. Let that go; assume my facts to be true.

A. Well, I don't think I can assume your facts to be true. I can't assume that the water is good to-day, because I do not think it is good to-day. I think that any water that receives the amount of human excrement, the amount of decaying and decomposing animal matter that this water is receiving, whether your chemical tests show it or not, whether your microscopical tests show it or not, that water is dangerous water; and whether you have an epidemic from it this year or next year, I think you are liable to have it at any time.

Q. Do you know how the health records of the cities and towns that have taken this water compare with those of the cities that take the Cochituate or Sudbury water?

A. I don't know what their death-rates are; at the present moment I don't recollect them; but death-rates are influenced by many things besides the water that is drunk, of course.

Q. Exactly. But assume that for the last ten years the health of the cities taking water from the Mystic river has been better than of that portion of the city of Boston taking the Sudbury or Cochituate?

A. I don't think that any one would receive that as a proof that Mystic water was necessarily better than Sudbury or Cochituate water, or that that good health was owing to the fact that they drank the Mystic water.

Q. It would be a fair conclusion that it was not very deleterious at present, would it not?

A. No, I don't think it would be necessarily, and I will tell you why, if you wish me to.

Q. Well, you may, if you desire.

A. Because the danger from contaminated water is either a general danger or a special danger. There is the general danger of a water which is contaminated with filth or decaying organic matter; and that general danger is one which affects the old, the young, or the weak, those who are prone to digestive disturbances. A strong and hardy population might be subjected to such a danger with impunity, where a weak one would not be. Then there is the special danger, which is always threatening, though it may never at any time come, of the contamination of such waters by the poison of specific diseases; and it is in such waters that those poisons find their most favorable conditions to develop. Now, it might be that the typhoid poison, which is always threatening us, might not get into that water, and might not get into the systems of those who drink that water; but they are always exposed to that danger; and if we had cholera here, which, of course, is rare, any such water would be a source of menace. And for that reason I say that the death-rate of such a community may not necessarily be an indication of the desirability of that water supply.

Q. Do you assume that the sewage of the inhabitants of those towns would flow into these waters?

A. Yes, sir; I don't see where else it can go.

Q. Directly?

A. Directly. When I was there there was sewage going directly into Town Meadow brook and into Russell brook.

Q. From what?

A. From water-closets; from privies.

Q. With a direct sewage outlet into those streams?

A. When I say "sewage," I mean human excrement and urine.

Q. Directly being carried into these streams?

A. Yes, and that at short distances.

Q. At how many places did you see anything of that kind along the line of that stream or the ponds?

A. Well, I could not say how many places, but then you could get exactly the number of places from the Water Board, and the precise number of people contributing to the pollution.

Q. You understand that they have the authority, and have had for years the authority, to stop it?

A. I understand that they have the authority to stop it, but I think the difficulty of controlling those things, where there is no other means of outlet, is very great indeed; and even if it were stopped, the only other way of getting rid of such refuse is by cesspools, and from the cesspools the refuse must leach through the soil, and it has got to go, either in a longer or shorter time, into those streams.

Q. Did you ever examine Pegan brook?

A. Yes, sir, I have; and I know the difficulties which the superintendent of that division has had in enforcing connections there, and in protecting that brook.

Q. The amount of deleterious matter that flows in there is infinitely greater than anything you have observed on the Mystic, is it not, and has been for years?

A. I was there last summer. It is not at present.

Q. It is not greater?

A. No.

Q. Is it as much?

A. I don't think it is as much at present.

Q. How many places did you observe during the time that you were up there, in those four hours, where there was any drainage running into these streams or into the lake, in your opinion?

A. I observed the drainage of three or four establishments, I think.

Q. Did you report them to the Water Board?

A. No, sir, I did not; but subsequently I did see a careful report made to the Water Board of all the places in this district which did turn into those streams.

Q. A year or two ago there was a large number flowing into Pegan brook, which is a source of supply on the west side of the city, were there not?

A. A year or two ago there were more than there are now. I understand that the Water Board, owing to a decision of the Court a year ago, received authority by which they were enabled to protect that brook to a degree that they had not been enabled to protect it before.

Q. Exactly, and they can do the same by the Mystic, can they not, if they want to?

A. I think it would be more difficult.

Q. Why?

A. Because the population is a denser one. You have a population in Woburn of 12,000; you have a population in Winchester of 4,500, and a population in Stoneham of about 6,000; and you have streams flowing directly through these towns and emptying directly into these water supplies, at very short distances.

Q. Then you mean to say that there is no way practically of testing whether waters are pure by chemical analysis, by microscopic examination, or anything else?

A. No, I don't say that. I say there is no positive way; you can approximate.

Q. Well, no safe way of getting at a conclusion in regard to it?

A. I don't think there is any safe way. There is no way in which you can be sure that even a water which responds favorably to the chemical test is not contaminated by specific poisons; and if you empty into a water supply (as has been proved over and over again), the discharges of a single case of typhoid fever, even where the dilution is so great that there is no way of proving that the poison is there, you may have an epidemic extending through the whole town. That is a matter which is to-day generally received and recognized.

Q. Are not the theories of medical gentlemen constantly changing in regard to the causes of disease?

A. We do make progress in that, as in other things.

Q. We are changing all the time?

A. We are making progress all the time.

Q. Do you remember an article that Dr. Bowditch published in the "Atlantic Monthly," three or four years ago, in which he stated his conclusion in regard to the possibility of medical men forming an opinion as to the causes of pneumonia?

A. I don't think I read Dr. Bowditch's article on pneumonia in the " Atlantic Monthly."

Q. Was it not his opinion that all these theories of medical men in regard to the causes of diseases were very uncertain?

A. I don't know what Dr. Bowditch's opinion may have been about what you call theories; and I don't care much about what is published in a popular magazine, but I state these things as facts. My position in regard to the possibility of producing an epidemic which will spread through a whole town, by means of the typhoidal discharges of a single patient into a water supply, where those discharges cannot be detected, — that is stated as a fact, not as an opinion about theories.

Q. You say the possibility of it is stated as a fact?

A. Well, that it does occur, that I state as a fact.

Q. That is, you think it occurs?

A. No, not that I think it occurs; I think it is as capable of proof as almost anything which we regard as proved. I think I could refer you to instances which would convince you that it does.

Q. Did you ever hear of any case of illness that has occurred from drinking the Mystic water?

A. I think that would be a very difficult question for me to answer. I don't remember of any.

Q. I simply asked you if you knew.

Witness. — What I wish to say is, that the fact that we have not heard of cases of illness would not in any way indicate that such cases have not occurred.

Q. I wish you would let us know, in the first place, whether you have heard of any, and then you can theorize about it afterwards.

A. I have not heard of any individual cases of illness from using the Mystic water.

Mr. BAILEY. — You do not practise anywhere where the Mystic water is used, do you?

A. I am one of the visiting physicians of the Boston City Hospital, and as such may be called upon at times to take charge of typhoid patients coming from Charlestown; but I think the gentlemen will readily see that it would be quite impossible for me to say whether those cases of typhoid fever were owing to the Mystic water or anything else; but otherwise, my private practice does not lie in Charlestown, and naturally I should have no opportunity to follow up such a case.

Mr. SMITH. — I should like to ask you if you found any trouble with the Sudbury system? Was that all right?

A. No, sir; that is, the Cochituate supply was not all right.

Q. Did you find the same difficulties with regard to the Cochituate that you did with regard to the Mystic?

A. We found difficulties similar in kind, but less in degree. But there is one difference, as I understand it, and that is, that the city has legal powers with reference to the Cochituate basin which they have not with reference to the Mystic, and if with these legal powers it is so difficult for them, and has been so far so difficult for them, to enforce the purity of that supply, I draw the conclusion that without them it will continue to be still more difficult for them to enforce the purity of the Mystic supply.

Q. Those are your inferences. I would ask you if, in view of the present condition of the Cochituate system, aside from the Shawsheen river, you would recommend that Cochituate lake be discontinued as a source of water supply, if it cannot be improved?

A. There is another difference. The volume of water is larger, and the population polluting is smaller, and naturally the dilution is greater. Of course, if the Cochituate cannot be corrected and a better water supply than the Cochituate can be obtained, which the city has a possibility of preserving in a pure state for a number of years, from a purely sanitary point of view, — not from the point of view of a tax-payer, but from a purely sanitary point of view, — I should say by all means have the water supply which is purest, and which can be kept purest the longest time.

Q. That is, you would recommend the abandonment of the Cochituate, provided it cannot be improved from its present condition?

A. I don't know what the present condition of the Cochituate is. I know that it has been improved since I was there very much.

Q. If that was susceptible of improvement, do you mean that to your knowledge the Mystic system is not equally susceptible of improvement?

A. No, sir; that is what I have distinctly stated, that I did not think it was equally susceptible of improvement, and I gave the reasons why I did not think so; but, of course, from the point of view of a sanitarian, no water supply can be too pure, and it is merely a question of limiting the danger.

Mr. BRUCE. — Doctor, did I understand you to assume, in your answer to Mr. Smith, that the water-shed area of the Cochituate was larger than that of the Mystic?

A. The volume of water is larger.

Q. The area is smaller, is it not?

A. The area of the Mystic, as well as I remember, is between twenty-seven and twenty-eight square miles. That is, the portion of the Mystic from which water is taken.

Q. That is it; and the area of the Cochituate is only eighteen square miles?

A. The area of the Cochituate may be smaller, but the volume of water is larger, and the number of inhabitants per square mile is, I fancy, less; that is, bearing upon that water supply. But in any case —

Q. There is the large town of Natick that is right on it?

A. Yes, sir, there is the town of Natick, but the city, as I understand it, has powers in protecting the Cochituate that it has not in protecting the Mystic.

Q. Would not the proper way to get a remedy, if they lack power, be for them to apply to the Legislature to get the same power that they have with reference to the Cochituate?

A. I don't know as they could. The Cochituate was taken years ago, and the city, as I understand it, has an ownership which it has not in the water-shed of the Mystic and which it cannot have.

Q. You think the Legislature cannot grant the Water Board of Boston the same powers over this system that it can over the Cochituate?

A. The Legislature can grant the whole State of Massachusetts to the Water Board if it wants to ; but I think, when you get the representatives of certain towns that are going to be granted away, or all their industries, they are not likely to vote for such a measure. There is the difficulty. If you can buy out all those manufacturers and clear the country, depopulate it, of course you will get a pure water supply eventually ; but you will not immediately then, because the country is saturated now with the pollution of refuse and sewage.

Mr. Poor. — Are you familiar with the Shawsheen?

A. No, sir. I do not appear here at all to give any testimony with reference to the Shawsheen.

Q. As a medical man what should you say would be the effect upon the health of the communities below this proposed dam if the waters of the Shawsheen were diverted?

A. I should prefer not to answer that question. I believe I was not called with reference to the Shawsheen at all.

Q. You prefer not to answer the question?

A. I would rather not answer such a question without giving it considerable attention.

Mr. Bailey. — Your committee, which made an examination of the Mystic basin, made a report to their societies, did they not, and called the attention of the Mayor to the subject?

A. Yes, sir.

Q. And urged upon him the importance of taking some means of remedying those difficulties there and procuring pure water?

A. That was the tenor of the report. That the condition of things, as we saw them, was dangerous.

TESTIMONY OF DR. HENRY J. BARNES.

Mr. BAILEY. — You are a practising physician in Boston?

A. Yes, sir.

Q. Whether or not you were one of this same committee that Dr. Shattuck has testified about?

A. I was.

Q. Whether or not you are acquainted with the water-shed of the Mystic?

A. Somewhat.

Q. And you are acquainted with the population and with the character of the industries carried on in that water-shed?

A. Somewhat.

Q. From the examination you have made of it, do you consider that territory such as should be continued to be used by the city of Boston for a water supply?

A. I look upon it as highly dangerous at the present time, or at the time I made the inspection last year.

Q. If the city of Boston could obtain a water-supply in the place of it that was free from pollution, whether you would deem it the duty of the city to obtain that and give up the Mystic?

A. In the present condition of the Mystic, decidedly yes.

Cross-Examination.

Mr. MORSE. — Do you know of any water-supply that is free from pollution?

A. Not absolutely free from pollution, but I think that a limited amount of pollution might be neutralized by living organisms in the water which would not make the water necessarily dangerous. I do not think there is any such thing as pure water.

Q. The question put you by Mr. Bailey assumed that it was practicable for the city to find a water-supply which was free from pollution, and your opinions were based upon that assumption, I suppose?

A. Yes, sir.

Q. You consider that any water supply into which any decaying or poisonous matter flows is polluted, of course?

A. No, sir; it depends upon the amount, I think; but to fix the line between danger and safety is a very difficult thing. I should make it as free from obvious pollution as possible.

Q. You recognize the impossibility of getting a supply of water from any place within a radius of twenty or thirty miles of Boston in which there will not be a certain amount of polluting matter, don't you?

A. Yes, sir; I don't know of any such supply.

Q. Are you familiar yourself with the Shawsheen?

A. No, sir.

Q. So that you do not undertake to say to the committee that that, in your judgment, would be free from pollution?

A. No, sir.

Q. And would be a desirable water supply for the city of Boston?

A. I have no knowledge on the subject. The most I know about it is from looking at the map.

Q. All the opinion which you intend to express is, that if the city of Boston can find a supply which is free from pollution, it would be a very good thing to take it?

A. I don't know anything about the necessity of Boston getting additional water.

Q. Have you ever made any examination which would enable you to express an opinion as to the danger of using the water now in use in Boston?

A. I have seen apparent causes of sickness in various sections of the city which would make me feel that I should not want to use the water. I can't say that I have made analyses of the water.

Q. What I mean is, are you aware of any cases of illness arising from drinking water in Boston?

A. I cannot recall any at this moment. I have a certain case in my mind, but I should not wish to testify upon it, because it is so imperfectly fixed there. It was some time since.

Q. Then you are not prepared to say that the existing pollution, whatever it may be, has affected either the water of the Cochituate system or that of the Mystic to such an extent as actually to injure health?

A. I should not want to wait for complaints. I should not

want to wait until an epidemic had spread over the city before I condemned the water.

Q. That is not the question. The question is, whether, at the present time, the water supply which comes from the Cochituate or the Mystic is, in your opinion, of a character to occasion illness?

A. I do not know whether it is or not.

Q. You are not prepared to say that it is?

A. No, sir, I can't say that it is.

Q. Suppose that the existing water supply of Boston could be kept as free from pollution as it is to-day, even supposing there was no improvement of it, do you apprehend any illness as likely to arise from it?

A. I think that possibly the troubles in the Mystic are not very great at the present time.

Q. I am not asking you what may happen hereafter. I am assuming that the Mystic water is to remain as free from pollution as it is to-day, that it is not to be improved at all, but kept in the condition in which it is, do you see any prospect of illness arising from its use?

A. I should not want to drink it myself.

Q. Pardon me, that is not my question. I do not know what your taste about water may be. The question is, whether you apprehend any danger coming from its use?

A. Certainly I do.

Q. Even assuming that there is no more pollution than there is now?

A. Yes, sir.

Q. Why, then, does it not cause illness now?

A. I suppose that no typhoid patient has happened to get his dejections in there up to the present time.

Q. Don't you think that, with all the excellent physicians in that region where they drink the Mystic water, some of them would have found a case of fever due to the water, if there had been any such case?

A. I think that I said that I did not know of any cases that had resulted from drinking the water up to the present time.

Q. Don't you think if there had been any such cases you would have heard of them?

A. I don't know. I might and might not. I can't say that I have the means of knowing.

Q. Were you a member of the committee that Dr. Shattuck has testified about?

A. Yes, sir.

Q. Are you testifying here to-day simply from your interest in these questions as a member of the society?

A. I was asked to appear here by Mr. Bailey.

Q. You come as an expert for the city of Boston, do you not?

A. Yes, I suppose so.

Q. And you expect to receive an expert's fee for attendance?

A. Yes, sir.

Mr. BRUCE. — Whether or not you have ever made a special study of water supplies, and of the danger to the public from their use?

A. I think I have given special attention to the subject, sir.

Q. Well, what? How familiar are you with the supplies of great cities?

A. Well, I have read some of the reports, that is, a very few of them. My own inspection has been limited.

Q. Your study of the subject has been rather limited, and your information upon it is limited?

A. Yes, sir.

Q. Do you know where London gets its water supply?

A. Only from reading on the subject.

Q. It comes from the Thames river, does it not?

A. A certain portion of it.

Q. Practically the whole of it?

A. I am not able to state that. I think they receive some from other sources, but the relative amount I am not able to state.

Q. The banks of the Thames are probably the most densely populated of any section, are they not?

A. What part of the Thames do you refer to?

Q. The whole of it?

A. It may be so. I rather think it is a densely populated district.

Q. The whole of it?

A. Yes, sir.

Q. Did you ever hear of any danger apprehended by any of the scientific men of London from the use of Thames water?

A. I think I have, but I am not able to fix the exact article.

Mr. SMITH. — I would like to ask a question with regard to your report. I read the report which you made with a great deal of interest, and, if my memory serves me right, you condemned the water supply of the Cochituate in the same way that you condemned the water supply of the Mystic, and for the same reason?

A. I should say in regard to that report, that it was written by one member of the committee, and, upon my motion, was accepted. I do not understand that it was adopted by the committee. For that reason I should not wish you to call it my report. There are certain things in the report which I am not able to substantiate from my own observation, but I do not raise any question as to the facts. I do not know that we condemned the Cochituate. We saw various sources of pollution there which were embodied in the report. That pollution has been corrected, to a certain extent, as I understand, at the present time.

Q. It was of the same character that you speak of; that is, the sewage, which can be taken out; there can be no question about that. You would not deny that the house sewage can be removed from those brooks?

A. I think that the character of the pollution in the two districts is quite different.

Q. That which would come from a fever patient, for example; all that you would say could be taken out readily?

A. Well, not readily; it can be taken out, I think.

Q. Does not the whole sewage of Marlboro' flow into Sudbury river?

A. No, sir; part of Marlboro' is on another water-shed. There is a great deal of time when Basin 3 of the Boston water supply is dry, and it is 7 or 8 miles from the water in the nearest basin.

Q. What I want to get at is simply this: It is not the amount, but the character of the sewage that goes into a water supply that physicians regard as the dangerous thing. Microbes, or whatever you call them, from a fever patient entering into water will be disseminated, and one patient will do the whole work as well as a thousand.

A. I think it is possible for one, but a thousand are a thousand times more likely.

Q. But the trouble lies in these patients?

A. Not alone, sir.

Q. Well, mainly?

A. I am not prepared to say that, sir.

Q. Don't your report say that?

A. It was not my report, as I stated to you.

Mr. POOR. — Are you familiar with the Shawsheen at all?

A. No, sir; only from looking at the map.

Q. Do you think that a diversion of the waters of the Shawsheen would injuriously affect the health of the communities below the proposed point of taking the water?

A. I really do not know how much they propose to take, nor anything about it.

Q. Suppose they take every particle of the water, do you think that would injuriously affect the health of the communities below the dam?

A. I think I should have to know what the nature of the country is there, whether there are mill-ponds below which would be constantly exposed; and there are a number of facts which enter into it.

Q. There are mill-ponds there. I will state that fact for your information.

A. I think if you should draw down a mill-pond in a thickly populated district there would be some objection at first to making that dry.

Q. You say " at first;" how soon would the objection be removed?

A. I think in one dry season there would be no serious trouble from it.

Q. Would it not be liable to cause sickness?

A. Well, it would be offensive, as the Boston water-basins have been when drawn down. I don't know as it would cause any sickness.

Q. Nothing more than offensive? Would it not be positively injurious to the health of the people?

A. I don't know. I live near the Charles river, and the smells are sometimes very disagreeable, but I do not leave that locality because I deem it injurious to my health. When the flats are exposed, the smell is offensive.

Q. But those flats are covered twice every twenty-four hours, are they not?

A. Yes, sir; still they smell.

Q. The Shawsheen flats would not be covered?

A. Then oxidation of the material by drying would soon take place, and I think there would be no decay of organic matter to make a disagreeable odor.

Mr. BAILEY. — They would be no worse off than if they had a mill-pond full every spring and dry every summer and those flats exposed?

A. No, sir; it would be the same thing.

Q. Would it be any worse to have the stream dried up in one season and never after that have water, than it would to have a mill-pond constantly in their midst that was full every spring and then laid bare every summer?

A. I think that would make a very disagreeable smell every summer.

Q. Whereas, if you did away with the stream, there would be one summer when it would be offensive?

A. Only one summer.

Q. Were not the pollutions of the Cochituate, that were anything similar in character or amount to those of the Mystic, confined entirely to what is called Pegan brook?

A. No, sir; Beaver Dam brook I think we found in an objectionable condition.

Q. Are you aware of the fact that the city of Boston is making every effort that it can to take both of those streams out of its water supply?

A. I am informed of that fact.

Adjourned to Wednesday, at 10.30.

THIRD HEARING.

WEDNESDAY, March 31, 1886.

The hearing was resumed at 10.30, Senator SCOTT in the chair.

The CHAIRMAN. — Since the adjournment yesterday we have received the remonstrance of Alexander Morrison and others, of Andover, against the taking of the waters of the Shawsheen.

Mr. BAILEY. — How many are there on there? I thought we had the whole population before.

The CHAIRMAN. — Eleven additional names.

Mr. BRUCE. — We can double it any time you want.

TESTIMONY OF DR. HAROLD C. ERNST.

Mr. BAILEY. — You are a physician?

A. Yes, sir.

Q. Practising in Boston?

A. Jamaica Plain.

Q. Were you on this committee that made an examination of the Mystic water-shed?

A. I was appointed on the committee, but I made none of the visits with the committee.

Q. Have you ever examined the water-shed yourself?

A. No, sir.

Q. Are you familiar with it at all?

A. Only from reading and from the maps.

Q. You have examined the subject, then, by reading and by a study of the maps?

A. Yes, sir, superficially.

Q. Are you acquainted with the fact that the water-shed consists of about 26 square miles?

A. Yes, sir.

Q. And that there are about 900 persons to the square mile?

A. I have heard it so stated.

Q. And that there are something like 100 large manufactories on it?

A. I think I have heard that statement.

Q. And that the greater part of the population is located in the immediate neighborhood of the source of the water supply?

A. It has been so stated.

Q. From that knowledge and from the examination that you have made, what is your opinion of that water-shed as a source of supply for a large city or for a large population?

A. I can only pass an opinion upon the knowledge that I have of the danger of organic material in a water supply ; and the danger from organic material is, so far as the scientific knowledge of the day extends, due to two causes. In the first place, there is the danger that that organic material offers for the nourishment of those lower forms of life which are known as bacteria, and which recent investigations show to be very intimately connected with the propagation of epidemic diseases ; and, in the second place, there are forms of disease due to organic material in water which are not as yet definitely connected with specific forms of bacteria ; and upon that basis, I should say that the introduction of a large amount of organic material into any water supply was a danger and a menace to the health of the population drinking that water.

Q. Then will you state whether it is or is not safe to use a water-shed like the Mystic, and which has no sewerage, for a source of water supply?

A. With the conditions as I understand them, I should say that it was not safe.

Q. If I remember rightly, you are the Professor of bacteria in the Harvard Medical School?

A. I am not a professor, but a demonstrator. I am the head of that department.

Q. In the Harvard Medical School?

A. Yes, sir.

Cross-Examination.

Mr. BRUCE. — Then the people who have been taking that water for the last ten years have been liable to be harmed by it?

A. If the amount of organic material present in the water has been as large for the last ten years as it is said to be at present, I should say they had.

Q. Have you any reason to believe that there has been any great change in the last eight or ten years in that valley?

A. Simply from the increase of population.

Q. Do you know what has been the increase in the last five years?

A. I cannot state that.

Q. Has not Woburn decreased?

A. I was not aware that it had.

Q. I believe such is the fact. Are you acquainted with Jamaica pond?

A. Yes, sir.

Q. That is right in the village or right near the village of Jamaica Plain?

A. Yes.

Q. Buildings all around it?

A. Not very thickly populated.

Q. Pretty thick, isn't it?

A. Not very thickly, no, sir.

Q. Do not houses line nearly the whole of the lake?

A. I can give you the exact number of houses if you would like to know.

Q. Let us have them.

A. There are 12 dwelling-houses, the nearest of which is within 25 feet, I should think, and the farthest is at least 200 yards.

Q. Do you know how many houses there are around Mystic lake?

A. No, sir.

Q. Does the water-shed run from the village of Jamaica Plain down towards the lake?

A. Distinctly not.

Q. No part of it?

A. No, sir.

Q. Do you know what the streams are that run into Jamaica pond?

A. There is only one, and that is about a foot wide.

Q. There are ice-houses around it, are there not?

A. Yes, sir. I spoke of dwelling-houses.

Q. I understand. But there are ice-houses in addition, are there not?

A. Yes, sir.

Q. Is that a safe source of supply of water?

A. I should think so ; yes, sir.

Q. No trouble about that?

A. Under certain conditions, — if the pond is not drawn down too low.

Q. No danger whatever from contamination of that from the houses about there?

A. Under present conditions, I should say not at all.

Q. Mystic Lake, you think, is different?

A. From what has been stated to me, I should think the Mystic water supply was different.

Q. From whom did you get the statement, — Dr. Shattuck?

A. I got it from members of the Committee, Dr. Shattuck among others.

Q. They gave you their opinion upon that?

A. Yes, sir.

Q. Did you sign the report they made on it?

A. No, sir, I did not.

Q. But if that section were properly supplied with sewers, and the houses drained into them, do you think the danger would increase or diminish if that remedy were applied?

A. I think temporarily it would be an improvement.

Q. No doubt about that, have you, that it would be an improvement?

A. I think not, if sewerage were properly introduced.

Q. There is no reason in the fact that there is a large number of people living along that water-shed why the water could not be kept pure for a large number of years?

A. I am not sufficiently familiar with that section to give any testimony upon that point which would be worth anything.

Q. You are not familiar enough with it to give an opinion of much value, any way, in regard to it, are you?

A. No.

Mr. Poor. — Doctor, are you familiar with the Shawsheen at all?

A. No, sir.

Q. Do you know anything about the waters of it?

A. Not from actual observation.

Q. You speak of the danger to health from using the water of Jamaica pond if it was drawn down too low : would the drawing off of the water have any other effect than to injure the health of those who drank it? Would it affect the residences there?

A. I think so.

Q. Then if the waters of the Shawsheen were diverted, and the flats and mud laid bare below the point of diversion, it might affect the health of the people below there, might it not?

A. I think so ; yes, sir.

Mr. BRUCE. — You would not advise its being done, would you?

A. I am not ready to give any advice upon that point at all.

Mr. SMITH. — Have you examined the drainage system as recommended by the commission appointed by the State?

A. I have been unable to obtain a copy of that report. I have only seen it for ten or fifteen minutes.

Q. From your general impression which you get from the newspapers, do you think, if that plan should be carried out, it would relieve in any way the condition of things on the Mystic system?

A. If it should be carried out, I should think that it would ; but I should think — that is all I care to say.

Mr. BAILEY. — The territory about Jamaica pond is completely sewered, is it not?

A. Yes, sir.

Q. And every house not only on the borders of the pond but every house in that neighborhood, enters into the sewer?

A. As far as I am aware.

Mr. BAILEY. — That is the fact.

Mr. MORSE. — Oh, no ; you are entirely mistaken when you say " every house." I live in Jamaica Plain, and have lived there all my life, and my house has never been connected with the sewer.

Mr. BAILEY. — Do you empty into the pond?

Mr. MORSE. — We do not empty into the pond, but we have an arrangement from which I have been afraid sometimes that there might be some percolation through the soil into the pond.

Q. You did not know that, did you, Doctor?

A. No, sir.

Mr. Morse. — Does Mrs. Frothingham's house enter the sewer?

A. No, sir.

Q. Does Mr. Parkman's house enter the sewer?

A. I am under the impression that it does.

Q. Mr. Perkins's?

A. I don't know.

Q. Mr. Gorham's?

A. I supposed it did.

Q. And Mrs. Spaulding's?

A. I supposed it did.

Mr. Bailey. — If none of those houses empty into the sewer, but drain into the pond, should you change your opinion as to that being a safe source of water supply?

A. I should.

Mr. Morse. — The city of Boston has asked for several years to be permitted to buy Jamaica pond for aqueduct purposes.

Mr. Bailey. — We have not asked for it for the purpose of taking the water.

Mr. Morse. — It is so stated in your bill.

Mr. Bailey. — We do not want their water, we want their pipe and franchise.

Testimony of Dr. E. Peabody Gerry.

Mr. Bailey. — You are secretary of the Suffolk Medical Society, if I remember rightly?

A. No, sir, I am not; I was secretary of this committee.

Q. You were secretary of this committee that made an examination of the Mystic supply?

A. Yes, sir.

Q. What was the result of your examination of the Mystic? Will you give it to the committee?

A. Well, the result was that we considered the Mystic supply, with the condition of the water at the time that we visited it, unfit to furnish water to be used for drinking purposes.

Q. How did you regard the dangers that surround the use of it in the future?

A. We regarded them as very grave.

Q. Is it a source of supply that, in your judgment, should be continued by the city of Boston beyond such time as may be necessary for them to get something better in its place?

A. No, sir; I have a very strong opinion in regard to it. I should consider that it would not be.

Q. Have you visited the place?

A. I have.

Q. You went all over the territory?

A. No, sir; I cannot say I went all over the territory. I made three visits there, and made a careful examination of that part of the territory that I went over.

Cross-Examination.

Mr. BRUCE. — Where do you live?

A. Jamaica Plain.

Q. How long have you resided there?

A. Over eleven years.

Q. When did you first go to examine the Mystic valley?

A. The 16th day of last June.

Q. You went with Dr. Shattuck and others?

A. Yes, sir.

Q. When did you go since?

A. I went last Saturday and last Monday.

Q. Who went with you the last time?

A. Doctors Henry J. Barnes, Arthur H. Nichols, and Joseph F. Withington.

Q. And you went as experts for the city of Boston, with the expectation that you would be called upon to testify here?

A. Yes, sir; that was the idea. Of course they did not send us there. We went to look the matter over.

Q. That is all I want to get at. You went with the idea of testifying as experts for the city of Boston?

A. Yes, sir.

Q. You signed that report which was drawn up by some person connected with the committee that was appointed by your medical society?

A. I think I signed it. I wrote it.

Q. That, I believe, condemned the Cochituate and Mystic systems both, did it not?

A. I think it did.

Q. When was that signed?

A. Well, there were two reports; one was in regard to the Mystic. the other was in regard to the Cochituate.

Q. When were they made?

A. One was made, I think, the 31st of August, the other somewhere within a week of that time. That is, the last of August and the first of September.

Q. When you made that report had you studied up the history of the condition of the Cochituate supply for a number of years preceding, and also of the Mystic?

A. Well, I can't say that I had studied the history of the Cochituate supply, but I was somewhat familiar with the condition of the Mystic supply.

Q. At the time you signed that report, you knew, did you not, as a fact that the conditions of Cochituate lake had been greatly improved from what it had been for a number of years preceding?

A. Yes, sir; I knew that through the exertions of the Boston Water Board they had obtained a law by which they were able to do that.

Q. Never mind about that; I am asking you about the improvement, not about the law. Do you know for how many years preceding the time you went there Cochituate lake had been in a far worse condition than it was at the time you went there?

A. No, sir; I don't know the number of years.

Q. Generally experience is a little better than medical theory, isn't it?

A. Yes, sir; I consider it so.

Mr. BAILEY. — You assumed something in your question that is not a fact.

Mr. BRUCE. — No, I didn't; I asked him if experience was not better than medical theory.

Mr. BAILEY. — You asked him before that if he could tell how many years preceding his visit the condition of the water had been worse than it was at that time. That is assuming that it has been worse.

WITNESS. — I knew something about it. I had read the report of the engineer, Mr. Fitzgerald, in regard to it.

Q. Was the sewage from the town of Natick flowing into Cochituate lake at the time you examined it?

A. I am very glad you have asked that question, because I wish to say that I did not make the visit to Cochituate lake; I was prevented from going by important business, and my duties as secretary of that committee were delegated to Dr. Arthur Nichols, and he wrote the report on the Cochituate.

Q. Then you did not know anything about it?

A. Well, I knew about it from the report he handed to me.

Q. You signed it?

A. Yes, sir, I signed it, and gave him credit for writing it.

Q. You agreed with the conclusions there expressed, of course, did you not?

A. I did; yes, sir.

Q. And you wrote the part of the report relating to the Mystic?

A. I did.

Q. Now, did you at the time you wrote it know what had been the condition of the Mystic supply for the ten years previous to that date?

A. Well, I knew it as a matter of public notoriety. I knew what Mr. Cutter had said about it; I knew what a great many of the people of Somerville thought about it, and I knew what every one who knew anything about it thought about it, as far as I had been able to judge from published reports, documents. etc., and from conversation with people living in that neighborhood.

Q. Did you live in the neighborhood of Mystic lake?

A. I had lived in Somerville. I did not live in the neighborhood of Mystic lake.

Q. That was eleven years ago, though, I understand?

A. That was eleven years ago.

Q. You mean you formed your opinion that you have given while you were living in Somerville?

A. Yes, sir.

Q. You examined the Mystic water?

A. Well, I knew what was said in Mr. Cutter's report and I knew what was said by other people.

Q. You have said all that; I want to know whether you did form an opinion about the Mystic supply during your residence in Somerville?

A. Yes, sir.

Q. From what people said about it?

A. From what people said about it there and from what I saw of it while I was there.

Q. Whether or not the condition of it at the time you examined it was better or worse than the time you formed your opinion about it when you were residing in Somerville?

A. Well, of course, my opinion is that it was.

Q. That it was worse?

A. Yes, sir; it was worse last summer by eleven years than it was before.

Q. Any time before that?

A. I don't see how it could help being.

Q. What is your opinion about the effect of the construction of sewers through that valley and the introduction of a system of sewerage in the villages of Winchester and Woburn?

A. I think that would relieve a large part of the trouble, but not—

Q. Wait a moment. You can say it would relieve a large part. Now, what part of the trouble cannot be relieved by the introduction of a proper system of sewerage?

A. Well, there are one or two things. In the first place, there is a territory which is becoming thoroughly saturated by the sewage which has been poured into it and allowed to run on to it, and in my judgment it is going to take years before that can be eliminated.

Q. Eliminated from what?

A. Eliminated from the soil. Of course, we understand that the ground is full of what comes, not only from the human product, but from the product of the manufactories, and it is going to take a great while, to say the least, before that country can be freed from what has been poured into it or on to it. That is what I mean.

Q. That, then, is the only trouble that they cannot be relieved from?

A. No, sir; that is not the only trouble.

Q. Let us have the whole of it.

A. Another trouble is that as yet there has been no system devised by which. for instance, the surface-water and the storm-water have been provided for.

Q. Have not been, but they can be, can they not?

A. I suppose they can be. That is a matter that an engineer would have to tell you about; I cannot tell you.

Q. I am assuming that the right system of sewerage is adopted. That would relieve all that difficulty, wouldn't it?

A. Yes, sir, if a perfect system of sewerage was adopted.

Q. Then the only trouble that would be left would be that arising from the fact that the earth has already been contaminated and the source of supply is liable to be affected by that fact, would it not, doctor?

A. Well, that is assuming that a perfect system of sewerage is adopted.

Q. I put it so. That would be all there would be left, would it not?

A. Yes, sir, to answer that question.

Q. Now, if you knew that, as a matter of fact. during the last ten years the water of Mystic lake and that supply had been improved instead of injured, would you not scientifically draw the conclusion that there really was not much danger from that cause of which you speak, — the impregnation of the earth with animal matter?

A. Yes, sir; I should say so. Of course, it is a question of degree. It is not a question of absolute statement; it is a question of degree, as I look at it.

Q. You have never heard of anybody living in that district being injured from drinking Mystic water, have you?

A. I never have heard of any case.

Q. And if a new system of sewerage should now be applied, the danger in the future would be less than it has been in the past?

A. Yes, sir, of course.

Q. If there has been any danger in the past it would be reduced pretty near down to the minimum, would it not?

A. I think there has been danger in the past.

Q. Do you know anything about how far it takes water in an impure state moving through earth to purify itself?

A. No, sir, I do not; but my belief is that it will never purify itself.

Q. But you don't know anything about that, nor do you know what the opinion of scientific people is upon that subject, do you?

A. Yes, sir, I do.

Q. What is the opinion of scientific people upon it?

A. Well, the opinion of scientific people is that the earth is a purifier, but that the purifying element of the earth is very liable to be overbalanced by the impurities that are put into the earth or put on to the earth. It is very well demonstrated, I think, that such is the fact. If I remember rightly, there was a gentleman read a paper last year before the Massachusetts Medical Society in regard to cremation, in which he spoke, if my memory serves me rightly, in regard to persons who had died of cholera, for instance, and had been buried in the cemeteries in London, and that when those cemeteries came to be done away with for the purposes of business, sinilar epidemics to the original broke out, if not identically the same.

Q. That is hardly a direct answer to my question, I think, which was, how long, in the opinion of scientific men, does it take water to course through the earth before it becomes purified?

A. Well, how long it takes I suppose is —

Q. How far does it have to go through the earth before it becomes purified?

A. I should say it would have to go a long distance.

Q. Well, "a long distance" may mean one thing in your mind and another thing in another man's mind. How far?

A. I can't tell absolutely how far; I don't know.

Q. I ask you for the opinion of scientific men, not your knowledge, and you tell me you don't know.

A. Well, my opinion is, that the opinion of scientific men (I adhere to that statement) is that the purifying effect of the earth is not as great as we have been led to suppose.

Q. Will you refer me to the scientific men whose opinions have ever been given in reference to that question?

A. I refer you to Dr. Marble's paper last year.

Q. That is all you can give me information about?

A. I should refer you to that as being the best.

Mr. Poor. — You practised in Somerville at one time?

A. No, I did not. I was a medical student when I lived there.

Q. While you were a medical student there did you know of any case of sickness arising from the use of Mystic water?

A. I can't say that I did.

Q. Have you known of any case since?

A. No, sir; I have not known much about that section.

Q. Is not this largely a matter of theory rather than experience?

A. No, sir; I don't think it is. I do not so consider it.

Q. Do you know anything about the Shawsheen river?

A. No, sir; I do not.

Q. Have you any opinion as to the effect on the health of the people of laying bare the bed of that river by the diversion of the water?

A. I have not. I should agree with Dr. Ernst in regard to that.

Q. That it would be injurious?

A. For a short time, I should say.

Q. For how long a time?

A. Well, I could not state, sir, for how long a time.

Q. A number of years?

A, No, sir, I should not think a number of years; I should say perhaps a number of seasons, or one or more.

Mr. Bruce. — On that point, doctor, supposing that each season, in the spring of the year, there was just water enough flowing down the river, at times of high water, to fill the usual course of the stream, and then every year it was bare by reason of taking away the water from the stream, would it not each year be likely to injure the health of that community?

A. Well, I must say that it is the prevalent opinion that low water is injurious to the health of a community.

Q. It would be your opinion that it would be likely each year to endanger the health of the community?

A. I should say so.

Mr. Smith. — You say that you were the secretary of this commission from the association of physicians: What was the origin of this commission? How did it come about?

A. Well, sir, I can tell you about that, because I knew of it. Last year, in May, we had the annual meeting of the Norfolk District Medical Society, and my friend, Dr. Ernst, who has just testified, read a paper on the cholera. After the discussion of that paper the water supply of different cities and towns was brought up, and after that discussion, knowing or feeling that the condition of the Boston water supply was not, perhaps, what it should be in case of the advent of cholera, I made a motion that a committee be appointed to investigate the condition of the water supply of Boston, in order to see, if it was not what it should be, if we could not, perhaps, see to its improvement. That committee was appointed, and the suggestion was made that the Suffolk District Medical Society be invited to join us with a committee. That plan was followed out, and Dr. Shattuck, Dr. Barnes, and others were appointed at a subsequent meeting of the Suffolk District Medical Society, and they were united with our committee. That is the history of the matter. It was simply and purely for scientific and sanitary purposes, for the good of Boston and the neighborhood about Boston.

Q. There was no outside intimation?

A. Not at all, sir. There was no outside intimation to me, and I was the one who suggested it. Nothing at all, from any source. In fact, at that time I was not acquainted with a single member of the Boston Water Board except Dr. Blake, whom I have known for a good many years, — been a student under him. And as far as the city authorities were concerned, I did not know any of them except, of course, the people from my ward and a few others through the city, but none that had anything to do with the question officially. I knew nothing about those gentlemen; hardly knew them to speak to them.

Q. You wrote one of the reports, and another was written by another physician?

A. Yes, sir.

Q. Both of those reports were about equally severe in their arraignment of the Boston water supply, were they not?

A. Yes, sir, they were.

Q. And a pretty severe arraignment, too?

A. I believe it was so considered.

Q. Do you know anything about the proceedings before legislative committees on the part of the city of Boston to secure authority for relieving the Cochituate system of the filth that was poured into Cochituate lake?

A. Only by report.

Q. You are not aware, then, that the statements that were made before the committees in 1883 and 1885 represented that that pollution was about as bad as could very well be made?

A. What pollution?

Q. Pegan brook; that that was about as bad as it could very well be made. And the representations of the experts and physicians called on the part of the city, who stated the condition of things as exceedingly bad, and such as would justify the report which your committee made with regard to the condition of that water?

A. Yes, sir, I was aware of that from the reports and from what I had heard gentlemen say who were posted.

Q. That that condition of things had existed for many years, and Boston had been unable to get relief from the pollution that came from Natick, both from privies and from manufacturing establishments there. Now, doctor, do you know of any single case of disease that has occurred from the pollution of Cochituate water or of the Mystic?

A. No, sir, I have no knowledge of any specific case.

Q. Is it not a fact that this filth, that theoretically may produce disease if it is put into a water supply, when it is put into a large body of water, comes to be perfectly innocuous?

A. I don't believe that theory, and that is not considered to be the opinion of scientific men.

Q. Does not the experience of Boston in this case justify the supposition, at least?

A. I don't think it does.

Q. You say that you do not know of any case of disease growing out of this impurity that has been put into the water supply of Boston for years and years?

A. I think it would be very dificult to follow up any such case. It would be utterly impossible.

Q. You mean that you do not know of any decided case that you could put your hand on?

A. No, sir, I don't.

Q. Are you not aware, also, that there has been great impurity in the Boston water system on account of the plan upon which their basins were built?

A. I have no personal knowledge on that subject.

Q. Are you not aware that during the summer season you could hardly go within a dozen rods of the basin at Framingham on account of the noxious smells that originated there from decaying vegetable matter, which is certainly more injurious than domestic excrement?

A. I have no personal knowledge of that. I know of it, as you do, from reports and newspaper articles.

Q. I know from testimony.

A. Well, I don't; I have not heard any such testimony.

Q. As a scientist and as a physician, which would you say was the most deleterious to health, the pollution that comes from decaying organic matter or the pollution that comes from a privy?

A. I should say that the privy was decidedly the worst, because that contains, or is supposed to contain, organic matter from an animal source.

Q. Well, you get organic matter, don't you, from decaying vegetables?

A. Yes, sir, but you don't get animal matter.

Q. Is it not a fact that the privy sewage, when it passes into the mains of a city drainage, is hardly distinguishable three rods from the house? Has that not been testified to over and over again?

A. I presume it has; I can't say.

Mr. BAILEY. — When you say that the Cochituate and the Mystic water systems were "condemned," do you mean that they were actually condemned, or only that the Pegan brook part of the Cochituate and the Mystic water were condemned?

A. You mean last summer?

Q. In your report.

A. Nothing was said about Pegan brook in our report, for the reason that Boston was trying to do so much to improve the condition of Pegan brook at the time that the committee did not think it advisable to stop there. As I understand it, they did not visit Pegan brook at that time.

Q. They did not examine it?

A. No, sir.

Q. I want to get at what you condemned. In answer to a question put to you by Brother Bruce you said they were "condemned." I ask you what you meant by "condemned"?

A. Well, the word "condemned" is rather a strong one. I said "yes" in reply to Mr. Bruce's question, and he used that word. If I had been going to state it in my own way, I should have said that attention had been called to what might be termed the bad condition of both supplies.

Q. Was the condition of the Cochituate and Sudbury systems, in your judgment, anything like the condition of the Mystic system?

A. Yes, I think it was, as far as my opinion went. Of course, my opinion was formed from the report of the gentlemen who went there. I did not make a personal visit. I wish that distinctly understood in regard to the Cochituate.

Q. But you did make a personal visit to the Mystic?

A. Yes, sir.

Q. With regard to the other you got the report of Dr. Nichols?

A. Yes, sir.

Q. Was not that report practically confined to the Pegan brook part of the system?

A. No, sir, not to the Pegan brook part.

Mr. BRUCE. — I understand that you thought the Cochituate was equally bad with the Mystic, — I am right there?

A. That was my personal opinion. I don't know anything about the opinion of the other members of the committee in regard to that.

Q. And that opinion was formed from an examination of the Cochituate supply, leaving out of the examination Pegan brook, which was the worst source of pollution of all? That is the fact, is it not?

A. Not from my examination.

Q. We understand that; I will exclude that always. But from the report that you got you formed the opinion that the Cochituate was worse than the Mystic, or as bad, didn't you?

A. Yes, sir; I would like to tell you why.

Q. Wait a moment. And the examination of the Cochituate on which that report was based was an examination which left out the Pegan-brook pollution?

A. Yes, sir, it did.

Mr. BAILEY. — Now tell why you formed the opinion that the Cochituate was worse than the Mystic, if you want to.

A. What I should say in answer to that question of the reason why the Cochituate, in my mind, at that time, was equally bad with the Mystic is simply this : That there seemed to be, as far as I could make out from the report, as large or larger per cent. of fœcal matter being poured into the Cochituate supply than there was into the Mystic supply. But I wish to say, that since reading Mr. Clarke's report as carefully as I could, and following up the condition of things as he reports it at the Mystic as regards privies and that sort of thing, and also knowing of the efforts that the Boston Water Board (both the preceding one and the present one) have made on the Cochituate, I think they have been able to improve the latter source of water supply very much. There has been a great deal done since that report was written, six months ago or more.

Q. Now I want to get clearly before this committee the distinction which I want to draw. I am not asking you whether you condemn the water of the Cochituate, or whether you consider the water of the Cochituate as bad as that of the Mystic ; but I am asking you whether the water-shed of Sudbury river or of Cochituate lake is as bad for the purposes of a water supply as the Mystic?

A. At that time?

Q. No, sir ; whether it is now. Not the water itself, but whether the water-shed is as dangerous on the Cochituate or the Sudbury as it is on the Mystic?

A. I think not. From what I can learn from the authorities I believe not.

Mr. Bruce. — And that conclusion you have arrived at since your examination of the Mystic last fall as one of this committee?

A. Well, I have arrived at that conclusion because I have had time to think it over and investigate it.

Q. Let us get at it. You have changed your mind since your examination of the country last fall as one of that committee, have you not? I am fixing the time now.

A. Yes, sir, I have. It is on record that I have.

Q. And solely from what somebody has told you?

A. Well, yes, sir, either by reports or word of mouth. I have not examined the Cochituate ; I don't pretend that I have.

Mr. BAILEY. — Did the report which your committee made deal at all with the water-shed, or simply with the water?

A. With the water. Nothing was said about the water-shed.

TESTIMONY OF DR. J. G. BLAKE.

Mr. BAILEY. — You were formerly a member of the Boston Water Board?

A. Yes, sir.

Q. For how long?

A. Two years and a half.

Q. During that time was it your special duty as a member of the Board to look after the sanitary condition of the water?

A. It was.

Q. Did you examine very carefully and to a great extent the water-shed of the Mystic?

A. I am familiar with it. I have visited it a number of times.

Q. What was the result to which you came in regard to the continuance of that basin by the city of Boston as a source of water supply?

A. Well, from the purposes to which that valley had been devoted, the nature of the business and the increase of business, I felt that if the time had not come it would come very soon when the safety of the community supplied by that water would require that another source should be sought.

Q. Did you think that by any system of sewerage that could be put into that basin, or was likely to be put into it, the territory could be preserved as a suitable water-shed to supply the city with water?

A. I suppose a very thorough drainage, taking in every factory and every house, removing both those classes of impurities, would very much improve the quality of the water-shed. The water itself is intrinsically pretty good in Mystic lake.

Q. Would a territory of twenty-six square miles, with 22,000 or 23,000 people living on it, and the population constantly increasing, be, in your judgment, a proper territory for a source of water supply?

A. If I had the choice between that and another territory, looking at the best interests of the people there, I should choose the other.

Cross-Examination.

Mr. BRUCE. — You only mean to say, in a general way, that, all other things being equal, if you had a source of supply that nobody lived near, you would prefer it to one around which a number of people were dwelling?

A. I should not only prefer it, but I would make every effort to obtain it, in the interest of the water-takers.

Q. What years did you make up the report as a member of the Boston Water Board in regard to the condition of Mystic water?

A. We made up last year's report, the year before that, and the year before that.

Q. For three years?

A. I think so. Our predecessors had not written their report. We made up that report and the reports for the two following years.

Q. In the report for 1884 you said the Mystic water was "abundant and quality excellent," didn't you?

A. Quality very good.

Q. "Excellent" is the word.

A. Well.

Q. The year before you said it was good.

A. Yes, sir.

Q. And the year before that.

A. Yes, sir.

Q. All the time you were a member of the Water Board, as a matter of fact, the water of the Mystic was good?

A. During certain seasons of the year.

Q. Was it as good as the Cochituate?

A. I hardly think it was at certain times. May I explain?

Q. No; let us get at some facts that we want, and then you can explain afterwards. There would be times in the year when the Cochituate water was bad? Is that so?

A. During the dry season there would be times, yes.

Q. And there would be times when the Mystic water was better than the Cochituate?

A. Certainly.

Q. And times when the Cochituate was better than the Mystic?

A. I beg your pardon; I said certain other times. Of course, during the rainy season, when these pollutions and defilements are very largely diluted, when the water is constantly and frequently renewed, then the water is safe, unless we should have an epidemic of some disease, like the cholera. At other times, in midsummer, when the water is not constantly renewed, when the pollution continues to go on and is not diluted as it is when there is a larger supply of water, at that most critical time of the year, when we want pure water, then we are compelled to use what we might term dregs.

Q. The water is not so good then as it is at other times?

A. No, sir.

Q. That is true of all water supplies when they are drawn down low, is it not?

A. Yes.

Q. It would apply to one system as well as another?

A. It would apply particularly to a system situated in such a manner as to receive the drainage and waste of houses and the waste material from manufacturing establishments.

Q. During the three years that you were a member of the Water Board whether or not you made any recommendations or took any steps towards going to the Shawsheen?

A. We examined the Shawsheen and —

Q. Just answer my question.

A. No, I don't think we did. Yes, we did take steps. We recommended that action be taken in our reports.

Q. Did you ever recommend that the Mystic water supply should be abandoned?

A. Not until we had another to replace it.

Q Well, did you ever recommend that it should be abandoned, anyway?

A. We said that the time was rapidly approaching when, the Mystic being insufficient in quantity and poor in quality, we should be compelled to seek another supply. That is in our report written by a member of the Board while I was a member.

Q. That is, the time might come by-and-by?

A. Yes, sir.

Q. If there was introduced into Winchester and Woburn a complete system of sewerage and all the tanneries and houses entered into it, in your opinion as an expert it would preserve the purity of the Mystic water for a long time, would it not?

A. I think it would tend to improve it very much.

Q. If it is " excellent" now, and you improved it very much, what would be the term you would apply to it?

A. Well, as has been testified here, in the case of any water supply situated as that is, with its surroundings devoted to manufacturing purposes, there is naturally a saturation of the soil which will require a good many years to cure.

Q. You say a " good many years"; how many years? Don't you think that, with a perfect system of sewerage introduced into those towns, the Mystic supply might last for a period of twenty-five years?

A. The quantity would give out. The water of Mystic lake itself, cutting off all the sources, I should think would be pretty good.

Q. Pretty good for twenty-five years?

A. Yes, sir.

Q. There is no reason why you could not have the Abbajona river for a new supply that would be good for twenty-five years, on the same conditions, is there?

A. You mean with additional sewerage?

Q. Yes.

A. I suppose not.

Q. In other words, by building additional sewers there, with the conditions I have mentioned, you could keep the Mystic supply up to what has been stated here, about 15,000,000 gallons, if you wanted to, and the quality of the water would be good for a period of twenty or twenty-five years?

A. That would be a question for engineers.

Q. I mean, as far as quality is concerned, it would be good for twenty or twenty-five years?

A. Yes.

Mr. Poor. — Did you ever know of any case of illness traceable to the use of Mystic water?

A. No; but I will tell you, if you want my opinion as a physician —

Q. No; I simply want to know if you know of any case?

A. No, I don't know of a case. If you want me to give the effect of drinking-water of that character —

Mr. Poor. — No, I don't care about that.

Mr. Bailey. — That is what you want.

Mr. Poor. — No, sir, that is not what I want.

Witness. — Perhaps Mr. Bailey wants that.

Mr. Poor. — Mr. Bailey is very apt to get what he wants. He will ask it before he gets through, if he wants it.

Mr. Loomis. — Have you examined the Shawsheen basin?

A. Yes, sir.

Q. Will you state whether there is any natural cavity now existing near the old Middlesex canal, in Billerica, which could be filled by any proposed reservoir?

A. I understand that the City Engineer and my associates on the old Water Board were of the opinion that there was, and that was pointed out by the late Mr. Wightman as the site of the intended reservoir, and then we could use the bed of the canal as a conduit or location for the pipe.

Q. What is the present condition of that territory which it is proposed to use as a reservoir?

A. It is sparsely settled. There is undoubtedly bog ground there, which perhaps would make the water a little high-colored, but would not contaminate or impair its quality to any marked degree. It would give us something like the water taken from the upper Sudbury, and free from the dangers which attend the lower part of Sudbury river. It is sparsely settled, and if the city took it, it could now protect it. That is the great point in favor of the Shawsheen. It is comparatively free from sewage contamination, and if the city took it now it could insure that for the future.

Q. As far as vegetable matter goes do you think there would be danger of a large amount of that coloring the water?

A. It might color the water, but it would not seriously impair its quality as drinking-water.

Q. Whether, from the conformation of the basin, the water that is stored in it must not be collected in the spring and kept through the summer until it is used? In other words, whether there is any large constant flow through that stream?

A. I understand from engineers that the yield of the river is 20,000,000 gallons a day. Of course, we could not collect all the water in the spring; but it is better, I think, to let water stand for a while before using it. The longer it stands the more thoroughly it becomes freed from these vegetable contaminations.

Q. A swamp, then, would be perhaps the most valuable source of supply; that is, water that has been kept in vegetable accumulations?

A. I have no doubt that that matter would be all removed. They would probably prepare the basin as they prepared basin No. 4; that is, all the peat, etc., would be removed.

Mr. SMITH. — I would like to recall your mind to the drainage system that is proposed by the State Commission. Do you think that that would be an adequate plan for removing the difficulties connected with the sewerage of the Mystic system?

A. Well, I am sorry to say I have not read it. I cannot answer that question.

Q. I have understood you to say that you thought there could be a system devised which would be a satisfactory protection for that system?

A. I think a very complete system of sewerage, which would take the sewage, drainage, and waste from all the houses there and all the manufacturing establishments, would very much improve the quality of the water, of course.

Q. Now with regard to the quality at the present time?

A. The quality at the present time, as shown by chemical analysis, — which, of course, is not quite reliable as showing the absolute purity and healthfulness of water, — compares favorably with the Cochituate.

Q. It is as good as the Cochituate?

A. I think it is.

Q. Then it is about good enough for Boston?

A. It is good enough for Boston if we are compelled to use it and cannot get better; but it is not good enough for Boston if we can get better.

Q. Then you think it would be wiser for Boston, when you come to that matter, to go farther and get a larger supply and better quality?

A. If we can carry out the law which we secured a couple of years ago, which will take very many years, I think we can protect our water so that our citizens can drink it with comparative safety.

Q. The Mystic system and all?

A. Yes, sir.

Q. Don't you think that it is equally desirable for Woburn, Winchester, and all those towns bordering on the Mystic system, and in fact necessary for them, to have a complete system of drainage, as it is for the Boston water supply from that system?

A. If I were a member of the Legislature I should grant no town a right to put in water without it also put in a sewerage system. That is my sentiment on that.

Q. You agree with me, then, in the idea that the necessity has come for those towns, aside from the protection of the Boston water system, to have a complete system of sewerage for their own health?

A. Yes, I think they ought to protect themselves.

Q. So that when you unite the interests of Boston and the interests of those towns, you have a pretty strong team in the way of providing a suitable system for the protection of that water?

A. If the team will pull, I think they will accomplish a great deal.

Q. Are they not obliged to pull or die?

A. They have not been up to date, — no. That is just the trouble. The difficulty is in getting them to coöperate.

Mr. BRUCE. — Are there not many wells still in use up through Winchester and all along that valley?

A. I don't know.

Mr. BAILEY. — Now, will you finish the answer you were going to give to brother Poor when you said that you would tell him what the effect was of drinking-water impregnated with sewage, or what the danger was of drinking such water?

A. The danger from our water supply, aside from the danger attending epidemic diseases, is the danger which comes from drinking this water, as we are compelled to do, during hot weather. I think any intelligent physician in practice in this city would say that if he had the choice between giving water like the Poland-springs water, to children sick with cholera infantum, or with any disease of the alimentary canal, and giving our city water, he would very much prefer the former. It is impossible for anybody to say that the drinking of water taken from an impure source at such a time is not the cause either of disease or the continuance of disease.

Q. Would anything less than such a complete system of sewerage as you have mentioned ; that is, a system that should take the refuse of every house, of every manufactory, and all the surface drainage into the sewers, render that a fit source of water supply, in your judgment?

A. Well, it is a very hard matter to supply a system of sewerage that will attend to all the surface drainage.

Q. Where a territory is as thickly settled as the Mystic district, would anything less than that make it a safe system?

A. I should prefer to have that, if possible. We might, perhaps, get along with a very thorough system ; but that, of course, would make it more certain.

Q. Let me ask you this: Is it not a fact that it is not safe to drink well-water in the city of Boston?

A. It is a notorious fact that it is one of the causes of disease.

Q. And yet every house in Boston probably enters into a sewer, and no sewage gets into the earth ; but the ground has become so impregnated that it is dangerous to use the water that percolates through the ground into wells?

A. Yes, sir.

Q. And that is always the case where there is a thickly settled territory?

A. Yes, sir.

Mr. BRUCE. — Are there not a large number of wells on Beacon Hill which are used at the present time?

A. I think not.

Mr. BRUCE. — I was in Mr. Thayer's house, and they told me that all the water used for drinking and cooking purposes came from a well in the yard.

WITNESS. — There is a well in Staniford street, you know, that caused the death of five people there from typhoid fever.

Testimony of Arthur L. Plympton.

Mr. Bailey. — You are connected with the City Engineer's Department of the city of Boston?

A. Not at the present time.

Q. You have been?

A. Yes, sir.

Q. Whether or not you made an examination of the Shawsheen basin?

A. Yes, sir.

Q. With what view?

A. The directions I had were to look over the valley thoroughly, to ascertain any possible sources of pollution on the whole drainage area.

Q. Were you also instructed to find out the number of dwellings there?

A. No, sir.

Q. The number of factories?

A. I was directed to ascertain the sources of pollution. That would include, in certain cases, houses.

Q. What did you find there actually existing as sources of pollution?

A. Of course, as sources of pollution, they would vary in degree. I have briefly summed them up and divided them under three heads. The positive sources of pollution in the whole valley number ten; probable sources of pollution, nine; and possible sources of pollution, twenty-five.

Q. That was after making a thorough examination of the whole water-shed?

A. Yes, sir.

Q. You did not examine the Mystic, I believe?

A. No, sir.

Cross-Examination.

Mr. Smith. — I would like to ask you if you have been employed by the city of Boston to look up any other water supply, and see if there is any water supply that could be made available for the city?

A. No, sir.

Q. As far as you know, Boston has confined itself strictly to the Shawsheen river?

A. The Shawsheen is all I know anything about, and that is the only supply that the city has in view that I know of.

Mr. BAILEY. — That is our case.

OPENING ARGUMENT FOR THE REMONSTRANTS BY ROBERT M. MORSE, Jr.

Mr. CHAIRMAN AND GENTLEMEN : — This is the fourth attempt to take the Shawsheen river. In 1881 the city of Cambridge came to the Legislature with an application to take 8,000,000 gallons a day from the Shawsheen. While that petition was pending, the representatives of the city of Boston presented their petition to be permitted to take the residue of the river. The two petitions were heard together before the committee at great length. The result of the hearing was the defeat in the Legislature of the joint bill which the cities finally concurred in asking.

In 1882 the city of Cambridge and the city of Boston applied again to the Legislature. The committee of that year reported that in their judgment the city of Cambridge had shown the need of an additional supply of water, but that it was not apparent that it was necessary to take the Shawsheen in order to give them that supply. They reported further that the city of Boston had not shown the need of an additional supply of water; and upon the whole subject they reported leave to withdraw to both cities. The matter was fully discussed in the Legislature, especially in view of the fact that the representatives of the city of Cambridge made a very urgent appeal, showing the necessities of their case, as they regarded them, and an attempt was made to substitute a bill for the report of the committee, — " Leave to withdraw." That attempt was unsuccessful, and the final result was that the cities again had leave to withdraw.

In 1883 both cities came again. They went through another hearing, and the result was the same. In the course of those hearings two things had been demonstrated, both of which have proved of very great value to both cities, and they could well afford to pay

all the large expenses to which the remonstrants have been put
by these varied applications, in view of the benefits which they
have obtained. The able and experienced engineer. Mr. Crafts,
who will appear before you at this hearing, and who has testified
at previous hearings, demonstrated, not only to the satisfaction of
your predecessors, the committees who heard these petitions, but,
what is more remarkable, to the satisfaction of one of the petitioners, that they were taking a wrong course in their own interest
in seeking to get the Shawsheen, and that their true relief lay in
appropriating the water of Stony brook, in Waltham. The result
of that investigation by him, conducted in the first place at the in
stance and at the expense of one of the remonstrants, was to satisfy
the authorities of the city of Cambridge that Stony brook furnished
the best and most economical water supply ; so that, in 1884, the
Legislature, upon proper consideration of the question, granted to
Cambridge the right to take property in order to avail itself of that
supply. Later in the year the necessary steps were taken by the
city, the construction was begun, and the city of Cambridge has
now near at hand, and it will get within a few months, an abundant
supply of good water from a source nearer to the city than the
Shawsheen, and at a very much less cost than it had expected to
incur. It is one of the most striking illustrations of the benefit
that may be derived from a full discussion of such questions, that
that source of supply was pointed out to the city of Cambridge by
an engineer employed by the remonstrants in these hearings, and
that, as I say, he convinced not only the committee, but the city
of Cambridge, that they were taking a wrong course in trying to
get the Shawsheen. The result is that the city of Cambridge has
dropped out of these proceedings altogether ; the city of Boston
remains.

What benefit has the city of Boston acquired from these hearings? Perhaps the most important one is that it has been
impressed with the necessity of economy in the use of its present
water supply. When our hearings begun, in 1881, it was stated
by the chairman of the Water Board that the consumption of
water in Boston, which at time was an average of eighty-seven
gallons per day for each inhabitant, was a reasonable consumption. He was just as confident that that rate could not be

reduced as Mr. Brackett has been during the present hearings before the committee that the present rate cannot be reduced. At that time the system of meterage had been used in Boston to only a slight extent, and the waste-detectors, which have been described before you, were not, I think, in use at all. The system of house-to-house inspection had not been undertaken upon as large a scale as it is now, although that scale can certainly be very much increased. That discussion, the testimony of the witnesses, the comments of counsel, and the conclusions of the committee, satisfied the authorities of Boston that they had been remiss. During the last three or four years there have been very important changes in the constitution of the Water Board of the city ; new systems have been adopted, and the result is that to-day the consumption of water averages per head seventy gallons, as against eighty-seven gallons five years ago. I do not speak of seventy gallons as a minimum with which the city of Boston should be satisfied ; I only mention it as showing the progress that has been made during the five years. Other results incidental to these discussions have followed, which will be referred to, I think, by one or two of the witnesses. It is sufficient for me to say that these hearings have benefited everybody but these remonstrants. The remonstrants are compelled, year after year, to come here and oppose these applications, to produce evidence, and make suggestions of one sort or another for the benefit of the petitioners. If this is to continue, I trust that some provision will be made by the Legislature for the payment of their expenses. I think that the city of Boston is indebted to them very largely for what they have done so far.

The application of the city of Boston is for the right to take a river which has its rise in the towns designated upon this map, made up from the confluence of several small streams, running finally into the Merrimac. The plan proposed is to divert the entire waters of that river at a point some twelve miles from its mouth, — a plan which is without a precedent in this Commonwealth. No city or town in this State of which I am advised has undertaken the serious business of utterly annihilating a river in order to obtain a water supply. There are cases in which the supplies are taken from important streams ; but in none of them has the proposition been made to destroy a river, to destroy the natural drainage system of a considerable region, to destroy an important feature of the natural scenery, to destroy a source of profit and benefit to the inhabitants along its borders, and all the manufacturing interests which have grown up by it, and which can alone be supported by its existence. The scheme is to take the whole of that river, making no provision whatever for the people below the dam, and to turn it all into a conduit which is to carry it to Boston. Such a plan involves, of course, the exercise of the right of eminent domain, the right to take private property for public uses, which exists only in the Legislature as representing the sovereignty of the State, and can be delegated by nobody but the Legislature to any of the citizens. The tendency of legislation during the last few years has been towards greater caution in the exercise of that right. The Legislature requires, very properly, that a strong case shall be made out before it will give to anybody the power to condemn private property, the property of individuals or of corporations, and to destroy manufacturing interests and industries at a single blow. That such a power exists everybody concedes; the Legislature is all-powerful in that respect; it can annihilate Andover, it can destroy its manufacturing establishments, it can send its operatives abroad, undoubtedly. But, before it does so, we ask your patient and and candid consideration of the objections that will be presented.

The great problem which the city of Boston is to solve in respect to water supply is to provide for a sufficient time in advance enough water of good quality for all proper purposes, for the inhabitants not only of the city of Boston, but of those cities which it has undertaken by contract to supply. Perhaps the most satisfactory way to deal with this matter will be to consider what the city of Boston must provide in order to meet those demands. The present population of Boston and these three other places, in round numbers, is 465,000. Upon the estimate of increase which has been shown by Mr. Crafts in a pamphlet to which I shall call your attention, the population of the same region in 1900 will be 640,000; in 1920, it will be 930,000; and in 1925, it will be 1,000,000. It will take, then, about forty years for that region to grow up to a population of 1,000,000. If the average supply per inhabitant be taken at sixty gallons, which I shall show you is a reasonable supply, it is evident that, upon a basis of population of 1,000,000, which will be the population in 1925, a daily supply of 60,000,000 gallons will be sufficient. The present supply from the Sudbury and Cochituate is 30,000,000 a day ; 5,000,000 gallons in addition will come from the new basin in course of construction, making 35,000,000 gallons ; 7,000,000 additional will come from the other basins which have been projected, making a total of 42,000,000 on the south side of the city. The present Mystic supply gives 7,000,000 gallons a day ; the additional basins which have been projected will give 10,000,000, making 17,000,000 on the Mystic side. Adding together the possible supply from both systems, you have 59,000,000 gallons a day, or, in other words, an ample supply for the population which will exist here in 1925. The present system, therefore, by the adoption of the basins which have been projected, will give all the water which the population of that district will need upon any fair basis of comparison for the next forty years.

This estimate is based upon certain assumptions. I ask the committee to consider for a moment whether those assumptions are sound. The important element is as to the amount required for daily supply. When we use these figures, 50, 60, or 70 gallons a day per individual, I think we hardly appreciate what that means. The water that is used in the city of Boston is used mainly for other purposes than drinking. It is used to water streets, to extinguish fires, to make steam ; and for all these purposes it makes no sort of difference whether the germs of disease lurk in the water or not. The quality of the water, whether it is of the best or not, is not material, although an abundant supply is necessary. It has been estimated by Mr. Crafts, as he will show you, that the amount of water that is used for domestic purposes each day does not amount to more than 250,000 gallons a day ; and, in forty years from now, when the population of this district is increased to 1,000,000, it will not then consume, for any purpose for which pure water is necessary, more than 600,000 gallons a day ; 59,000,000 gallons will be flowing in through the conduit and the pipes to supply the inhabitants, and 600,000 gallons will be all of that 59,000,000 which will be drunk. When you consider those figures you are impressed with this fact, that science may devote itself, perhaps, with more success to removing all unhealthy elements in the water in this comparatively small amount that is drunk rather than in attempting to deal with the whole problem of purifying the great supply of 59,000,000 or 60,000,000 gallons which may be pure or impure, so far as its use for general purposes is concerned.

But, assuming for one moment that we are dealing with this water supply in the mass, without attempting to distinguish between what is used for drinking purposes and for other purposes, I ask your attention to the point as to what is a proper allowance to be made. Of course, Mr. Chairman, some estimate must be made. It is idle to talk about a supply of water as if it should be unlimited, as if it should be so large that every man may turn the cock in his pipe and allow the water to run freely. There must be some limit, and that limit can only be ascertained from the experience of various communities which have water supplies, and of persons whose duty it has been to inspect the various systems for preventing waste. Mr. Brackett says that, in his judgment, of the 70 gallons per day per head which are consumed in Boston, at least 20 gallons run to waste. They run to waste by reason of defects in the main pipes, accidental leaks in house-fixtures, or careless opening of faucets. In some way or other 20 gallons a day at least of the 70 run to waste. I have no doubt that more careful observation would increase that estimate very much. But, even taking his estimate of 20 gallons, it will be seen at once that if as much attention is given to prevent waste as is given to seeking out sources of water supply, the probability is that a very large part of this 20 gallons of waste can be prevented. Boston has been for many years one of the most extravagant cities in the world in its use of water. I make no comparison between Boston and cities on the western lakes, because the nature of the systems there is such as almost inevitably to lead to waste. When a man knows that he is drawing from the lake through one pipe, and is discharging the water by another pipe into the lake, he is very apt to think that it does not make much difference what he uses, or how much runs to waste. The cost of pumping is the only cost to the city of Chicago; and that is true in regard to the other western cities that get their supplies from the lakes. I exclude, therefore, from the comparison that class of communities. If you come now to other cities, you will find that the practical experience of some of the largest cities has been that a much smaller consumption is possible than in Boston. In Cincinnati the consumption in 1883 was only 55 gallons per inhabitant, and that had been reduced from 87 gallons in 1881 ; in other words, Cincinnati in 1881 consumed as much water per inhabitant as Boston did. Boston in five years reduced its consumption from 87 gallons to 70 gallons ; Cincinnati in two years reduced its consumption from 87 to 55 gallons. In Worcester the average consumption was 50 gallons or so in 1880. These figures are taken from the reports of that year. In Providence, in the same year, it was 35 gallons ; in Lowell, in 1880, it was 37.9 ; in Lawrence, the same year, it was 47.5 ; in Taunton, the same year, it was 34 ; in Fall River, the same year, it was 36 ; in Cambridge, in 1882, it was 45 ; in 1877, it was 55. I may remark, by the way, that when we had the hearing before this committee, two or three years ago, the Cambridge parties took pains to prove that their rate of consumption was small, and that they had exercised the utmost economy in caring for the water supply they had. In Philadelphia, in 1880, the consumption was 70 gallons *per capita;* what it is now I do not know ; perhaps that will be shown you. In St. Louis, in the same year, it was 71 gallons. That shows that five years ago, before the invention of some of the systems that have been since successfully adopted, the consumption in those cities (Philadelphia having a population almost double that of Boston) was considerably less than it was in Boston.

The experience of cities abroad is in the same direction. A table of English cities prepared by Mr. Crafts, including London, Sheffield, Manchester, and Leeds, shows that the average consumption in 1870 was only 31.8 gallons for each inhabitant. In the city of London, with the densest population in the world, the average rate of consumption is only 35 gallons per inhabitant ; in Scotland the average rate is only 42 gallons ; and in the principal continental cities, including Hamburg in Prussia, Berlin, Leipsic, Paris, Marseilles, Angiers, Toulouse, Ghent, Lyons, Genoa, Geneva, and Madrid, the average rate is only 26.4 *per capita.* This review shows that in Boston, until within the last three or four years, sufficient attention had not been given to the important duty of economizing the water supply, and that we have not now reached the lowest limit by any means.

In addition to this experience of other places we have the judgment and opinions of competent authorities. So far as Boston is concerned, I should not need to go farther than to cite the opinions of Mr. Wightman, the City Engineer of Boston until his recent death, who has testified more than once before committees of the Legislature that in his judgment 60 gallons per inhabitant is a sufficient allowance. That is the opinion of a number of competent men, some of them putting the estimate very much below that.

The point for which I am contending is, that, for the purpose of an estimate, 60 gallons per inhabitant is a sufficiently liberal allowance, and that even that includes, upon the basis of Mr. Brackett's statement, at least ten gallons of waste. It is not right or expedient for the city of Boston to make any of its calculations or provisions upon any larger allowance than that. If it does so they are excessive. Neither the Water Board nor the city government would be justified, in the face of the experience of other cities, and of the positive and clear opinions of competent engineers, in making provision for the future upon any larger computation than 60 gallons per inhabitant. If you assume that as being the proper allowance, you will have as the result the figures that I have given, showing that so far as supply goes the city of Boston will have sufficient for the next forty years.

It is interesting to note that the city has several sources of supply already authorized by law. As a matter of convenience to the committee I will refer to the acts under which the city has from time to time obtained authority to take water.

Originally, as perhaps the committee may not know, the water supply of Boston came from Jamaica pond, and that was the only source of supply until Lake Cochituate was taken. When at last that was secured it was thought that there was an ample supply for an indefinite length of time, and the city was illuminated, processions went about the streets, and the President of the United States and the Governor-General of Canada came here to celebrate the introduction of an unlimited quantity of pure water. But in the course of time that was found insufficient; and a supply from the Sudbury was authorized by the Act of

1872, Chap. 177. The city of Charlestown was annexed to Boston in 1874, and it brought with it, among other blessings, the Mystic water supply, which it had obtained under acts authorizing that city to take the water. There is also an act, to which no reference has been made during this hearing, authorizing the town of Brookline to sell water to the city of Boston. That is Chap. 127 of the Acts of 1875, being the act under which the town of Brookline was authorized to take water from Charles river. So that it is a fact that if any great water famine should come, or if any pestilence should be threatened by reason of the use of any one of these different systems, the city of Boston has authority at present to obtain from Brookline the entire supply from the Charles, or as much as it needs.

Mr. BAILEY. — No; Brookline is only authorized to take 1,500,000 gallons. All we can buy from her is what she has within that quantity that she does not want.

Mr. MORSE. — I am not prepared to dispute that statement, if you say that is the precise limit. I do not doubt, however, that it would be perfectly easy to obtain from the Legislature authority to take more water from Charles river.

Mr. BAILEY. — We should have more mill-owners objecting on the Charles river than we would on the Shawsheen.

Mr. MORSE. — Not at all. At all events their position would not be as strong as ours, since nobody would propose actually to annihilate the Charles river. The reason why our opposition has been pretty steadfast so far, and pretty successful, also, let me suggest, has been because this plan would annihilate the river, — take the whole of it. I said, and I say again, that the Legislature would be much more likely to increase the authority of the town of Brookline, if it should become necessary for the city of Boston to take water from Charles river, a large river, than to allow the entire waters of the Shawsheen to be used.

There is plenty of legislation at present authorizing the city to get an abundant water supply. There is no doubt that the city is entirely safe against any sudden famine in that direction. The question of quality is a separate question, which I will deal with presently, but, as far as quantity goes, there is at present, in the systems which are now authorized, ample security against a water famine ; and if there is not, I maintain that through a connection which may be easily made with the Brookline water pipes, — indeed, has been made, I believe, on some occasions, — it is possible for the city of Boston to get water from Charles river.

Mr. BAILEY. — The connection which has been made will not give us the quantity we want, because those are only small pipes.

Mr. MORSE. — Then you can put in larger ones.

Mr. BAILEY. — Certainly, we can do all those things.

Mr. MORSE. — Now, I think I have established the proposition pretty well that there is enough water for the next forty years for all this district. There remains the question whether its quality can be kept sufficiently good for use. I may start with the assumption, Mr. Chairman, that whatever may be the serious polluting influences at work upon any or all of these sources of water supply, — for I am not here to deny that they exist, or that they are serious, or that they need the constant and vigilant oversight of the Water Board and of the other authorities of the city of Boston, — still I may assume that if the quality of the water can be kept as good as it is now, there is no reason to apprehend any danger to the health of the inhabitants who use it, and there is no especial objection to drinking the water. There is no such thing as absolutely pure water in its natural state. No rain falls anywhere which does not come in contact with substances tending more or less to pollute it ; and even should the city of Boston go to the Shawsheen, which, I will agree, merits all the commendations which Mr. Plympton has given it as being the nearest to absolute purity which can be found, still, in the course of time, there will be more or less disturbing influences at work to affect the quality of the water. But, Mr. Chairman, no city or town should give up an expensive system which it has entered upon, after consideration and at great cost, without very great effort to relieve itself from the difficulties. The city of Boston has never admitted that it is not possible to protect its water supply. Whatever my brother may think it necessary to say or to offer to prove in this hearing, the city of Boston does not go to its customers and tell them that its water is not fit to drink, and that it is unhealthy to use it. The Legislature has been very liberal in respect to laws on this subject. The Public Statutes, Chap. 80, Secs. 96 to 98, contain provisions in regard to the pollution of streams or ponds, the water of which is used for drinking purposes. It is not necessary for me to read them; they are familiar to some, at least, of the committee. I only refer to them as showing that as far as the law is concerned there is ample power conferred upon the authorities interested in the protection of any water supply to prosecute persons who defile the streams. The city of Boston, moreover, obtained in 1875, by Chap. 202 of the acts of that year, authority to construct a sewer in the Mystic valley for the purpose of taking the drainage and sewage in that region, and so preventing contamination of the water supply there, and in that act is a distinct provision, that all parties discharging offensive sewage shall be compelled to discharge it into this sewer. The city of Boston is clearly bound to enforce that law; and if there are people who are discharging sewage into the Abbajona river, or anywhere else, in the manner that has been described by some of the witnesses for the city of Boston, they are doing so in violation of the Act of 1875, and can be prosecuted under it by the able and zealous City Solicitor. Moreover, in the recent decision of our Supreme Court, in the case of Martin v. Gleason, 139 Mass., 183, the court laid down the broad and important proposition that the city, in taking rights, whether of land or of water, in connection with providing a water supply, is entitled to take prescriptive rights to defile or to pollute streams.

Mr. BAILEY. — I know you do not mean to misstate the law, and I would like to say one word.

Mr. MORSE. — I do not object in the least.

Mr. BAILEY.—We have not taken any water rights on the Mystic; we have on the other streams.

Mr. MORSE. — Why don't you ask the Legislature for the right to take them?

Mr. BAILEY. — Because we don't know that it would be worth anything if we got it.

Mr. MORSE. — The question whether it would be worth anything is one question; whether you have the right or can get it is another.

Mr. BAILEY. — That is what I am calling your attention to.

Mr. MORSE. — That is not the subject I am talking about.

Mr. BAILEY. — You said we had a right to protect our water rights, and I was simply saying we had not taken any.

Mr. MORSE. — The decision I have cited refers to the Sudbury. If my brother says that the city has not the authority at present to take the same rights on the Mystic system, I shall of course accept his statement of the law, as he is more familiar with it. But I say that the Legislature would not hesitate, in my opinion, to give the city of Boston the same right upon that side that it has upon the other. I do not know that any such rights exist. It has not been shown at this hearing that there are any prescriptive rights to pollute the Mystic or its source of supply; but, even if that is so, there cannot be any doubt that the Legislature would give the city the same power over those rights that, by the decision in this case of Martin v. Gleason, the court has held that the city of Boston has over the rights on the Sudbury.

In addition to the attempts that have been made by the Legislature in its general laws, and by the city of Boston in its special Act of 1875, we have, as has been pointed out to you, the report of the Drainage Commission of this year, in which that commission advises the adoption of a large and comprehensive system for the drainage of the Mystic valley. It recommends it on the ground that it will benefit the towns which will use it, and will also protect the water supply. Some difference of opinion has been expressed among the scientific gentlemen here, as to the effect of the adoption of that system upon the water supply from the Mystic. Dr. Blake, who brings to this subject the largest practical experience of any of the physicians who have testified before you, says that in his opinion if that system should be carried out it would materially and sensibly affect the quality of the water of the Mystic system. Now, it is too much, it seems to me, to assume that a Commission which has investigated that subject as fully as did that Commission, is not going to have the serious ear and attention of the Legislature. It may not be that this year or that next year the system will be adopted, but nobody can read that report without being impressed with its general thoroughness and wisdom, and there cannot be a doubt that in the course of a comparatively short time its main recommendation will be adopted, and the Mystic valley is perhaps the first place in which its plans will be carried out. Can anybody doubt that the present system of sewerage which the city of Boston itself has adopted, and the adoption, within a reasonable time, of the plans of this Drainage Commission, will keep the quality of the Mystic water at least as good as it it is to-day? If not, if the experience of the next ten or twelve years should show that that cannot be done, and if by that time the additional supply which can be obtained from the Sudbury alone shall prove insufficient for the population which will then exist (although upon these tables and figures I do not understand that it will be so), the city may have to meet the problem of what additional supply shall be had. When it comes to deal with that, however, it will do so, I submit, upon altogether larger grounds than have been presented here. If the city shall have eventually to take any other source of supply than what it is now authorized to take, it will, in the judgment of those men who have given the most thought to this matter, go to some considerable distance, perhaps to Lake Winnipiseogee ; at all events, to some source of supply which shall be ample for a long period and where the quality of the water will be permanently good. Indeed, if this act should be passed by the Legislature it would be, in my judgment, impossible to induce the city government of Boston to incur the expenditure of the four or five millions of dollars which this system would cost, in the face of the overwhelming testimony that would be produced of the temporary character of the relief that the act would give.

I have taken your time, Mr. Chairman, in discussing the reasons why, in the interests of the city of Boston and of that large community, and of those large industries for which the city of Boston stands, it is not desirable that the Legislature should pass this act. It is not a kindness to the city of Boston to help it to a course of action which will prove in the end very false economy. The passage of such an act, it may be urged, will do no harm, if no action is taken. It will do this harm, that it would undoubtedly lead to agitation, and there would be, of course, the possibility of some city government adopting the plan. It is not in the interest of the future prosperity of this city and this large population that expenditures in this direction should be encouraged.

There is another side to this question, Mr. Chairman. Even if the needs of Boston were great, and it were shown that something should be done in the way of procuring an additional water supply, I should still submit with confidence that these needs were not so great as that any injustice should be done to the large interests which are represented at Andover. This is not a case of disposing of manufacturing establishments alone. It has been sometimes rather flippantly said in the Legislature that, if a community needs a water supply for domestic purposes, the interests of the manufacturer and the mill-owner should not be regarded at all. In one sense that is true. If the safety and the life of human beings are on one side, and the mere question of carrying on certain business enterprises is upon the other, of course the last should give way. But if the necessity does not exist in the sense in which it is represented to exist, and if it be shown that the damage to be done is one that cannot be met by compensation in dollars and cents, you have then a very different problem to solve. The manufacturing interests upon the line of this stream are large. They represent a great many hundreds of thousands of dollars; they give employment to a great many people, — several hundreds of them, — who have found their homes in that valley, and they make use of the water of this river not simply for making steam or for water-power, but for bleaching and washing purposes, where pure water, clean water, is necessary, and no compensation in money can make good that loss to them. The bill, if it should be passed and accepted by the city of Boston, would take away the life-blood, so to speak, of large enterprises, so that those enterprises themselves must go down. There are the establishments of Mr. Bradlee, at Ballardvale, to which your attention will be called; the establishment of the Smith & Dove Manufacturing Company, lower down upon the stream, and the establishment of Mr. Stevens. At Mr. Bradlee's mills a quality of flannels is made which has a reputation all over the world, identified with that locality as the " Ballardvale Flannels; " at the Smith & Dove establishment twine and shoe-thread are made; at Mr. Stevens's woollen goods, — all of them requiring the water of the Shawsheen as essential to their business. There are employed at Mr. Bradlee's establishment 200 operatives; at Smith & Dove's, 350; at Mr. Stevens's, 200; and these operatives, who have found pleasant and profitable employment at these mills, must all be driven away and the establishments themselves closed. The question is, whether Massachusetts is prepared to adopt legislation which will annihilate three important industries like these.

But it is not simply the destruction of manufacturing establishments ; it is taking away from the region some twelve miles in length of a natural watercourse, a stream which gives beauty and picturesqueness to the landscape, which is the natural drainage for the territory, and which, as Dr. Gerry and some of the other physicians have said, is essential to the health of the people. Is it not more important to keep for these people a stream which is essential to their health and life than it is, upon the theory that the present water systems of Boston may not be sufficient, or of a proper quality, in ten or fifteen years from now, to take it away from them and give it to the city of Boston ?

These considerations have been so often presented in previous years that I shall take up no more of your time in stating them. Indeed, I should not have said as much as this if it were not that the city of Boston appears this year to be somewhat in earnest in this application. In former years it has seemed to be masquerading before the Legislature. When the city of Cambridge came in and asked for the Shawsheen, and the city of Boston turned up and asked for it also, it looked very much like an attempt to " euchre" the city of Cambridge. It succeeded in that very well in those years. The city of Boston then wanted to sell water to the city of Cambridge, and proposed to sell it.

Mr. BAILEY. — Oh, no, nothing of the kind.

Mr. MORSE. — It proposed to sell water to the city of Cambridge, and it said in the first hearing that took place here that it had sufficient water to supply Cambridge ; and part of the argument which I had the honor of submitting to the committee five years ago was that the city of Boston had sufficient water to supply itself and the city of Cambridge, and that it had legal authority to sell.

Mr. BAILEY. — That was your argument, but we never said so.

Mr. MORSE. — That was my argument, and a very convincing one, so the committee thought. For two or three years the city of Boston came up before the Legislature really looking after the

city of Cambridge, to see that Cambridge should not get the
Shawsheen. Boston, for a while, was really our ally in defeating
the application of the city of Cambridge. But now, as I have
said, it seems to have come here in sober earnest, and it has got
these medical gentlemen, who spent two or three hours one day
last summer upon the Mystic, to come before this committee, and
advise them that it is essential that the city of Boston should have
the Shawsheen.

Mr. BAILEY. — Perhaps I went too far in one statement I made.
I do not want to give the impression that we have not any right
to protect and purify the Mystic more than we have done. What
I mean is, that when the city of Charlestown took its water supply it
simply took the waters of the Mystic upper pond, and did not take
any water-rights ; therefore, the decision of the Supreme Court in
Martin v. Gleason will not apply to that case.

Mr. MORSE. — You reserve the right, I suppose, to claim hereafter before the court that it does apply ?

Mr. BAILEY. — I should not want to waive it.

Adjourned to Thursday, at 10.30 A.M.

FOURTH HEARING.

THURSDAY, April 1, 1886.

The Committee met at 10.30, Senator SCOTT in the chair, and the remonstrants proceeded to put in their evidence.

TESTIMONY OF J. PUTNAM BRADLEE.

Mr. BRUCE. — Mr. Bradlee, you are a resident of Boston?

A. Yes, sir.

Q. And have been for how many years?

A. Ever since 1817.

Q. Are you the owner of the Ballardvale mills?

A. Yes, sir.

Q. And of water rights upon the Shawsheen river?

A. Yes, sir.

Q. How long have you been connected with those mills?

A. Ever since 1841.

Q. Are you now the entire owner of the Ballardvale mills?

A. Yes, sir.

Q. And have been for how many years?

A. I have had the entire control since 1852, and the actual possession of the property since 1866.

Q. What goods do you manufacture there?

A. Fine white flannels.

Q. Are there any others of the same kind manufactured in the country?

A. Mr. Gilbert, of Ware, manufactures something similar, in fact the same thing. We are rivals to some extent. We make only whites; Mr. Gilbert makes a few whites, the rest colored goods.

Q. What proportion of all the goods of that class used in the United States are manufactured by you at Ballardvale?

A. Well, sir, all excepting what Mr. Gilbert makes. There is no other manufacturer.

Q. How does the manufacture of these goods compare with yours in quantity?

A. I suppose he is running about three sets now.

Q. And how many do you run?

A. We call our sets seventeen.

Q. Practically, do you manufacture about four-fifths of the entire product of that class of goods in the country?

A. Yes, sir, I should say we manufacture four-fifths.

Q. You use the water of the Shawsheen both for power and for scouring your goods, do you not?

A. Yes, sir.

Q. And whether or not purity of water is a necessity in the manufacture of your goods?

A. Pure water is essential. Without it we could not manufacture those goods.

Q. Are your goods known as the Ballardvale Flannels?

A. Yes, sir.

Q. And how long have they been known as the Ballardvale Flannels?

A. My predecessor, the one who established the mill, began in 1836, and he was the first man in the country that ever made goods by double-spinning.

Q. Whether the trade-mark is of very great value to you?

A. Yes, sir, everything to me.

Q. Whether or not it would be possible to carry on the manufacture of those flannels at your mill provided this request of the city of Boston to take all the water of the Shawsheen should be granted?

A. Well, sir, that is an end of me.

Q. It ends the mill, does it not?

A. It ends my mill for this kind of work.

Q. Do you know of any other kind of work that could be put in there in competition with the great mills of Lowell and Lawrence?

A. No, sir, I do not.

Q. In other words, you would abandon the manufacture at that place entirely if the river was taken by the city?

A. If that was taken away from me.

Q. What is the population of Ballardvale?

A. Between eight and nine hundred now. Eight hundred, certainly.

Q. How many people have you in your employ?

A. Two hundred.

Q. What is the value of the annual product of your mill?

A. About four hundred thousand dollars. If we had good times we might get up to half a million. As I have stated before, between four and five hundred thousand dollars. It certainly ought to be four hundred thousand in a good season and fair prices.

Mr. GAMWELL. — I understand that to mean gross.

A. Yes, sir, gross.

Mr. BRUCE. — What is the character of the population that you have collected around your mill?

A. I consider them first class.

Q. Have you a large number of mechanics there whom you have induced to come into your employ, and who have purchased property at Ballardvale, and own their houses?

A. A great many of them own their own houses.

Q. What would be the effect of the destruction of this water power on the property of these men who are in your employ?

A. I should think that to leave all those flats bare would have the effect to create malaria and make it very unhealthy.

Q. Would those people be able to get employment in Ballardvale if your mill was destroyed?

A. I cannot tell what my mill might be turned into by somebody else, but these people I have got have been educated to nothing else, and have been with me so long that any other business might not be suitable to them.

Q. Would it not very materially injure the value of the property owned by those employés of yours?

A. It seems so, decidedly.

Q. How many churches are there in that little village?

A. Three, sir.

Q. What have you done towards building them up? .

A. I have helped them whenever they wanted me to, in fitting them up.

Q. All of them?

A. All of them; yes, sir.

Q. These churches are of what denominations?

A. Methodist, Orthodox, and Catholic.

Q. Is there a library there?

A. Yes, sir.

Q. How large?

A. 1,500 volumes.

Q. Who furnished it?

A. I did.

Q. Open to all the people of that village?

A. Yes, sir.

Q. Free?

A. Free.

Q. Have you a hall there?

A. Yes, sir.

Q. Who furnished it?

A. I did.

Q. To whom is it open?

A. It is open to the people for lectures, concerts, or anything.

Q. And free?

A. Free, sir.

Q. You furnish courses of lectures?

A. Yes, sir.

Q. Free?

A. Yes, sir.

Q. And are there other things that you have procured and furnished for your employés there to which I have not alluded?

A. Yes, sir.

Q. What?

A. Bowling alley and pool-table.

Q. And those are free also?

A. Yes, sir.

Q. You have never had any strike there at your mill, have you, captain?

A. No, sir.

Q. You have been for a long time, have you not, in the city government of Boston?

A. Yes, sir. I served the city of Boston twenty-one years.

Q. Whether or not you have considered the question of a water supply for the city of Boston?

A. Yes, sir, as it has come along from time to time.

Q. In your opinion, is it good policy on the part of Boston to go to the Shawsheen river and take a small supply like that?

A. Decidedly not.

Q. Do you think the people of Boston would favor such a scheme?

A. I should hardly think they would if they understood it thoroughly.

Q. Is there anything else you want to say to the Committee in opposition to the request of the city of Boston to take this water power of yours?

A. Nothing, except in general terms.

Q. Well, you can say anything you want to in general terms?

A. I have said nearly all I wanted to say in answer to the questions you have put to me. I have built up that property and have been connected with it so many years that I should like to keep it the rest of my days, if I could. I should think the Committee would feel that it was pretty hard to destroy a whole village like that.

Cross-Examination.

Mr. BAILEY. — Capt. Bradlee, what was the value of your product in 1882?

A. I can't remember so long back.

Q. Can you give it to me in 1883?

A. I can't remember back.

Q. Can you give it in 1884, the year before last?

A. I don't remember it.

Q. You can furnish from your books the gross value of it for the last three years?

A. Yes, sir; I can.

Q. Will you do so by-and-by?

A. Yes, sir.

Q. What is the water used for by you in your mill?

A. When we have enough of it we use it for power; when there is not enough of it, we use it for steam, and for scouring purposes.

Q. Those are the three purposes?

A. The first thing we look after is water for scouring. If there is an abundance of water, then we run the whole mill by water power. As I explained in my previous testimony before the committee some years ago, we try to keep our head up so that we shall have cold water, and then when the water falls we take off a wheel, and when it still further falls we take off another ; so we nurse the water from time to time to make it piece out.

Q. Yes ; but those are the three purposes for which you use it — for steam, for water power, and for scouring?

A. Yes, sir.

Q. Do you know how much is required to run your mill by water power?

A. No, sir.

Q. Do you know how much water is required for scouring purposes?

A. No, sir.

Mr. BRUCE. — It requires a large amount of water, does it not?

A. Yes, sir.

Q. I suppose you are not able to use it for scouring your finest goods through the entire year?

A. No, sir ; we have to look out for the seasons. We make our fine goods in the winter, when the water is high, and lay them by.

Mr. BAILEY. — How many of your fine goods do you make in the winter?

A. We begin in October to make some of our finest goods, — ones and twos.

Q. And continue up to what time?

A. We don't make any of them in the works after the 1st of April.

Q. So that really the great bulk of your work is done between the 1st of October and the 1st of April?

A. No, sir ; these very fine goods that I speak of comprise but a small portion. We make a great many other goods, coarser goods. Those we make later in the season.

Q. But the fine goods are made between the 1st of October and the 1st of April?

A. Yes, sir, generally.

Q. What proportion of fine goods do you make as compared with all the goods you manufacture?

A. I can't tell you that without looking.

Q. Will you furnish us with those figures, — whether three-quarters, seven-eighths, one-half, or what proportion?

A. Yes, sir.

Q. During what months do you manufacture the other goods?

A. The rest of the year.

Q. All the rest of the year?

A. Yes, sir.

Q. Do you make your flannels during the summer months?

A. We keep our mills going all the year round.

Q. Have you ever stopped your mill?

A. Only for repairs.

Q. During the last year has it been necessary to stop it for any other purpose except for repairs?

A. This last year we stopped during the months of July and August to make general repairs.

Q. That was simply for repairs?

A. Yes, sir. I put in a dam and a stone wall in front of the mill.

Q. But you have never had to stop the mill at any time on account of the scarcity of water?

A. No, sir, because we have helped it out by our engines.

Q. I mean, you have had plenty of water for scouring purposes all the time?

A. We have had to stop scouring.

Q. For how long?

A. Perhaps two or three days, when all the ponds were low, and everybody was suffering.

Q. During how many years have you had to stop scouring for two or three days at a time on account of want of water?

A. I don't remember. It was merely a bagatelle.

Q. When you stopped for those two or three days you did not scour again until your mill-ponds got full?

A. Until I got enough to do my scouring.

Q. Until water had accumulated in your ponds so that you could do your scouring?

A. Yes, sir.

Q. Then you resumed?

A. Yes, sir.

Q. Do you know the capacity of your mill-pond?

A. No, sir.

Q. Can you give us that in any way?

A. I cannot.

Q. Is there any way in which you can give us an opinion as to the amount of water required for doing the scouring in your mill?

A. Not without getting an engineer to examine it and tell you.

Q. You never made any estimate, then?

A. No, sir.

Mr. BRUCE. — It is a large amount, is it not?

A. Yes, sir; it must be.

TESTIMONY OF WILLIAM L. STRONG.

Mr. BRUCE. — Where do you reside?

A. City of New York.

Q. What is your business?

A. Domestic commission business.

Q. What is the name of your firm?

A. W. L. Strong & Co.

Q. Are you the selling agents for the Ballardvale flannels?

A. We are.

Q. How long have you been?

A. Since '59.

Q. You are familiar, I suppose, with the Ballardvale mills, their product, and also with the market for flannels in the United States?

A. I think so.

Q. Do you know what proportion of the whole product of flannels in the United States is made by Capt. Bradlee at his mills?

A. Of this particular class of goods, — just the class that he makes, — I suppose he makes fully three-quarters of all the goods that are sold in the United States.

Q. Whether or not there are any persons manufacturing the finest quality of goods, such as are manufactured by Capt. Bradlee?

A. George H. Gilbert & Co., of Ware, are the only manufacturers in the United States of the same class of goods.

Q. Whether or not the stamp, " Ballardvale Flannels," is a trade-mark of great value, and well known to the trade throughout the United States?

A. As well as the A, B, C are to anybody in the trade.

Q. Are you familiar with the Ballardvale mills?

A. I think so. I have been going there once a month for fifteen or eighteen years. I think I ought to be.

Q. Whether or not the use of pure water is an absolute necessity in the manufacture of these goods?

A. It is.

Q. Without it they cannot be manufactured?

A. They cannot.

Q. What is the value of the product of that mill yearly?

A. About $450,000.

Cross-Examination.

Mr. BAILEY. — Are you at all acquainted with the manufacture of flannel?

A. I am not.

Q. You do not know how much water it takes for scouring purposes, or anything like that?

A. No, sir. I said the yearly product was about $450,000. I think the product from 1882 to now has not varied $10,000 from $400,000. It might run one year as low as $386,000 or $387,000.

Q. So that the average for the last four years has been about $400,000?

A. Yes, sir. They carry over from $40,000 to $50,000 worth of goods, so that the product is about $450,000.

Q. That makes the annual product about $400,000?

A. No, sir, the product is about $450,000 a year. Sometimes we get our sales up to $425,000 or $430,000.

Q. How can the product be that?

A. Because we carry over $50,000 or $60,000.

Q. If you have $50,000 or $60,000 in stock one year, and the next year have the same, is not your actual product about $400,000?

A. No, sir. Some years we have sold as high as $440,000 or $450,000. The last three years which I have been taking now have been the most disastrous years for manufacturers that we have had for the last twenty.

Q. What has been the product of those mills for the last three years?

A. I think it will average in the neighborhood of $410,000 or $415,000, if you take in four years.

Q. I see, Mr. Strong, on these different samples of flannel, the words "Japanese," "Chinchilla," "Asia:" what is that for?

A. That is to distinguish the particular fabric.

Q. Is it not the name of the flannel?

A. No, sir. We have above that "Ballardvale Mills."

Q. It is not the name of the flannel at all?

A. No, sir. We have the stamp "Ballardvale Mills" and "J. P. Bradlee." Between those two stamps are these different names. It is simply to distinguish the fabric. There is one line of goods manufactured there on which we put nothing but "Ballardvale Mills."

Q. Have you a trade-mark in the term "Ballardvale?"

A. We have, sir. The goods are Ballardvale goods — "Ballardvale Flannels."

Q. Have you ever had a decision that you can use that name as a trade-mark, to the exclusion of everybody else?

A. I believe there has been a decision of that kind in our State.

Q. Do you think you can use the name of the place to the exclusion of everybody else manufacturing in the same place?

A. No, I think not.

Mr. BRUCE. — There is where my brother makes a serious mistake. The place has not given the name to the flannel, but the village takes its name from the flannel.

Q. Have you any idea that you can use the name of the village as a distinguishing trade-mark to the exclusion of any other person in that same village, or in any other village, who sees fit to use it?

A. I can answer that question by saying —

Q. Have you ever had any suit upon it?

A. I know of a suit of that kind. The Amoskeag Mills sued Garner & Co. of New York for using the label "Amoskeag

Prints" on goods that were manufactured in Cohoes, N. Y., and the court held that Garner & Co. had no right to use that name.

Q. That was in the New York court, was it?

A. Yes, sir.

Q. If that is the case, there is no trouble in taking that same name wherever you go?

A. They did not allow Garner & Co. to use the mark "Amoskeag."

Q. You could manufacture this same class of goods, couldn't you, in any other city or town and still keep your trade-mark?

A. Not according to that decision in our courts.

Mr. BAILEY. — I think you can.

Mr. BRUCE. — I do not dispute that they could do it, but Capt. Bradlee says he shall not do it.

Q. I understand you to say that you have never had any practical experience in the manufacture of flannels.

A. Not with the details of the manufacture.

TESTIMONY OF N. HENRY CRAFTS.

Mr. BRUCE. — What is your business?

A. Civil engineer.

Q. How long have you been such?

A. Since 1849 or '50.

Q. Were you at one time city engineer of the city of Boston?

A. Yes, sir.

Q. How many years?

A. About nine years.

Q. And what time, thought, and investigation have you given to the question of water supplies for cities and the construction of water works?

A. Well, that was a branch of my duties and profession while I was city engineer; since then that has been almost exclusively my business, — water works and sewerage.

Mr. GAMWELL. — You live in Boston?

A. Yes, sir, I live in Boston.

Mr. BRUCE. — What years were you city engineer of the city of Boston?

A. From 1864 until the close of 1872.

Q. Whether you have given special attention to the question of a supply of water for the city of Boston?

A. I have made it more or less of a study, have been interested in the matter, and have kept up my interest in it ever since I left there.

Q. Have you made a general study of the subject of water supplies to cities so as to take in what has been done not only in this country but in Europe, to a greater or less extent?

A. I don't profess to be very familiar with the water systems of Europe except by reading.

Q. I mean by reading, — the examination of reports.

A. Yes, sir.

Q. Now will you give to the committee the results of your experience, judgment, and investigation in regard to what is a proper supply for a city like Boston, — how many gallons *per capita?*

A. My own judgment is that a liberal supply for a city like Boston, or any large city, is forty gallons per day for each inhabitant, — that is, under strict regulations as to waste, and so on. Making a fair allowance for waste, I should say fifty; but in looking for a supply I think I should go beyond that and estimate as high as sixty.

Q. And would you consider it wastefulness on the part of a city to allow a consumption greater than sixty gallons *per capita?*

A. I should, decidedly.

Q. Now will you state what has been the opinion of different engineers of the city of Boston in regard to it? Mr. Davis was the city engineer at one time, was he not?

A. Yes, sir.

Q. Whether or not he is considered one of the most eminent water engineers in America?

A. I believe he has that reputation.

Q. Do you know what his opinion upon that subject was and is?

A. Mr. Davis, in 1873 (City Document No. 29 of that year, being a " Report on an Additional Supply of Water for the City of Boston ") adopted as the standard sixty gallons per inhabitant. In 1879, after he had built the works which he designed at that time on the basis of sixty gallons, in a report on waste, which is

City Document No. 79 of the year 1879, p. 45, he said: "We are now using eighty gallons of water per inhabitant. There is plenty of evidence to prove that one-half of this quantity is a liberal supply for all useful purposes." That shows that he had changed his mind, bringing his standard down from sixty gallons, when he planned the works, to forty after he left them.

Q. When did Mr. Davis resign as engineer of the city of Boston?

A. My impression is it was in '79 or '80.

Q. He was followed by Mr. Wightman, was he not?

A. Yes, sir.

Q. A man of considerable eminence as an engineer?

A. Yes, sir.

Q. Do you know what his opinion was, as expressed in his reports, as to what was an abundant allowance *per capita* for a population like that of Boston?

A. Mr. Wightman testified at a hearing here in 1881 upon this very question of taking the Shawsheen (p. 54 of the printed evidence) that sixty gallons per head was a liberal allowance.

Q. Have you prepared a table this year giving the amount *per capita* used by the different cities of the United States and also in Europe?

A. Yes, sir.

Q. I would like to have you state what they are, if you have them before you.

A. I will state that the tables which I have prepared give the consumption of certain English cities in 1870. The average daily supply of London per head was 35 wine gallons; Sheffield, 35; Liverpool, 32; Manchester, 29; Leeds, 28; being an average of 31.8 for those different cities. I think I might say, in addition to that, that taking London later than that, say ten years later, in '81, when the population of London was given, I think, as 4,600,000 the amount of water used was 140,000,000 gallons, of which 68,000,000 came from the Thames river and 72,000,000 from other sources. That would make the average a little higher, I think, than what I have given.

Q. Have you prepared a table of the consumption of the cities of the United States? If so, will you give it to the Committee?

A. I have prepared a table, not of all of them, but a certain number. In Boston, in 1882, the consumption under the Cochituate system was an average of 93.6 gallons *per capita* per day; in '84, from the same system, it was reduced to 68. In 1880 the consumption under the Mystic system was 81 gallons per inhabitant per day; in '84, 71 gallons. In Worcester, in '80, the average *per capita* rate was 50 gallons; Providence, in 1880, 35 gallons; Lawrence, in '80, 47 1-2; Taunton, in '80, 34; Fall River, in '80, 36; Cambridge, in '77, 55; in '82, 45; Lowell, in '80, 37.9; in '77, 83; New York, in '80, 80; St. Louis, in '80, 71; Philadelphia, in '80, '70; Cincinnati, in '81, 87; in '82, 69.7; in '83, 55.

Q. Do you know anything of the history of the reduction that took place in Cincinnati from '81 to '83?

A. I merely know that it is claimed to have been reduced by the use of a system I think called the Bell Waterphone, or some system of waste detection.

Q. Are you familiar with the history of the attempts made here in Boston to reduce the *per capita* consumption of water?

A. Yes, sir.

Q. Will you give the result of your study of the question to the Committee?

A. Well, to state it in brief, the importance of the question of waste was recognized by the Water Board as far back as 1850. There was at that time a large waste of water, and from that time down to the present that matter has been discussed in almost every report of the Water Board, and measures at different times have been adopted to reduce the waste. The most marked reduction by the use of inspection alone I think took place in 1884 and 1885. At that time the supply of water from Lake Cochituate ran low; the Water Board issued cautionary notices to the people, and early in 1865 they put on inspectors. The result was that in 1865 the waste had been reduced from 16,000,000 for the year previous to about 12,000,000, and remained at 12,000,000 as long as that inspection was kept up. I do not know how long it was kept up; I think two or three years. It remained at about that figure for two or three years. Then, as the system of inspection was relaxed, the consumption was increased. The reports of the Water Board show that this question of curtailing the waste of water by the use of meters is one that has been talked of and discussed a great deal. The objection at the start was that no reliable meter could be found, and the first reliable one that was found was so expensive it could not be brought into general use. I think the records will show that the Water Boards all along through from as far back as 1850 have been desirous of getting hold of some water meter that would be reliable by which the waste of water could be curtailed. I have a statement here of the number of meters in use at different times and the effect of the meters. Going as far back as 1863, the number of meters at that time was 254. It gradually increased up to 1869, when there were 1,089 meters in use. In 1871, two years later, the number had increased to 1,091. This was the time when the question of a new supply began to be agitated, and there was nothing further done in regard to adding meters for about nine years. In 1880 there were 1,097 in use, showing that there had been no increase to speak of in that nine or ten years.

Q. What effort since then has been made, and with what results? Give them as briefly as you can.

A. Well, a great change in this respect took place upon the advent of Messrs. Simmons, Hobbs, and Blake in the Water Board. They took hold of the matter in July, 1883, I think, in earnest, both as regards putting in recording meters, putting in waste meters, or what are called " waste detectors," the Deacon meter, and also increasing the force of inspectors. That policy was inaugurated under their administration in 1883.

Q. With what result?

A. In May, '85, the number of recording meters had been increased from 1,097 in '80 to 4,439, and the reports of the Board show the effect both of the application of meters and of the system of inspection. Pretty much all that is contained in this pamphlet[1] is extracts from the published reports.

Q. In those sections of the city where the system was generally applied what was the result?

A. Well, in Boston, between May 4 and November 18, '81, experiments were made in the Charlestown District with the Deacon meter and waste detector. The population affected was 21,760.

---

[1] " The Water Supply of Boston," by N. Henry Crafts, C.E.

The *per capita* rate was reduced from 58½ gallons per individual to 37.7. This meter or waste detector is an instrument which has been used in European cities with great success, among others in Liverpool and Glasgow. The city of Glasgow takes its supply from Lake Katrine by gravitation, and the supply is supposed to be practically inexhaustible. This detector was applied there, and in a district containing 81,289 persons the daily *per capita* rate was reduced from 58.8 to 38.4, which is substantially the same result which was accomplished in the Charlestown District. In East Boston these detectors were applied to twelve districts, comprising a population of nearly 26,000. The percentage of reduction varied in different districts from 22 per cent. to 47. Section 12 included what is called the high-service district of East Boston. The reduction there was from 53.3 to 26.6. The *per capita* rate in the whole of East Boston was estimated at about 48 gallons per day, including the shipping, manufacturing, and business purposes. In the city proper, nineteen sections, with a population of 34,900, had their daily rate reduced from 89.8 to 49.6. In South Boston, seventeen sections, with a population of 41,445, had their rate reduced from 50.2 to 39.1. This general system was inaugurated in July, 1883, and has been continued to the present time. In May, 1885, the detectors had been applied to one hundred and thirty-seven districts, containing a population of 360,000. In the Sudbury and Cochituate systems, the daily per head rate was reduced from 91.5 to 68, equal to 25.6 per cent. In the Mystic system the rate had been reduced from 82 per head to 71, equal to 13.4 per cent.

Q. Do you have any doubt that it is perfectly practicable to reduce the consumption of water below sixty gallons per individual in the city of Boston?

A. I have no doubt of it.

Q. Do you think it ought to be done?

A. I think so.

Q. Now, you understand thoroughly the Cochituate and also the Mystic systems, do you not?

A. I am more familiar with the Cochituate and the Sudbury than with the Mystic.

Q. What would be the expense of making a connection at the pumping station of the Mystic with the Cochituate system?

A. It depends upon the size of the pipe. I estimate that a thirty-inch main connecting Chestnut-Hill reservoir directly with the Mystic pumping station would cost about $250,000, and that that size of pipe would be capable of delivering about 13,000,000 gallons a day.

Q. And that is about the present consumption of the Mystic district, is it?

A. Yes, sir.

Q. ·Were your estimates carefully made, Mr. Crafts, upon that basis of a thirty-inch pipe?

A. Yes, sir, I think so. It is based upon the experience we have had in laying the same size pipe in the city of Cambridge.

Q. Do you know what were the estimates of Mr. Francis and Mr. Kirkwood with reference to getting an additional supply from the Mystic that should be equal to about 17,000,000 gallons? Do you remember what their estimates were? or can you refer to them?

A. Their estimate is contained in City Document No. 85, for the year 1875.

Q. State what it is.

A. They estimated that the storage might be increased to 2,250,000 gallons; and with that increase, the supply, in a dry year, would amount to 17,000,000 gallons per day; and that the expense of securing this storage would be $994,562; also, that at an expense of about $800,000 the storage might be increased so as to add 5,000,000 gallons, making a total of 13,000,000. Their estimate of the capacity of the Mystic system as it at present exists was 8,000,000 gallons, instead of what has been put in here as 7,000,000.

Q. You know Mr. Francis, do you not?

A. Very well.

Q. And Mr. Kirkwood?

A. Mr. Kirkwood I know only by reputation.

Q. You know the repute of these men as skilful engineers upon these subjects, do you not?

A. Quite well; yes, sir.

Q. What is it?

A. I suppose they stand at the head of the profession; there is no doubt about that, sir.

Q. Now will you state what is the capacity of the water rights developed which the city of Boston has acquired on the Sudbury river and the Cochituate?

A. You mean as they exist to-day?

Q. As developed; that is, existing, and the rights that they have under the law now by building their additional basins, — what would be the result?

A. I do not put my hand on the figures now, but my recollection is that my estimate of the supply available from the south-side works, including Basin No. 4, was about 50,000,000 gallons a day; that is, taking the Sudbury and Cochituate together. I reckon the Sudbury at 38,000,000, and the Cochituate at 12,000,000 gallons. I would state, however, that that estimate was based upon a calculation of twelve inches of rainfall.

Q. Whether you think that is a correct basis?

A. I think it is. It has been shown that the amount collected in the different basins has been as low as ten inches. That is an extremely rare occurrence, and, as Mr. Brackett stated the other day, the amount held in store from previous years to be carried over will often make up the difference between an excessively dry year like that and what we call an average year. In fact, until recently twelve inches was considered an excessively dry year; that is, when only twelve inches were collected.

Q. And with proper basins could not that amount be secured, in your judgment?

A. I think so.

Q. I think you also made up a table giving the estimated population of the cities within the Mystic, Cochituate, and Sudbury districts for a series of years?

A. Yes, sir. On p. 13 of this pamphlet will be found a table of the population of the districts now supplied by the south-side and Mystic works; that is, by the Cochituate, Sudbury, and Mystic, which includes Boston proper, East Boston, South Boston, Roxbury, West Roxbury, Dorchester, Brighton, Charlestown, Chelsea, Somerville, and Everett. The population of this district from 1850 to 1880 was as follows: —

In 1850 the total population was 182,692.
" 1855   "   "   " 215,479.
" 1860   "   "   " 268,916.
" 1865   "   "   " 292,488.
" 1870   "   "   " 327,918.
" 1875   "   "   " 388,133.
" 1880   "   "   " 413,165.

The census of 1885 should be added, but it is not in the book now.

Mr. WILSON. — It is 451,000.

The WITNESS. — On the following page, p. 14, I have made an estimate of what the future population of that district will be ; and the basis upon which that estimate is made is as follows : The present rate of increase, twenty-five per cent., should be assumed for the first two decennial periods, and twenty per cent. for the next two. Then follows a table which upon that basis shows that, calling the population 413,165 in 1880, in 1925 it will amount to 1,023,326.

Q. And with the development of the rights which the city of Boston now has, for how a long period of time have they a sufficient amount of water for the inhabitants of the two districts?

A. That depends upon the rate of consumption.

Q. Put it on your own rate. I ask your judgment now about it.

A. On p. 36 I make this estimate : The population to be supplied at the end of forty years will not be over one million. The daily *per capita* rate need not be over fifty gallons. If the rate be kept up to fifty gallons per head, I estimate that the present south-side supply will be ample until the year 1915, say thirty years ; and at seventy gallons, the present rate of supply from the Sudbury and Cochituate sources, calling it fifty millions of gallons a day, would supply a population of 714,000, which would be the population in 1905.

Q. Now, as an engineer, do you think it is good policy on the part of the city of Boston to go to Shawsheen river, even if they had the right to do it?

A. No, sir, I do not.

Q. You would not recommend it, then?

A. No, sir.

Q. Do you think there is any necessity for an increase of the supply of the city of Boston at the present time?

A. I do not.

Q. Whenever the time comes for an increase of the supply of the city of Boston, in your opinion, would it be good policy for them to take the Shawsheen river?

A. No, sir.

Q. What course would you recommend the city of Boston to take in reference to obtaining an additional supply?

A. I am not prepared to answer.

Q. That is, you do not say which would be best?

A. I think there are a number of problems connected with the water supply and drainage, not only in Boston, but what we call the metropolis, which require considerable study and time ; and my view of the matter is, that the wisest policy is to make what we have go as far as we can, go slow, and take time to study this matter. I am not prepared to say what should be the policy of the future in regard to this matter, but I do decidedly think that the policy of taking a small stream here and there to make up for the abandonment of existing sources is bad policy, and I believe that we should endeavor to maintain the purity of what we have, keep the waste down to as low a figure as possible, make it go as far as we can, and take time to study the problem in all its bearings.

Q. Now will you give us an estimate, as near as you can, of the amount of water that is at present consumed in the city of Boston for manufacturing purposes?

A. I have a statement prepared from the Water Registrar's Report of 1885 which gives a statement of the amount of water sold by meter measurement, and for what purposes. This table of course assumes that that covers the great bulk of all the water used for manufacturing purposes. The items are as follows : —

Steam railroads	23,002,380 cubic feet.
Sugar refineries	28,594,000 " "
Factories	22,770,098 " "
Iron works and foundries . . .	4,402,173 " "
Carried forward	78,768,651 " "

Brought forward	78,768,651	cubic feet.
Mills and engines	2,672,000	" "
Marble and stone works . . .	2,275,700	" "
Gas companies	9,044,432	" "
Breweries	7,626,000	" "
Oil works	1,690,000	" "
Chemical works	2,801,000	" "
Laundries	326,000	" "
Steamers and shipping . . .	7,526,000	" "
Elevators and motors . . .	12,824,833	" "
Electric lights	3,248,874	" "
Miscellaneous	1,116,667	" "
Total	129,920,157	

Calling the population 353,000, it amounts to seven and a half
gallons per head per day. That includes all the consumption for
manufacturing, shipping, and other purposes that is measured by
meter.

Q. Is there any way by which you can get at the amount of
water consumed in Boston for power purposes? I mean, where it is
used as a direct means of power.

A. Well, I presume the item under the head of "Elevators and
Motors" would give that.

Q. What is that amount?

A. That for the whole year amounts to 12,824,833 cubic feet.
It would be between ninety and a hundred million gallons for the
year.

Q. How much a day?

A. Not a very large amount. You can divide it by 365 and
you will get it.

Q. Whether or not you were the person who, at the expense of
Capt. Bradlee, pointed out the source of supply for the city of
Cambridge which was finally adopted?

A. Yes, sir.

Cross-Examination.

Mr. BAILEY. — Do you think, Mr. Crafts, that it would be safe
for any city to go to the expense of furnishing itself with a water

supply on a less estimate than that of sixty to seventy gallons per inhabitant?

A. Sixty gallons I think would be very liberal.

Q. Would you recommend their going into any expense on a less estimate than sixty gallons?

A. I think I stated before —

Q. No; I ask you now, would you recommend their going into the expense of supplying themselves with water from any source upon a less estimate than sixty gallons per inhabitant?

A. No, I think not.

Q. Do you know of any city in the United States of the capacity of Boston that has ever got along with less than sixty?

A. I think the recent experience of Cincinnati shows about fifty-five; a little less.

Q. Is there any other city that you know of with anywhere near the population of Boston that has got along with less than sixty-five?

A. No, I think not.

Q. Now about foreign water works: do you know anything about their construction, or about their system of supplying their people with water?

A. Not in detail. I know that in London the water is supplied entirely by water companies.

Q. Do not most of the companies supply water during a portion of the day, and then shut it off, and allow no water to run for a long time?

A. Part of them do.

Q. Those companies that practise that method are the companies whose estimates you have got in here, are they not?

A. I have the gross estimate for London.

Q. Some of them are taken in there in making that estimate?

A. Certainly, they are all taken in.

Q. Now, are not the gallons that are used there smaller than the gallons that are used here?

A. I have reduced it to wine gallons.

Q. So that the gallon is the same capacity that it is in this country?

A. Yes, sir

Q. But that is the fact in regard to the different methods of the use of water there?

A. It is in London, I think. I think that part of the companies there supply what they call constant service; they are getting into that system; they will soon be out of the other.

Q. Part of them now supply water on one system and part of them the other?

A. Yes, sir.

Q. Don't you understand that a different system prevails there from that in use here?

A. No, sir. I understand it is the water-closet system, substantially the same as here.

Q. A great many of the large consumers of water use driven wells, do they not?

A. In London and other places a large proportion of them do not use any other than the water that is got from these water companies.

Q. Some of them use wells?

A. Possibly they may.

Mr. BRUCE. — They do here.

Mr. BAILEY. — I don't know that they do; they have tried to, but couldn't.

Mr. BRUCE. — They do at Squire's slaughter-house, I understand.

Q. In all places, both in England and Scotland, and in the United States, the uses for water are constantly increasing, are they not?

A. Well, I can't say that they are.

Q. How many years ago is it since the first water elevator was used?

A. Well, it is quite recent.

Q. Is not that fast assuming a very important position in the consumption of water?

A. It may be, but it ought not to.

Q. Well, it is, isn't it?

A. It is in Boston.

Q. Is it not in other large cities?

A. I presume so.

Q. So that it is a fact that the purposes for which water is used are increasing?

A. I think so, to a certain extent.

Q. And where they do increase they use very large amounts of water. Now, you say you are familiar with the Mystic valley?

A. I said I was not, only in a general way; not as familiar as I am with the old works.

Q. You are familiar enough with it to state in your paper here that you deem it for the best interests of Boston to seek to protect the purity of the water itself rather than seek to obtain new supplies in its place, do you not?

A. I do, decidedly.

Q. Have you made sufficient examination of the Mystic water-shed to be able to give your opinion on this matter, as an expert and an engineer, whether the purity of that water-shed can be preserved for any length of time?

A. Not from personal examination.

Q. So that you would not undertake to contradict the witnesses here who have given it as their opinion that it was not a fit supply for the city of Boston, would you?

A. Well, I should say in reply to that, that what opinion I have formed in regard to that district has been mainly formed from the reports of the city officials of Boston who have charge of that district. It has been obtained from the Water Board Reports, and not from personal examination. I think I should rely more upon the reports of the Water Board than I should upon the opinion of the experts who were here yesterday.

Q. That is not an answer to my question. Are you prepared to say, in contradiction of what they have testified to, that it is a fit territory to use for a water supply of a large community like Boston?

A. No, sir, I am not.

Q. Have you ever been over the territory that composes the water-shed?

A. No, sir.

Q. Have you ever been over the Shawsheen valley?

A. Portions of it; I have been over it from the place where you propose to build the dam, — down, not up.

Q. So that you can't testify at all in regard to the character of the water-shed?

A. Not from any personal examination. I have no question it is very pure water — a very good supply.

Q. Your opinion is that a supply that is capable of furnishing 20,000,000 gallons per day, and a very good supply, from a territory of thirty-four square miles, populated by 4,200 people only, is not a desirable supply to take and utilize for the purposes of a water supply?

A. Not for the city of Boston.

Q. Is it for any city?

A. I should suppose it might be for some smaller place.

Q. For a population of about how many would it be an adequate supply?

A. Well, a population of two or three hundred thousand.

Q. For a population of two or three hundred thousand it would be an adequate water supply, would it not?

A. It would be for a population that should remain at that figure.

Q. If a city with a population of two or three hundred thousand had an opportunity to get such a territory as that, and buy land, and protect it in the condition in which it is, would you not think it was a very advantageous and proper thing for that community to do?

A. Yes, sir, I should think it would be.

Q. Is it not a fact that the longer you wait in this age of the world, and let a territory of that kind remain idle, it is constantly becoming more contaminated, and the chance of protecting its purity in the future less?

A. I think so.

Q. And the longer you delay to avail yourself of a territory like that the less chance you run of getting a good, pure territory, don't you?

A. I think so.

Q. Now in regard to waste : is it not a fact that in some seasons of the year you must have a smaller consumption than fifty or sixty gallons to get a daily average consumption of fifty or sixty gallons?

A. Yes, sir.

Q. Therefore, if the daily consumption is seventy gallons during some seasons of the year, there must be a consumption, at times, of about forty gallons, must there not?

A. Possibly ; possibly less.

Q. Now, is it not a fact that this small consumption is in summer?

A. I think the summer consumption runs, in very hot weather, nearly as high as it does in winter.

Q. Then during the spring and fall months it is less?

A. I think the spring and fall months always show a less consumption.

Q. Therefore, during the spring and fall months, the consumption would be about forty, if the daily average is about seventy?

A. Well, the reports show that.

Q. Now, is it not a fact that these different appliances and contrivances for discovering the waste of water cannot be used in the winter?

A. I don't know why not.

Q. Do you know about the construction of the Deacon meter?

A. I am not very familiar with it. I never saw one of the meters. I only know what results are claimed for them.

Q. If Mr. Brackett should testify that their construction was such that it was not practicable to use them during the winter months, you would say that that statement was correct, wouldn't you?

A. I should say this, that I should not doubt Mr. Brackett's word.

Q. Do you know any other person in the United States who has had more experience in trying to prevent the waste of water than Mr. Brackett?

A. With that particular means, I do not.

Q. Whether or not you are aware of the fact that he has had charge of this attempt of the city of Boston during the last five years to stop the water waste?

A. Yes, sir, I am.

Q. Knowing that he has had that experience, do you know of any other engineer in Boston who has had any greater experience in that line?

A. No, sir, I can't say I do.

Mr. BRUCE. — Whether or not you ever estimated what was the amount of water that a population of a million would use for purely domestic purposes? I mean by that culinary purposes and to drink.

A. I think Mr. Morse, in his statement yesterday, rather misconstrued what I said. I did not intend to convey the idea that a quarter of a million gallons is a supply for a million persons. The language may perhaps bear two constructions; but my intention was that a quarter of a million gallons would be ample for the present population. For a million people my estimate was a million gallons, in round numbers.

Mr. BAILEY. — Have you made any examination of the flow of the Shawsheen river?

A. No, sir.

Q. Have you made any examination of the consumption of Capt. Bradlee's mills?

A. I made an examination a few years ago, with reference to the amount passing through his mills when the wheels were running; that is, the total amount of water used to run his whole establishment, that is all.

Q. At what season of the year?

A. That was at a time when there was water enough running for the whole establishment. I have forgotten now what the figures were, and have not my notes with me. It was several years ago. My recollection is that the total amount required to run the wheels to their full capacity and do all the work (and this gauging was a rough gauging) was about 40,000,000 gallons a day.

Q. Forty million gallons a day to do all the work that is required?

A. Yes, sir.

Q. Now can you tell us the amount required to run the mill separate from the scouring?

A. I could not.

Q. Did you ever make any examination so as to satisfy you that there were 40,000,000 gallons a day running down that river?

A. Yes, sir.

Q. There are 40,000,000 gallons running down that river daily?

A. At certain seasons, yes, and more too.

Q. For how long a time?

A. I can't tell you that.

Q. For a month? Can you give us anywhere near the time?

A. I have kept no regular gauges. I should say so.

Q. Is there for two months?

A. I should think likely.

Q. Give us some idea. Is it for six months?

A. I should not say quite as long as that.

Q. Is it for four months?

A. Probably; that is guesswork. I don't like to give an estimate that may be wrong. I have not gauges enough extending through the whole year to be able to say.

Q. You think it is not for six months?

A. I think it is hardly for six months.

Q. Are there any times when more than double that goes down the river?

A. Yes, sir, more than three times.

Q. Are there any times when there are more than 200,000,000 gallons running down that river daily?

A. I should think not. I will state in regard to that, that I cannot answer these questions definitely; but the minimum flow in streams of that size, in a dry time, that is, taking it for a month together, would be a quarter of a cubic foot per second for each square mile; and there are somewhere about sixty square miles above Mr. Bradlee's place. That is a matter of computation; I think I called it fifty-seven. That was by a rough estimate.

Q. If you had the flow of the Sudbury river at a certain point during the dry season would that be a fair basis on which to determine what the flow of the Shawsheen would be?

A. Yes, as fair any anything, I think, except actual gauges.

Mr. BRUCE. — My brother wants to know about the flood tide in this little stream. In the flood tide of the Sudbury how many billion gallons of water run to waste in one day?

A. I think I have stated that. I don't think we ever had any freshet that would compare with what we had this spring.

Q. Taking that basin as the basis of comparison, and finding the number of square miles of the Shawsheen, could you find the same thing?

A. You could approximate it. There would be a difference, according to the topographical features of the basin.

Mr. LOOMIS. — Before we proceed with other witnesses, there is one question I would like to bring to the attention of the Committee and to that of the City Solicitor. That is, as we have no draft of the proposed bill, but simply the statement of the city that they desire to take everything, I deem it desirable that some statement be made in regard to the taxable property which they propose to take in the towns of Billerica and Bedford; that is, whether they propose to take property and pay taxes on it to these municipalities, or whether they propose to practically deprive these two municipalities of so much taxable property, although the damages are paid to individuals.

Mr. BAILEY. — We ask to be allowed to take land not exceeding one hundred rods on each side of any pond or stream that we take in that valley. We have not proposed to put in any requirement in regard to taxes. That will be a matter for consideration hereafter. We do not absolutely oppose taxation of the property.

Mr. LOOMIS. — In other words, you would consent to a tax, if it is put on a reasonable basis?

Mr. BAILEY. — Yes, if the Committee think that is a proper thing to do.

TESTIMONY OF HENRY W. WILSON.

Mr. MORSE. — What is your profession?

A. Civil engineer.

Q. Where have you been engaged in it?

A. I have been engaged in and about Boston principally, but in every New England State, New York, Delaware, and California.

Q. Have you had any connection with the city government of Boston?

A. Yes, sir.

Q. In what capacity?

A. I was assistant city engineer five years, from 1858 to 1863 ; I was a member of the Common Council in 1867, 1868 and 1875, and was upon the Water Committee of 1868, and also in 1875 at the time the additional supply was talked of.

Q. Have you given special attention to the water supply of the city?

A. I have, yes, sir, as much as a private individual can do.

Q. Have you studied the present situation?

A. Somewhat, yes, sir.

Q. Will you state to the Committee your views as to the advisability of the city taking the Shawsheen, or making any other provision, and if so, what, for a future water supply?

A. I do not think it is advisable to extend the works of Boston in the direction of the Shawsheen. If the problem was submitted to me of erecting new works on the Mystic system now, if it was to be a new undertaking, it would be one problem ; but having works costing, I believe, nearly $2,000,000, I should hardly advise their abandonment when the records of all the medical fraternity and all the engineers show that the quality of the water as regards pollution is being improved steadily. The Mystic system reached its lowest state of depravity, if I may so call it, previous to the introduction of the new intercepting sewer, which was completed about 1879. There is no doubt at all that at that time the water of the Mystic was positively unwholesome. It was not unwholesome to that degree that it bred contagion, possibly, but to invalids and people in depressed health it was not quite wholesome water to drink at that time. Nevertheless, the water, by analysis (and that is the only means by which the relative purity of water can be determined), was just as wholesome, by all medical and chemical tests, and twice as pure, as the water supplied to over three million of the inhabitants of London. By the same process of comparison, the death rate in the districts supplied by that system, at the same time, was less than the death rate in Boston proper, which is another test of the comparative purity of the water. Still, there were times when the quantity of albuminoid ammonia (which is a more refined and modern mode of comparison) showed that it was well nigh what is called the limit of safety, and the result was that in 1874 the city made an effort to build that intercepting sewer. There was a violent contest. It happened to be my fortune at that time to be chairman of this Committee on the part of the House, and I remember distinctly the contest that was made over it, and the agreement which was finally arrived at as the result of the contest.

Mr. BAILEY. — In what year was that?

A. That was in 1874. That was the first bill; and the bill was so loosely drawn that the city had a right to build sewers, but had no right to discharge them, and that rendered the whole thing nugatory. Then they came to the Legislature the next year and got the right to have an outlet for their sewers. Mr. Healy drew the bill, I think, which enabled them to lay sewers, but did not give them the right to discharge them anywhere. At any rate, at that time it was shown conclusively that the sewage and offensive mechanical refuse could be completely diverted. The great conflict that had always been in that valley grew out of the towns insisting upon the city of Boston maintaining their general sewerage system as well as diverting these impurities which naturally tended toward the streams, both towns and individuals claiming prescriptive rights of drainage.. The matter lingered along until finally the city of Boston got the right to divert these impurities and build the sewer without any regard to the towns. I think that that was an unfortunate thing for the city of Boston ; that the asperity and discourtesy which marked the agents of the city at that time prevented a combination of interests.

Mr. BAILEY. — Well, this is funny! How does he know that the discourtesy was on the part of the city authorities? It was just the other way.

Mr. MORSE. — You can state your views by and by. Mr. Wilson is making his statement to the Committee now.

The WITNESS. — I was asked how this thing came about. I will stop if it is desired. I am not reflecting upon any of the city officials. I was about to say that it was a misfortune that the city of Boston did not have the present Water Board.

Q. That they did not have the present amiable and pleasant men upon the Board?

A. Exactly. You have stated it in a briefer and more effectual way. In 1875 I happened to be a member of the committee that reported in favor of an appropriation of $250,000 to build the Mystic sewer, and it was my duty to examine the territory. In fact, in '74 we went over it; in '75 we went over it again repeatedly, and visited the sources of pollution. I cannot enumerate nor specify them now, because that was eleven years ago; but the general impression remains upon my mind that I got at the time as to the amount of pollution which was pouring into that system. If my memory serves me there were some thirty-two manufacturing establishments, twenty of which were tanneries, the waste of which was then discharged into streams tributary to Mystic pond. There were one hundred houses the fœcal discharges from which were practically all discharged into those streams which were tributary to the Mystic. When the work was completed the bulk of that matter, amounting to anywhere from 300,000 to 500,000 gallons a day of a fluid that will carry at times ten or eleven thousand parts per million, was taken round the upper pond and discharged into the lower pond, in Somerville and Woburn, and the purification of that water begun which is now being done after a manner. That is, at the present time the reports of the Water Board show that the water that is supplied by the Mystic system is more wholesome water than is supplied by the Sudbury system, by all the chemical tests that can be applied, excepting that there remains the general idea that water that receives pollution is to be regarded with suspicion.

The CHAIRMAN.—You did not quite complete your statement, Mr. Wilson. You spoke of opposition to the plan of the city to discharge the sewage into Mystic lower pond. What did you do?

A. They were allowed to so discharge it for one or two years — I cannot give the exact time, but for a certain interval — until legislation could be obtained to restrain them. They discharged it then as a separate stream below the upper pond, and the effect was to cause the water in the lower pond to become greatly polluted and very offensive.

Mr. MORSE. — The question of the Chairman was, " What was done to remedy the trouble?"

A. There were settling-basins of moderate size built, and a long ditch, perhaps from eleven to thirteen hundred feet in length, in which this matter was allowed to pass along, with some percolation into the gravel and some subsidence of the solid products, and a stream of sewage running at times as high as 4,000 parts of impurities per million was discharged into the lower lake.

Q. It is a system of purifying the sewage?

A. It is not a system of purification at all; it is nothing more than subsidence in a long ditch, or in tanks that are limited in capacity. I won't attempt to state the capacity of the tanks, but I think they are about 20,000 gallons, and have since been doubled.

The CHAIRMAN. — Those basins are on the banks of the lake?

A. No, sir; they are retired somewhat from the banks of the lake, on the border of the railroad, near the Mystic station.

Q. Its liquid portion runs into the upper pond?

A. No, sir; into the lower pond.

Mr. BAILEY. — It soaks in there?

Mr. BRUCE. — No, sir, it does not.

Mr. MORSE. — What, in your judgment, is the practical result of this system of sewerage, as regards the condition of the Mystic supply at present?

A. I think that the practical result has been satisfactory, has justified its expense, and is showing a marked improvement in the quality of the water.

Q. You say that the present reports indicate a higher quality of water in the Mystic supply than in the Sudbury?

A. They do, decidedly.

Q. Is there any present necessity, then, in your judgment, for abandoning the Mystic system?

A. No, sir, I should not advise its abandonment at all.

Q. What would be your judgment as to the advisability of the city making additional basins on the Mystic?

A. I really think it would be the most economical and satisfactory plan to erect basins there. It would be preferable to making this large expenditure in going to the Shawsheen, because the interest on this proposed expenditure of $3,500,000 in a few years would provide the means of building the basins.

Q. You have paid attention, I suppose, to the report of the Drainage Commission, have you not?

A. I have examined it; yes, sir.

Q. What is your judgment as to the effect of the adoption of the system recommended for the Mystic valley on the purity of the Mystic water supply?

A. It would still further facilitate the course of improvement which is shown to be going on there in these waters. There are, of course, many sources of impurity which are not reached by the present intercepting sewer that would be provided for by that system. They can be provided for otherwise, but if that should be undertaken, of course the difficulty would be met adequately.

Q. What is your judgment as to the necessity of the towns in that valley adopting that system or some system of the kind?

A. I think there is a necessity for the towns in that valley and for all the towns in this metropolitan district to provide for some system of drainage for the health of their own people. I do not indicate precisely what system, but some system. There may be modifications of the plan reported by the commission which will be rendered necessary ; I think there will be.

Q. How long, in your opinion, Mr. Wilson, would the present water supply for Boston, reckoning into it the additional quantity that can be obtained by a development of the rights which it has now, be sufficient for the district which is now supplied by the city?

A. I think the present sources of Boston are adequate for forty years.

Q. In your judgment, is there any necessity at present for making additional provision?

A. I do not see any.

Q. If that subject were to be considered at all, have you any opinion as to the true policy for the city?

A. Well, sir, that is coming close home to a question which cannot be thoroughly opened up without investigation. An engineer may have an opinion as to the advisability of an investigation ; though nothing but investigation can give him the facts which will justify an opinion ; but I have, and have always had, a decided opinion as to what the policy of the city should be.

Q. Will you state what it is?

A. Well, sir, I am hardly prepared to state that now, because it would only give rise to the criticism that is customary in such a place as this,'and I have not the means, by surveys and data, which can only be got by investigation, to sustain myself. I do not wish to do it.

Q. You are not prepared, however, to adopt the policy of taking a comparatively small supply, like that of the Shawsheen?

A. I think that the city of Boston should consolidate its supply where it can have it well in hand. I think that one of the greatest mistakes we have made in the past has been in continually taking small pieces of territory, a slice here and a slice there, and antagonizing the surrounding and neighboring towns. I think that the city of Boston, as a municipality, is thoroughly detested by about all the towns in Eastern Massachusetts. That has been my experience in the Legislature, and was my experience while on the Committee, and it is simply the result of their course in grasping here a slice and there a slice, and then being brusque in their treatment of people after they have got the rights which they sought. I hope, under the new *régime*, that this course will be discontinued. I think that the true source of water supply for Boston lies to the west, and not to the north. The whole of the eastern part of Massachusetts, in my opinion, is destined to be densely populated.

Mr. BAILEY. — And, therefore, unfit as a source of water supply?

A. And therefore unfit, yes, sir, for gathering grounds for water. I will put right in here — which, perhaps, may not be drawn out by any question, but it is a subject to which I have given a great deal of attention, and for the last two or three years it has been brought to my attention more than ever before — a new source of defilement that is endangering us in this district, and that is what arises from the extension of what is called " high farming," or market gardening. Few people have any idea of the extent to which the soil is enriched by the cultivation of our market-gardens. There are men in Arlington who put upon their soil every year thirty-seven cords of manure per acre; and there are farmers in that town who put 2,500 cords of manure a year upon farms of less than seventy-five acres; and if you go there in the spring-time, when the frost is coming out of the soil, and the whole surface of the ground is in a pulpy and semi-fluid condition, you will see the water, in the condition of liquid manure, running off in streams into the low grounds and into the ponds. And that is one of the causes of the abandonment of the proposed plan of Cambridge to introduce Spy pond as auxiliary to their other source of supply at Fresh pond. They obtained the right to the water, and after making considerable expenditure they found that, although the water on the surface of the pond was pure, so that ice cut upon it in winter had a worldwide reputation for purity, upon examining it below they found that this water was tainted by all these nitrogenous depositions, really a saturation of the water with nitrogen, so that they abandoned the project. Now, the demand for land for market gardens is increasing, and they are pushing over into the region of the Shawsheen. The prize cabbages, the prize turnips, the prize squashes, the prize melons at the Horticultural Exhibitions last autumn were raised on the borders of the Shawsheen valley, and, as I say, they are pushing in there rapidly. They are being forced out by the building of dwellings in Arlington and Belmont, and those men must find land for their market gardens elsewhere. Now, that is a source of defilement that is rapidly increasing, and cannot be provided for by drainage, or by taking land unless the whole area be taken. The city of Boston, if they take this district, must take the whole of the land.

Mr. BAILEY. — We would like to do it, if the Legislature will give us authority.

The WITNESS. — The time is coming when it will not be considered safe to take as gathering ground for water for a city any territory where they cannot own it and control its management and cultivation.

Q. What do you say to Mr. Bailey's proposition to take a hundred rods on each side of every pond and stream?

A. I should think that would amount to a confiscation of nearly the entire area of the whole water-shed of the stream. If they are going to take one hundred rods on each side of the river and on each side of every brook, that would take practically the whole area, as nearly as I can estimate, as the plan lies in my mind. Portions of Lincoln and Lexington are in this basin. I saw one large field, which must have contained forty or fifty acres, that is drained land and highly cultivated. That was the last time I was up through that district. I had no idea of this matter in my mind then ; I only saw it casually.

Q. You think that an amount of taking like that would be substantially the destruction of all the available land in that territory?

A. If they are to follow up all the tributaries to their source, it would be taking the largest portion of the territory, I should say. At the same time, that is a mere impression. The map is here and you can see.

Cross-Examination.

Mr. BAILEY. — Those prize cabbages, etc., were raised by Mr. John Cummings, were they not?

A. No, sir.

Q. By whom were they raised?

A. By Mr. Hartwell, of Lincoln.

Q. Can you point out on the map where his land is?

A. Yes, sir. It is right up on the water-shed. It is on Tarkiln brook. (The witness pointed out the location of Mr. Hartwell's farm on the map.)

Q. In your opinion, the high cultivation of land like that makes the territory unfit to be used for a water supply?

A. I don't say that it is unfit now ; I say that is a result to be expected in the immediate future.

Q. Then if the city of Boston is ever to be granted the right to take it, now is the time?

A. I confess it, " now is the accepted time." I will say this : there will never be in the experience of men now living any time when it will be so desirable to take that water as at the present time.

Adjourned to Friday, at 10.30.

FIFTH HEARING.

FRIDAY, April 2, 1886.

The Committee met at 10.30, Senator SCOTT in the chair.

HENRY W. WILSON, *recalled.*

Mr. BRUCE. — What uses of the soil lying on a water-shed are most deleterious to water?

A. The most deleterious use of the surface of the ground, I suppose, is the high enrichment produced by market gardening.

Q. That is the worst?

A. Yes, sir.

Q. And from your knowledge of the Mystic valley, whether or not you think there will be any difficulty in maintaining the present quality of the water of that system?

A. Not if the ordinary means are available of removing the excrementitious matter from the household, which forms the pollution of the natural use of the surface.

Q. Have you prepared a map that you will show the Committee which will illustrate the taking suggested by Brother Bailey?

A. Yes, sir.

Q. I would like to have you show it to the Committee.

(The witness exhibited a map to the Committee, which he explained, and stated that the proposed taking would take over twenty-seven square miles of the area, the whole being thirty-four.)

Mr. BRUCE. — That includes one hundred rods on the margin of all the streams. That is what Brother Bailey wants to take.

Mr. BAILEY. — I said we were willing to take the whole.

The CHAIRMAN. — It comes clear up to Bedford Spring station.

The WITNESS. — Here are the tributaries laid down on the map. I will not vouch for their accuracy. They ought to be accurate : there has been money enough spent on it. But laying off one hundred rods on the margin of all the tributaries, following the line around, and showing the limits of the water-shed, it leaves only these little portions colored with a lighter tint excluded ; the rest, with a darker color, comes within that limit.

The CHAIRMAN.—It will take the whole village of Lexington, then.

A. Yes, sir; it takes substantially the whole business portion, and it takes to the further line of the Middlesex Central Railroad.

Q. Whether or not you have the reports of the investigations of the Mystic water in the years '74, '79 and '83?

A. Yes, sir.

Q. By whom made?

A. In '73 and '74, when the preliminary discussion of this question took place, which led to the legislation for the construction of the intercepting conduit or sewer, there were some investigations made by Prof. Horsford. He made very elaborate investigations, and in his report (City Document No. 134, for the year '74, p. 70) he pronounces the Mystic water to be a safe and salubrious drinking water. This was before anything had been done in the way of sewerage. In the same document, p. 28, Messrs. Francis and Kirkwood said that the impurities could be intercepted and taken to tide water. That was their report.

Q. That was James B. Francis, of Lowell?

A. James B. Francis, of Lowell, and J. P. Kirkwood, who was the engineer of the Brooklyn Water Works, New York.

Q. Those men are among the eminent engineers of the country?

A. There are none more eminent.

Q. And among the oldest?

A. They are the oldest. I have known them nearly thirty years.

Q. Whether you have some further and later reports?

A. In the report for the year 1879, No. 79, p. 44, Prof. Woods, who had made an examination of the waters of the Mystic and the Sudbury by the most delicate modern tests for free ammonia and albuminoid ammonia, reported that he found in the Mystic the free ammonia was 0.0141 parts per million. In the Sudbury, the free ammonia was 0.0064 parts. Of albuminoid ammonia, which is the dangerous element, he found the Mystic contained 0.0115 parts as against 0.0195 parts per million in the Sudbury.

Q. What year was that?

A. That is in the report for 1879. I think it is a report of the Water Board.

Q. Anything later?

A. Yes, sir. In 1883 I have the reports of the investigations that were made at Chestnut-Hill reservoir and at different points in the distribution, and also in the Mystic system. The comparison is as follows : —

Prof. Woods' report of the relative purity of the Mystic and Sudbury waters 1879, in parts per million.

	Free Ammonia.	Albuminoid Ammonia.
Mystic	0.0141	0.0115
Sudbury	0.0064	0.0195

By the same authority (see Report Boston Water Board for 1883, City Doc. 173, p. 5), parts per million : —

	Free Ammonia.	Albuminoid Ammonia.	Volatile.
Chestnut-Hill reservoir . . .	0.0019	0.0246	3.00
Service, Warren and Dudley streets,	0.0021	0.0276	3.80
Medical College, Boylston street .	0.0037	0.0248	4.40
Service, 453 Hanover street . .	0.0011	0.0244	3.10
Service, 4 Thompson street, Charlestown, Mystic	0.0005	0.0208	4.20

All of the investigations and reports show that the Mystic has less indications of contamination from sewage and is far within the recognized limits of safety.

Q. Now if you have anything further to say upon the question of waste of water by the city of Boston you may put it in.

A. The element of waste includes also, of necessity, the element of consumption. Of course, we cannot say that there is anything wasted until we know what the limit of necessary consumption would be, and then take that from what is used. In order to ascertain what is the necessary amount for domestic use in a family, Mr. Ebenezer Johnson, who was president of the Water Board in 1861, had a meter put into his house in Chestnut street. He was a man who lived in good, liberal style, and it was supposed that the wants of his family would represent at least the wants of the average family. The result showed a consumption of 14 gallons by each member of his family, including eight persons. To show how much the consumption can be reduced when people know that they must husband their resources, I will state this fact: That an accident took place in 1869 which affected the entire community at once, caused by the fracture of the main at the westerly end of the bridge across Charles river. It broke on a Tuesday morning, about seven o'clock. At the time of the breakage of course they cut off the entire supply. There were about 100,000,000 gallons that were available for distribution in Boston. Immediately notices were sent to the citizens to limit their consumption, stating the fact that a breakage had occurred, and for five days Boston depended upon its reserve. I have the consumption here as it went down. It is interesting to note that the first day after the break the consumption was 56 gallons *per capita* the next day, 45; the next day, 34; the next day, 22; and on Saturday, the fifth day, 19.6 gallons *per capita*. There was a suspension of some manufacturing uses, but water was furnished for steam boilers. That showed that when an entire community is aware of the fact that water is a precious thing and must be taken care of, the use is restricted to the minimum limit. That cannot be accounted for by any consideration of diminution in pressure, because the reduced head at the Brookline reservoir, which, if my memory serves me, was the only source, was only about seven feet. Yet the consumption in the five days was only about one-third of the amount on storage.

Q. You are of the opinion, I believe, that anything more than sixty gallons per head is pure extravagance?

A. I think anything more than forty gallons per head is extravagance; I think that we might reasonably calculate on fifty, including eighteen gallons *per capita* for daily consumption other than for domestic uses. I think that sixty is the outside limit in the computation of sources.

Cross-Examination.

Mr. BAILEY. — It is a fact, is it not, that chemical analysis fails to detect all the impurities in water?

A. Chemical analysis is the best known standard by which to compare one water with another.

Q. Now, will you answer my question?

A. Wait a moment. I am answering your question. But there are in water the well-known germs of certain forms of epidemic and other diseases, called, sometimes, zymotic diseases, which analysis will not detect. That we understand. But they all go through the alimentary canal of human beings, and if proper means are taken to exclude excreta from these waters, that source can be eliminated.

Q. Now I will put the question again. It is a fact, is it not, that chemical analysis fails to detect all the dangerous elements that there may be in water?

A. Yes, sir; *all* of them. I have mentioned one which it cannot detect.

Q. So that water may be absolutely dangerous to life and chemical analysis fail to detect it?

A. That is conceded and understood, yes, sir.

TESTIMONY OF HARLOW COLBY.

Mr. LOOMIS. — You reside in Billerica?

A. Yes, sir.

Q. You are one of the committee appointed by the town to oppose the taking of the Shawsheen river by the city of Boston?

A. Yes, sir.

Q. Will you state the character of the land, if you know it, which will be occupied by this basin, as to whether it is productive land or not?

A. Well, sir, the Shawsheen meadows are some of our best land. It is grass land; we get a crop of grass every year, without any extra effort. It fertilizes itself, and the land is very valuable to the farming interests of our town.

Q. Whether this land is owned in small sections by farmers all over the town?

A. It is mostly, sir.

Q. And the hay is used for the purpose of keeping stock over the winter?

A. Yes, sir.

Q. And especially for milk stock?

A. Yes, sir.

Q. It makes a good quality of hay for the production of milk, does it?

A. Very good quality. The Shawsheen meadows furnish the best quality of grass ; it is of better quality than the grass produced on the Concord-river meadows.

Q. Whether the proposed reservoir, by soaking, will injure adjacent lands, which are used for producing English grass, so as to injure the whole grass yield of the town, as well as the land directly affected by the overflow?

A. I don't know as I could say that the flowage would damage the English hay in any great measure.

Q. If a hundred rods are taken on each side of this proposed reservoir and all the streams flowing into it, as suggested by the counsel for the city, whether it will take away a large and important area of arable land from the town, and so materially injure the interests of the inhabitants?

A. If that is taken, it will take a good deal of the land.

Q. Now, as regards Mr. Clark's mill, which is to be a part of this reservoir, will you state whether that mill, which is used for grinding grain and for sawing logs, is very important or not to the whole community in the part of Billerica which is near to it?

A. Well, it is a fact that we are under the necessity, and have been for the last twenty-five years, of going to that mill to have our grain ground and logs sawed ; not the whole of the logs, for we have another mill in town, but that section of the town that the Shawsheen goes through. There is another mill in town, in another direction, but that part of the town is accommodated, and it is the only grist-mill that we depend upon, and has been for the last twenty years.

Cross-Examination.

Mr. BAILEY. — You are one of the assessors of Billerica, are you?

A. No, sir.

Q. Do you anything about the value of land along this stream?

A. The most that I can say about that is that I have paid taxes for several years at a valuation of $100 an acre on my meadow.

Q. Where is that?

A. On the Shawsheen.

Q. Anywhere near where it is proposed to put this basin?

A. I don't know as you could tell by your map here. There is a book running through my meadow into the Shawsheen. It goes through Henry Magee's farm above it.

Q. You consider your land about as valuable as any in town, don't you?

A. I do.

Q. Is not the taxable value of the land all the way from $25 to $100 an acre?

A. I am not able to say, not being one of the assessors.

Q. Is not that generally understood to be the value of land there?

A. I presume it is.

Q. If this grist-mill should be run by steam it would be just as good a mill for all purposes as if it was run by water, would it not?

A. I don't know why it wouldn't, if we only got our grain ground.

Testimony of Oliver J. Lane.

Mr. Loomis. — You are chairman of the selectmen of the town of Bedford?

A. Yes, sir.

Q. And have been at various times for twelve or fifteen years?

A. Yes, I have been on the board the last five years in succession, and have been on the board at other times.

Q. Will you please state to the committee the directions in which the town and community will be injured·by the proposed action of the city of Boston in taking this river and the land about it? What is the character of the meadow land in this basin? Is it permanently fertile, or not?

A. Certainly it is; and, as I understand it, if they propose to take a hundred rods on either side of every tributary of the stream, they go in every direction through the town, and certainly they will take one-third of the amount of taxable acres and a vast amount of valuable land. These brook meadows are considered as valuable as any land we have, because they yield great quantities of grass, and it costs nothing to keep them in condition yearly. Of course the grass would not command the price that English hay would in the market, but it is used extensively by the farmers. Our people are mostly milk raisers; they use this grass to keep their stock, and consider it very valuable.

Q. Then would it practically destroy the milk interest of a large portion of the town if this land should be taken?

A. I should judge it would. If the people who now own it were not allowed to cultivate this territory which is proposed to be taken of course it would lesson the productive land very much.

Q. It appears from the map that the head of the basin will be in the upper part of Bedford, and the dam down in the eastern part of the town. If the plan of the city, which consists in filling up a large basin in the winter and drawing it off gradually in the summer season, leaving a large area of land exposed, should be carried out, whether, in your opinion, the health of the inhabitants would suffer materially from the exhalations from the marsh lands exposed?

A. As far as my experience has ever led me to notice, of course when land is drained after it has been flooded for months, and the water is taken away from it, there always rises more or less miasma, that we do not consider very healthful.

Mr. BAILEY. — Brother Loomis, we have been doing that for years upon the Sudbury, and if you can find anybody who finds any fault with it bring him in. This is not a matter of theory, it is a matter of practice; we have been doing it for years.

Mr. BRUCE. — How would the same argument apply to the Mystic water? People have been drinking that for years, and nobody can point out a case of sickness that has been caused by it.

Mr. BAILEY. — I propose to address the committee upon that when I get to it.

Q. Whether or not Bedford has been one of the healthiest towns in the State hitherto?

A. I think Bedford ranks No. 2 in regard to health, and has for years past. I think Lincoln is called number one, and Bedford is considered next to it.

Q. Then you would regard it as endangering the health of the town if the city of Boston should take this large area of land?

A. I should judge it would be.

Q. Now I want to ask you in regard to the mill property of Mr. Clark. Is that water power the only one that is available on this stream?

A. That is the principal water power. There is a power on what is called Vine brook, which is used, I think, slightly.

Q. The city proposes to take Vine brook also, and to take that water power?

A. Mr. Clark's is the only mill within quite a circuit, a number of miles, where there is very much business done. He has for years past done a great deal of business.

Q. Sawing logs and grinding corn?

A. There is usually a large amount of lumber sawed in the spring.

Q. Whether the Western corn ground there is very extensively used by the farmers in raising milk, which is the principal industry of the place?

A. Thousands of bushels. Mr. Clark could answer that question better than I can; but he is selling grain all the time, — has quite a large sale, I should judge.

Q. Then as to people coming into the town: Is it true that the town has recently had two railroads built into it, one from Lexington up to Bedford, within ten years, and an extension from Lexington to North Billerica, so as to bring it on to the through line from Boston to Lowell, within the last year; and whether the town as a place of suburban residence will be injured by creating this large basin?

A. Well, of course we have had two railroads. The Middlesex Central was built through the town in 1872, and there is a branch that runs now to Billerica, opened last year. We were supposing that it would help our town very much, but if we are going to have anything taken from the town to injure it a great deal more than that would help it, I should suppose we would be in the background.

Q. Now, as to the question of drainage: If the city should be allowed to take Shawsheen river, where would it be possible for our town to be drained? How could it be drained?

A. Really, the only chance we have to drain the village is towards Shawsheen river. Concord river lies to the west of the town, but the fall would be so little that it would be no use to think of carrying the sewage from the village that way. This is the only direct way that the village ever could be drained.

Q. The natural drainage of the village now runs to the Shawsheen?

A. Runs into the Shawsheen, and Elm brook, which is very near the main river.

Cross-Examination.

Mr. BAILEY. —What you mean is that the sewage soaks into this stream?

A. Yes, sir.

Q. You have not any sewers built in the town?

A. No, sir.

Q. It simply soaks through?

A. That is all.

Mr. LOOMIS. — There is one short sewer, that runs through the centre of the village.

Q. Will you tell me how the fact that that land is owned by the city of Boston will injure the town any more than if it is owned by private individuals?

A. Well, if the land is taken for this purpose, as I understand it, we lose the tax on this large amount of property.

Q. That is the only reason why you think it would injure the town?

A. I should think it would injure the town a great deal to have this land exposed where water is allowed to flow over it.

Q. That would simply apply to the land occupied by the basin, wouldn't it?

A. I should suppose it would be everywhere, almost, because it would flow up more or less from the tributaries, wouldn't it?

Q. That is where you think the town would be injured?

A. I think that the principal part of the town would be injured.

Q. The mere fact that the land is owned by the city instead of other parties would not of itself injure the town, would it?

A. No, not if the town should get the tax from the city, the same as it would if private individuals owned the land. What I understand is that it is going to injure our town in a great degree if they take it and we can't tax it.

Mr. Loomis. — If the city takes land which has heretofore been cultivated every year, and kept in a high state of cultivation, and allows it to go back into a state of nature, where it will not be manured every year, would not that injure the land?

A. I should suppose it would, very much.

Mr. Bailey. — I understood that you claimed that this land was particularly valuable because you did not have to manure it, and yet got good crops every year.

A. If you go one hundred rods each side of every tributary you go outside of what we call brook-meadow land. I have testified in regard to taking one hundred rods each side of every tributary.

Q. Has any question been asked you that you have answered with regard to anything but brook-meadow land?

A. I don't know that there has.

Mr. Loomis. — Will a hundred rods on each side of the stream include arable land as well as brook-meadow land?

A. Certainly, and a large number of buildings.

Q. What will be the injury to the town in regard to the arable land if the city should take it and prevent it from being manured?

A. Well, the experience I have had with land teaches me that it depreciates in its productiveness pretty rapidly when it is not manured.

Cross-Examination.

Mr. Bailey. — Do you tax land any higher if it is manured than if it is not?

A. The assessors are supposed to tax land on its market value.

Q. They don't propose to tax a man for every load of manure he puts on his land, do they?

A. I suppose not.

Q. If the city owns these lands, and rents them to parties who pay taxes on them, what difference does it make to the town whether the city owns them or somebody else?

A. Of course, if the town realizes the same amount of taxation that it does now, I don't know what difference it makes who owns it.

Q. You and Brother Loomis seem to go upon the idea that we propose to make a desert up there.

A. That is the way I look at it.

Testimony of Charles H. Clark.

Mr. Loomis. — Whether you are the owner of the mill property in Bedford which is proposed to be taken by the city?

A. I am.

Q. Will you state to the committee what injury there would be to the community, if any, by the taking of that mill property? What is it now used for, and to what extent?

A. I use it now for grinding corn, sawing logs, and running a cider-mill.

Q. Can you state the amount of business you do a year?

A. Well, I should think about $35,000.

Q. Whether you have built up a business there of grinding Western corn in addition to the former business of grinding corn produced in the neighborhood?

A. Yes, sir. There was nothing of that kind done when I took the mill.

Q. From what towns are logs brought to your mill to be sawed?

A. From Bedford, Carlisle, Billerica, Burlington, Lexington, and Lincoln.

Q. Whether it would be possible by steam power to grind up that corn and to saw those logs as cheaply as it is done now by water power in Bedford?

A. I have some steam power there, and I do not find it so profitable as I do to run by water; and in grinding the corn that the farmers raise there, I could not grind it by steam at the same price that I have for grinding by water; the business would not be worth anything to me. It is a harder corn than Western corn, and takes considerable more power to manufacture it into meal. And in regard to sawing logs, they are sawed by steam in some sections, but I claim that in that section, at that distance from the wood market, it is not so profitable as to saw them by water. At this distance from the market, the slabs and sawdust are something that can be disposed of, turned into ready money, whereas in some sections, where the mills are run by steam profitably, these go to waste and are not considered of any value. That is the difference that we claim in the location between running by steam and running by water.

Mr. Gamwell. — Is not this rather a matter of estimating damages than whether the city should be allowed to take the water or not?

Mr. Loomis. — We claim that it would be an injury not to the mill owner only but to the community, — that it would be a public injury to take away from us the only mill power that we have.

Mr. Gamwell. — He is stating the difference between steam power and water power in reference to sawing logs and grinding corn. I don't know but it may cost a little more to use steam.

Mr. Loomis. — I would suggest that the community has to pay the cost of these things eventually. If it costs more to grind by steam than by water, the town must pay for it in the end.

Mr. Gamwell. — There may be a remote element: I don't know.

Mr. Loomis. — It is on that ground that we introduce this evidence.

Cross-Examination.

Mr. Bailey. — For how many months in the year does your mill run by water power?

Q. That depends upon the amount of rainfall. It is something that is uneven ; but as a general thing, from year to year, it is from about September to into June that I have a pretty reliable supply of water.

Q. A pretty good supply of water from September to June?

A. Yes, sir. The summer months are uncertain.

Q. So that, with the exception of two months in the year, there is always plenty of water running in that stream?

. A. Not always.

Q. But there is commonly?

A. Yes ; from June to September. It is more uncertain in the summer months.

Q. Do you have an engine to help you out?

A. Yes, sir.

Q. How large is the engine?

A. Fifteen-horse power.

Q. That does all the work that the water power does?

A. No, sir.

Q. Well, why doesn't it?

A. It isn't large enough.

Q. Don't you run it during the time that there is not water enough running?

A. Yes, sir. I understood you to ask me if that did all the work that the water was able to do?

Q. That the water-power does, yes?

A. It doesn't.

Q. That is, you can't do as much work when you are running by steam as you can when you are running by water?

A. No, sir.

Q. How large an engine would you require?

A. I should require about fifty-horse power.

Q. That would do, ordinarily, would it, all the work that you are required to do?

A. Yes, sir.

TESTIMONY OF THE REV. M. J. MURPHY.

Mr. BRUCE. — You are the parish priest of Andover, in the Catholic Church?

A. Yes, sir.

Q. You have charge of the church at Ballardvale?

A. Yes, sir.

Q. The population of Ballardvale is about 900, is it not?

A. Yes, sir.

Q. What proportion of the population are members of your church, or attend your church?

A. About one-third, I should think.

Q. Do many of them own houses in Ballardvale?

A. Yes, sir.

Q. And are they all employed in the factory of Mr. Bradlee?

A. Many of them are.

Q. What would be the effect upon the population of the village of Ballardvale of the taking of the whole of this stream by the city of Boston?

A. I assume that the doing away of the mills would result from it.

Q. Is there any other employment in the village that these people could get who are now employed in Mr. Bradlee's mill if that mill was given up?

Q. There is another establishment there, but not many of the inhabitants of Ballardvale are employed there. There are more employed in Mr. Bradlee's mill.

Q. There is some other employment?

A. Yes, sir.

Q. But that population is there also?

A. Yes, sir.

Q. Now what would be the effect on the people owning houses in that village of the destruction of Mr. Bradlee's mill?

A. Those along the river it would affect considerably, because it would be unhealthy, and affect the value of their property.

Q. If a large proportion of that population were obliged to abandon Ballardvale in order to get employment, whether or not it would seriously affect the value of their houses and other estates?

A. Yes, sir; I think so.

Q. Now it is a very pleasant and flourishing manufacturing village, is it not?

A. Yes, sir; the people are all contented.

Q. They all like the employment of Mr. Bradlee and his men, do they not?

A. Yes, sir.

Mr. Poore. — Father Murphy, you are also pastor of the Roman Catholic Church in Andover, as well as of the church at Ballardvale?

A. Yes, sir.

Q. Is it not a fact that most of your congregation are connected directly with the manufacturing works there, — the Smith & Dove establishment and the Marland mill?

A. Yes, sir.

Q. So the manufacturing population there would suffer as much as the people in Ballardvale by the taking of the Shawsheen?

A. Yes, sir.

Q. Is it not also a fact that very many of your parishioners in Andover own their houses along the valley of the stream?

A. Yes, sir.

Cross-Examination.

Mr. BAILEY. — I don't want you to be misled, as I think you are being, therefore I will ask you if your opinions and the answers you have given are not all predicated on the idea that the mills are going to be discontinued, — that this damage would happen only if the mills were discontinued?

A. No, sir; I think that the value of the stream is so great that without it the mills would not be kept running.

Q. If the mills still remained there, and were kept running, it would not injure the people in the way you say, whether the water were taken or not, would it?

A. Oh, if the mills were kept running, that would be their own lookout.

Mr. BRUCE. — But if Capt. Bradlee gave up manufacturing at his mill, do you think it likely that anybody would carry on any kind of work there that would take the place of his mill?

Mr. BAILEY. — That is a matter that the committee know just as much about as Father Murphy.

Q. Capt. Bradlee has done a great deal for all classes of people in that village, has he not?

A. Yes; he has done considerable for them.

Mr. SMITH. — Is it probable at all, if Capt. Bradlee should be compelled to give up, that any other party would be found that would take his place in regard to the good treatment of the operatives, in your judgment?

A. In my judgment, they are so contented and prosperous now, that, looking at other places, I don't think it could be bettered.

Q. It could be made worse?

A. Yes, sir.

TESTIMONY OF JOSEPH SHAW.

Mr. BRUCE. — Where do you reside?

A. In Ballardvale.

Q. What is your business?

A. I have charge of the sorting, scouring, and drying at the woollen mills.

Q. How long have you been there in charge of that department?

A. Going on six years.

Q. How long have you been in the employ of the Ballardale mill?

A. Twenty-four or twenty-five years, certainly twenty-four.

Q. Do you own property in Ballardvale?

A. I own a piece of land.

Q. What, in your opinion, would be the effect on the value of landed property in that village of the taking of this stream by the city of Boston?

A. I think it would more seriously affect the property of those employed in the mill than it would the property owners outside of the mill.

Q. For what reasons?

A. Well, for the reason, as has been stated, that the supply of water would not be adequate for the woollen mill, and if it was turned into a cotton mill, — the help there have all been educated up to that business, and to put them into a cotton mill would be taking them right away from their regular line of business.

Q. Do you think that a cotton mill could be erected there that could successfully compete with the Lowell and Lawrence mills?

A. No, sir, I do not.

Q. And the plant that Capt. Bradlee has got there would not be at all adapted to a cotton mill, would it?

A. Not to compete with mills on other streams, — I will say at Lawrence or Lowell.

Cross-Examination.

Mr. BAILEY. — How much wool do you scour there in the course of a year, or per day either?

A. To-day we are scouring about 2,200 pounds.

Q. How much water does that require?

A. Well, it requires a great amount. I couldn't say just the amount.

Q. Don't you know about how much it requires to scoure a pound of wool?

A. No, sir; I can't say.

Q. Did you ever make any estimate of the quantity of water required?

A. No, sir.

Q. But that is the limit, — about 2,200 pounds a day?

A. Yes, sir.

Q. For how many days in the year?

A. Every day, except legal holidays.

Q. Did you find any difficulty in getting water enough to scour your wool the past year?

A. I will change that a little, and say except during the dry season : then of course we can't scour. Every day that we have sufficient water we scour that amount, and sometimes we have to run up to 2,500 pounds.

Q. During the past year did you scour every day?

A. No, sir.

Q. How many days were you obliged to refrain from scouring?

A. That I can't say. If the water is too low to thoroughly rinse the wool we stop scouring.

Q. Yes ; that is general ; but how many days were there in the last season that you could not do that?

A. I can't say that exactly.

Q. Have you any recollection at all about it?

A. No, sir ; I have not.

Q. Have you any recollection of having stopped an entire day during the past season?

A. Yes, sir ; I know that we did during the months of July and August.

Q. Can you give us any idea of the number of days that you stopped?

A. No, sir, I couldn't : I haven't any book ; I have only my time-book ; and when the help get through there and can't scour they go into the yard to work.

Q. Your recollection don't help you so that you can remember the number of days?

A. No, sir.

Q. Was it a week?

A. I can't say. I couldn't set any definite time.

Q. Was it two weeks?

A. That I can't say.

Q. You can't give us any idea whether it was one day or two weeks?

A. No, sir; I couldn't set any day, but I am certain we had to stop; I am positive.

Mr. SMITH. — I would like to ask you, Mr. Shaw, in regard not only as to the necessity of having a good supply of water but also as to the necessity of having a pretty strong head when you are scouring. Is not that necessary?

A. Yes, sir; it is.

Q. You want something more than the mere water, then?

A. Yes, sir.

Mr. POOR. — What you have said about the need of water would apply just as much to the Marland mills, Mr. Stevens, as to Mr. Bradlee's mill, would it not?

A. Yes, sir; it would apply to them; but still it is a greater necessity with us to have clear water than it is where they are manufacturing colored goods, because during the summer months, in July and August, when the water gets down low and sluggish, then it is very difficult for us to cleanse our wool thoroughly.

Mr. BAILEY. — There is nothing peculiar in the wool that you have to wash, is there, over any other wool that is washed?

A. Well, there is a peculiarity in it in this way, — that it is a great deal more difficult to make work of fine wool than it is of the coarser grades; and it is harder to scour, also.

Q. I admit that; but there is nothing peculiar about the wool that you manufacture at your mill, is there, that distinguishes it from the wool at any other mill where they manufacture fine flannels of the same kind?

A. There are very few manufacturers that do that.

Q. Never mind that. I ask you if there is anything peculiar about the wool that is used in your mill that distinguishes it from the wool used in any other mill where goods of the same class are manufactured?

A. If they have a good head of water they can get it just as clean as we can when we have a head of water.

TESTIMONY OF LAWRENCE WHITTAKER.

Mr. BRUCE. — Where do you reside?

A. Ballardvale.

Q. How long have you resided there?

A. Since 1839.

Q. What is your business?

A. In the furnishing department of the Ballardville mill.

Q. How long have you been there?

A. Six years.

Q. Do you own property there?

A. I do, sir.

Q. Own a house?

A. Yes, sir.

Q. What, in your opinion, would be the effect upon the people who own houses in the village there of the taking of this river by the city of Boston?

A. I should think the property would depreciate.

Mr. GAMWELL. — Is that a matter which needs pressing upon the committee very much? Might we not assume all that?

Mr. BRUCE. — I think so. I will stop right there.

Q. What is the character of the soil along the stream above your pond?

A. It is muddy, marshy soil.

Q. Whether or not, when the water is low, there is so much of this soil in the water as to render it unfit for use for scouring purposes?

A. At times, in a dry season, the water is not fit to use, because it is muddy, and will not cleanse the wool as we want it to.

Cross-Examination.

Mr. BAILEY. — There is water enough then, but it is not of the right quality?

A. We don't have enough in the dry season.

Q. Do you know how much it requires to scour your wool?

A. No, sir; I don't.

Q. Your remarks about the damage that will be done are all based upon the idea that the mills will have to be discontinued, are they not?

A. Yes, sir, that business.

Mr. SMITH. — It seems to be assumed that there is considerable water running in the Shawsheen river at Ballardvale in the summer season: Is there any reservoir owned by the mills that is used in addition to the river?

A. There is a small reservoir.

Q. That is what helps you out, not what comes from above?

A. Yes; we have to run by steam power.

Q. If the Ballardvale mills are stopped would you be under the necessity of leaving the place and seeking some other employment?

A. I should, sir.

Q. And that would be the case with others who are employed there as you are?

A. Yes, sir.

Cross-Examination.

Q. Mr. BAILEY. — Do you know how far below Mr. Clark's mill you are on the river?

A. I do not, certainly. I have heard statements made, but I don't know.

Mr. CLARK. — About ten miles, I think.

TESTIMONY OF GEORGE H. TORR.

Mr. BRUCE. — You are the treasurer and selling agent of the Smith & Dove Manufacturing Co., are you not?

A. I am.

Q. Will you state to the committee, in your own way, the character of the manufactures carried on by this company on the Shawsheen river?

A. The goods we make are chiefly shoe threads, sewing twines, and carpet yarns. Part are bleached and part not bleached. We use annually about 3,000,000 pounds of flax and flax-tow. We are employing at present a little over 300 hands, but in good times we could employ 50 or 75 more.

Q. How many mills have the company?

A. We have three mills at Abbott Village and two at Frye Village.

Q. How far are they from each other, and how far from Capt. Bradlee's mill at Ballardville?

A. I think it is about two miles to Capt. Bradlee's mill, and about a mile and a quarter between our upper and lower mills.

Q. What is the number of people in the employ of your company?

A. We employ a little over 300 at present. Sometimes we employ from 350 to 375.

Q. What is the value of the annual product of your mill?

A. It is from half to three-quarters of a million dollars a year.

Q. Will you state what is the necessity in your manufacture of a large supply of water?

A. Well, we use it for power, and we use it also for bleaching, and we are obliged to have pure water for bleaching.

Q. Could you get along without it?

A. We could not.

Q. Whether or not you could carry on the manufactures that you now do at your mills if the request of the city of Boston were granted to take the water of this stream?

A. I don't see how we could.

Q. Your opinion is, then, that the manufactures would have to be abandoned that are now carried on there?

A. It seems so to me.

Q. Now will you state how your mill would be affected even if you had a part of the water of the stream, taking into consideration the fact that Mr. Stevens' mill is above you?

A. Well, we would be affected chiefly in our bleaching, and if there was a small supply of water, our bleaching being at the lower mills, we would get all the dirt that comes from the upper mills and all the dyestuff that comes from Mr. Stevens' mill.

Q. And pure water is as much a necessity to you as to Capt. Bradlee?

A. Yes, sir.

Q. What is the capital of your corporation?

A. $500,000.

The CHAIRMAN. — Do you use other power than water power?

A. We have three steam-engines of about seventy-five-horse power each.

Mr. BRUCE. — Whether or not in the two villages where your mills are located quite a proportion of the people own their own houses?

A. Quite a proportion of them do.

Q. And they have been educated and brought up to the peculiar business carried on at your mills?

A. They have, yes.

Q. Whether or not, at the present time, at all seasons of the year, there is sufficient water power for the use of your mills?

A. We have not at all times sufficient for power.

Q. How long has your company been in operation on that stream?

A. We have been spinning flax there for a little over fifty years.

Q. Whether or not your company was the first to manufacture shoe thread in this country?

A. I think they were.

Q. Is there any other reason that you wish to give to the committee why this request of the city of Boston should not be granted, as far as it affects your mills? If so, state it.

Q. I think if the request was granted, as it is stated, it would stop our works.

Q. Do you think of any other particular reason excepting what you have given.

A. I don't think of anything else.

Q. Whether or not your goods have a name by which they are known to the trade?

A. They are known to the trade as "Andover Goods,"—Andover hreads, twines, and yarns. That name is of considerable value to us. We have kept up the quality of the goods so as to make the name valuable.

Cross-Examination.

Mr. BAILEY. — Has there been water enough running the past season to enable you to do your bleaching?

A. There has.

Q. All the last year?

A. I think so.

Q. How much water does it require to do your bleaching?

A. That I am not personally acquainted with. It was testified to as 2,000,000 of gallons. Less than one-half of our goods are bleached. If all the goods we spin were bleached it would take more than double that.

Q. That was based on the amount actually required, was it not?

A. On the amount required at that time, yes.

Q. What is the material that you use there that requires bleaching ?

A. Flax.

Q. How much flax do you have to bleach a day, on the average?

A. It depends on how business is pushing. We have other work that we can turn the hands on to if we are a little slack of work of that kind.

Q. What is the amount of flax you use?

A. We use about 3,000,000 pounds of flax and flax-tow. I am am not able to distinghish.

Q. It all requires to be bleached?

A. No, sir, not all of it.

Q. How much of it requires bleaching?

A. It is a variable quantity. We supply whatever the market calls for. They may call for a large quantity of bleached goods, they may call for brown goods.

Q. Would it be two-thirds, on the average?

A. I am not able to tell the average.

Q. Is that so pretty regularly throughout the year? As much so one day as another?

A. Yes, sir; we run pretty steady. If business is slack we pile up the goods.

Q. That would be about 10,000 pounds a day?

A. Yes, sir, of flax and flax-tow. Flax-tow is a product of flax, — comes out in preparing it.

Q. The works have run uninterruptedly all this last year?

A. Yes, sir.

Q. And the year before?

A. Yes, sir. I don't remember that we have ever been stopped for want of water.

Mr. BRUCE. — That, I think, closes our evidence.

Mr. POOR. — I do not propose, on behalf of Mr. Stevens, the proprietor of the Marland mills, to introduce any testimony at this hearing. I will simply state in his behalf that he has there a mill of fourteen sets, employing some 200 hands, with a large investment, — just how large I will not undertake to state; it has been stated at former hearings; but the buildings have been increased in number and size, and a very large business is done there in the manufacture of woollen dress goods. The annual product is somewhere between four and five hundred thousand dollars. The mill privilege is situated between Abbott Village and Frye Village, the two Smith & Dove privileges, and our objections to the taking of the water are the same as those of the other manufacturers. We need it for power, for scouring, and for all the purposes incident to manufacturing.

I do not propose to argue the case. You can readily see that the taking of the water will be a very great damage to us, and where the field of argument has been reaped by Brother Morse, as it has, and will be again by Brother Bruce, it seems to me to be foolish to attempt to glean between them. With this brief statement I shall rest Mr. Stevens' case.

Mr. BAILEY. — Can you tell us the amount of wool that is used there?

Mr. POOR. — I cannot. You can readily see that it is a large amount.

Mr. BAILEY. — I can't see anything about it, because I don't know anything about it. If you are going to claim that there will be any damage to that property, I want you to put in something about it, so that we can form some opinion when it comes to the question of damages.

Mr. POOR. — We will talk with you on figures when the time comes.

Mr. BAILEY. — If you are willing to leave it there, I am.

Mr. POOR. — We are willing to leave it there. We are forced to leave it there. We don't want you to come there. We don't want to lose our privilege. We don't want our water taken.

Mr. GAMWELL. — I understand that the whole product is between four hundred thousand and half a million.

Mr. BAILEY. — Yes, sir; but we want to know how much wool is washed there, and find out how much water is required to wash it.

Mr. GAMWELL. — I understand that the goods manufactured are all-wool fabrics?

Mr. POOR. — Yes, sir.

' Mr. BAILEY. — Will you furnish us with the amount of wool that you consume yearly?

Mr. POOR. — I won't agree to.

SIXTH HEARING.

MONDAY, April 12, 1886.

The Committee met pursuant to adjournment, Senator Scott presiding.

The CHAIRMAN. — I understand there is a committee here from Lexington, who would like to be heard. Would you prefer to go on, Mr. Bailey, or had you rather hear what they have to say before you proceed?

Mr. BAILEY. — I think I prefer to wait until they have been heard.

The CHAIRMAN. — Then we will hear the gentlemen from Lexington, if they are ready to proceed.

STATEMENT OF MR. WALTER BLODGETT.

Mr. Chairman and Gentlemen : — Lexington is particularly interested in that part of the water-shed of the Shawsheen river that is comprised in the valleys of the two brooks that run through her territory, one known as the North brook, which runs through the north side of the central village, and the other known as Vine brook, which rises in the meadows on the south side and runs through the village. Both of these brooks empty into the Shawsheen at or near Bedford. They have their sources in rich meadow lands, that are annually heavily manured, making their waters black with the sediment whenever there is a copious rain. It is manifestly important to the riparian owners that no town or corporation shall control these waters, or place restrictions upon the adjoining lands, as it would depreciate the value of their property to a large extent, and render these meadows, now susceptible of a high cultivation, valueless. This would be the case whether Boston takes one rod on either side, or one hundred, to secure the purity of the water ; for, in either event, she would virtually control that property.

Now, to show how important these brooks are to Lexington, especially Vine brook, it will only be necessary for me to state that upon three former occasions — twice when the town of Arlington proposed to take this brook for agricultural and domestic purposes, and once, no longer ago than last spring, when a private water company wanted it for domestic purposes — the town each time chose a committee to come here to defend her interests, and also the interests of the riparian owners. After the matter had been discussed in all its bearings the committee on water supply gave to those parties who sought to obtain this stream leave to withdraw. Thus heretofore Lexington's interest in Vine brook has been always acknowledged.

Now that water has been introduced into our town, it is felt that this brook is of more importance to the town than ever before, as the introduction of water necessitates a system of sewerage and drainage ; and as this brook is the only outlet which we have that could be utilized for this purpose, and as it at present receives the whole surface drainage of the thickly settled part of the town, it is evident that it is of the utmost importance to Lexington, for sanitary purposes, that no restriction shall be placed upon it by any other town or corporation ; for as soon as she is restricted of the privileges which she now enjoys it will force her to adopt some other and more expensive system of sewerage. It will probably be said in answer to this, that a committee has already reported a bill to secure the adoption of a uniform system of sewerage in this portion of the State. I will only say in this connection that this system has been examined into by several large towns already, and has been very strongly objected to on account of the great expense it would be necessary to incur in order to avail themselves of it.

Lexington has always been noted as one of the healthiest towns in the State, and this, together with the associations clustering around her, is attracting year by year more and more people from abroad to make permanent homes within her borders. We feel it would be a great misfortune to her welfare if anything should occur to hinder her growth or impair her present good sanitary condition ; and I think this would surely be the result if this petition prevailed.

Mr. BAILEY. — Is not Vine brook now used as a source of water supply for your town ?

Mr. BLODGETT. — No, sir.

Mr. BAILEY. — Where do they get their supply ?

Mr. BLODGETT. — They get it from wells.

Statement of Mr. M. R. Merriam.

I do not know as I have very much to offer in addition to what my colleague has presented to you, except to emphasize what he has said of the importance of the conservation of these tributaries of the Shawsheen to the town of Lexington. Those tributaries are the only effluents of surface and underground water that exist in the town. It is well known, I suppose, and yet it may be important to state it in its bearings, that Lexington is the highest land in the county of Middlesex, consequently its streams are diminutive, although numerous and somewhat lengthy, and ramify among the agricultural districts to a considerable length. But, certainly, it strikes a layman, who is not, perhaps, sufficiently posted to give an expert opinion, that the quantity of water available for purposes of a supply for a great city like Boston is entirely inadequate, proportioned to the damage which must individually accrue to the affected properties. Lexington is largely an agricultural town, to be sure, and it has a good deal of land that has been highly cultivated and underdrained, and is highly fertilized, as has already been said to you. This brook is the only outlet for the surface drainage, particularly in the village, and it has from time immemorial been used to a greater or less extent as an outlet for sewage ; and since the introduction of public waterworks it must inevitably be more used than before for this purpose. The retention of the sewage upon the land, which would inevitably follow the protection of these waters from pollution, must operate very disastrously upon the health of the thickly settled portion of the town. Already complaints have been made.

And aside from that, I regard the location, the trend of the land towards the watercourses, as such that retention of the sewage in the soil cannot avail much in protecting the water supply from pollution. A good deal of the ground is level, and the underground water stands high, and the sewage from our cesspools permeates that water, and is not deodorized, but soaks through and gets into the brooks and rivulets. Whatever may be the propriety of draining sewage into streams, nevertheless such drainage has always existed there, as in many other parts of the State, and it must necessarily. No human enactments can prevent it. As long as the soil adjacent to the streams is occupied the sewage of dwellings must inevitably soak into the ground, into the underground water; and unless that is aerated, of course we all understand it never can become deodorized, or proper for use for drinking. The time may come in the far future when the population shall have so increased that some such system as has been already proposed by the Commission on Drainage may include Lexington. But at present there does not seem to be a necessity for it, and the waters are adequate to take away the sewage without serious detriment to public health. I do not know as I have anything further to say, excepting that I believe that restrictions placed upon the borders of these tributaries would make an encumbrance upon the adjacent property which it is very difficult to estimate the amount of. It would certainly be very serious. A casual glance at a map which I have seen of these tributaries shows that the territory that would thus be sequestered and detached from the useful purposes which it now serves would be enormous. Moreover, there are tributaries to the waters which are not represented on the map which I have seen, which go through very valuable portions of territory in the town, and that necessarily carry with them a large amount of polluting substances. The volume of water might prevent them from becoming a public nuisance, but certainly it would be distasteful in sentiment, if not more than that. I do not know that I have anything further to add.

Mr. BAILEY. — Your remarks apply equally as objections to the city of Boston or the town of Andover taking the Shawsheen river?

A. Yes, sir.

Q. And I understand, as the result of the examination you have given the subject, on account of the liability of Lexington becoming thickly populated, you think that would not be a proper source from which to take a water-supply for a large community?

A. I think Lexington, as it exists to-day, vitiates it as a proper supply, whatever may be the prospective prosperity of Lexington.

Q. What is the population of Lexington that would naturally drain into Vine brook?

A. It drains both ways. There are two sources in Lexington, very narrowly separated: one the direct source of the Shawsheen,

and the other Vine brook, which ultimately empties into the Shawsheen at the limits of the town, separated only by a few rods.

Q. What is the population within that territory?

A. Well, it would be simply an estimate, but I should say the
population was 2,000.

The case for the remonstrants was closed at this point, and Mr.
Dexter Brackett was called by Mr. Bailey, in rebuttal.

TESTIMONY OF MR. DEXTER BRACKETT.

Mr. BAILEY. — Have you made any examination or inquiries in
regard to the amount of water required to wash wool, where it is
used for such products as have been described here by Mr. Bradlee and others?

A. I have, — for the purposes of washing wool, and of woollen
manufacturing.

Q. Where have have you made your examinations?

A. At Saxonville, on the Sudbury, and also I have made some
inquiries at Lawrence.

Q. In what mill?

A. The Pacific.

Q. Is that the largest woollen mill in Lawrence?

A. I understand it is.

Q. How much wool is consumed there?

A. About 4,000,000 pounds per year.

Q. That is about how much a day?

A. About 13,330 pounds per day.

Q. And what is the amount of water required for washing the
wool?

A. The entire consumption in the manufacture of the wool is
about 1,890,000 gallons per day, or about 140 gallons for each
pound of wool.

Q. How is it at Saxonville, — what is the amount used?

A. At Saxonville they manufacture between three and four
millions pounds of wool per year, and for a water-supply they have
1,500,000 gallons per day, which we allow to flow into the river,
and, also, what is gathered between our dam and Saxonville, which
would bring it, in a dry time, a minimum week, to only about
1,700,000 gallons.

Q. And with that they do all the operations required on between 3,000,000 and 4,000,000 pounds of wool?

A. Yes, sir.

Q. Now, sir, what would be the supply at Bradlee's mills, on the Shawsheen, after the part asked for by Boston has been taken out?

A. Well, on the basis of Mr. Crafts' testimony, of a quarter of a foot per second per square mile, it would be about 4,500,000.

Q. That would go past Mr. Bradlee's?

A. Yes, sir.

Q. And if the other mill is two miles down there would be still more, would there not?

A. There would be more.

Q. Have you made an examination of some of the statements in Mr. Crafts' pamphlet?

A. I have; yes, sir.

Q. Well, sir, will you state what you have to say with regard to the supply?

A. With regard to the available amount which can be depended upon from the different sources of supply, Mr. Crafts said that when Basin 4 is completed, as it is at present, the full capacity of the Sudbury river would be 38,000,000 gallons per day; and that Lake Cochituate will furnish 12,000,000 gallons more, making a total supply at present of 50,000,000 gallons. I would say with regard to the first statement of 38,000,000 per day from the Sudbury-river works, that when the present works, exclusive of Basin 4, were constructed, they were calculated to supply 20,000,000 gallons per day, and the experience of years since that time has shown that they could not be safely depended upon for more than that amount. In 1883, with a consumption of less than 20,000,000 gallons, all the storage reservoirs were emptied, so that the supply was exhausted. The completion of the additional basin — Basin 4 — has added about 5,000,000 gallons per day, so that the present full supply is about 25,000,000 per day, instead of 38,000,000. At Lake Cochituate the full supply, as estimated by Mr. Davis, was 12,000,000 gallons. But at that time the lowest recorded yield was 13,600,000 gallons; while since Mr. Davis' report was made there have been two years when the amount was only about

9,000,000 gallons per day. So that, even using the Lake Cochituate as a storage basin from the Sudbury works, as we do to a certain extent, it is not safe to consider that available for more than 10,000,000 per day, which would make the present total supply available 35,000,000 gallons, instead of 50,000,000 gallons, as stated by Mr. Crafts.

Q. This pamphlet was prepared by the city engineer and yourself?

A. Yes, sir.

(Pamphlet referred to, being an answer to a pamphlet prepared by Mr. Crafts, was put in evidence by Mr. Bailey.)

Q. Now let me ask you about the statement made by Mr. Crafts of the cost of connecting the Chestnut-Hill reservoir with the Mystic supply.

A. The statement was made that by laying a 30-inch pipe from Chestnut-Hill reservoir to the Mystic pumping-station, at a cost of $250,000, I think, the 13,000,000 gallons a day could be immediately made available for that supply. Well, in order to have that amount we should be obliged to build the additional storage basins on the Sudbury supply, at a cost of about, probably, $2,000,000 ; and the size of the pipe which Mr. Crafts has based his estimate upon, while sufficient to supply 13,000,000 gallons, would not supply a daily average consumption of 13,000,000, for the reason that in the winter season the consumption is sometimes double the average consumption. So that in order to supply an average consumption of 13,000,000 gallons per day, it would be necessary to have a pipe large enough to supply nearly double that amount.

Q. And the total cost would be how much?

A. I should say the total cost of supplying that 13,000,000 gallons per day would be at least $2,500,000 instead of $250,000.

Q. As much as it would cost to obtain a supply from the Shawsheen?

A. Yes, sir.

Q. Now, with regard to the proportion of the Mystic works that would be abandoned, in case the Mystic was abandoned as a source of supply, what would be the value of the part of the works that would be abandoned?

A. At present not more than $200,000.

Q. What would be the value of the part that would have to be abandoned ultimately, if we went on and built the additional basins on the Mystic, and then were compelled to abandon the works?

A. About $2,000,000.

Cross-Examination.

Mr. BRUCE. — You base your estimate of the amount of water used for scouring wool on what is used at the Pacific and the Saxonville mills?

A. Yes, sir.

Q. Do you know what kind of goods they manufacture there?

A. They manufacture worsted at Saxonville.

Q. All colored goods, are they not?

A. I think not, sir.

Q. Do you know?

A. I understand not.

Q. What do they manufacture at the Pacific mills?

A. They manufacture worsted goods.

Q. Aren't they all colored goods?

A. It may be.

Q. Now, do you know what the amount of water used for scouring the wool, for the purposes for which it is used at the Pacific and the Saxonville mills, is as compared with that used at Capt. Bradlee's?

A. Not except in a general way.

Q. You mean you can guess, don't you?

A. I mean from inquiries which I have made.

Q. From whom?

A. From people who manufacture woolen goods.

Q. Do you know of anybody in this country who manufactures goods like Capt. Bradlee's?

A. I am not acquainted with any one.

Q. Therefore you have made no inquiries as to the amount of water required to scour wool for the purposes of his manufacture?

A. I have understood, as I say, in a general way, that it might require from a half to three-quarters more water.

Q. You do not know but it would several times as much, do you?

A. Of my own personal knowledge, no, sir.

Q. You do not know?

A. No, sir.

Q. Do you know what would be the character of the water that would run down that little stream, over that muddy bank, if there was only the amount you specify?

A. I know there would be more running there than there is at Saxonville.

Q. That does not help us any. I did not ask anything about the amount of water; I asked you what would be the character of it.

A. I could not say as to the character of it.

Q. Now, you have figured the water-supply over on the Sudbury lower than it was ever figured by anybody before, haven't you?

A. I have it lower than it has been estimated.

Q. Has there ever been a statement by any engineer who has ever appeared, representing the city of Boston, before any committee of the Legislature, which has put the supply down to where you put it to-day?

A. I think probably not, for the reason —

Mr. BRUCE. — I did not ask you the reason; I simply asked you the fact.

Mr. BAILEY. — You can give the reason if you wish, now that you have answered the question.

WITNESS. — For the reason that the later records have shown that the amount which had previously been estimated upon cannot be depended upon.

Q. Now, what is the record, and of what year?

A. One in 1881, and one in 1883.

Q. Those are the two records you rely upon?

A. Yes, sir.

Q. Was not Mr. Wightman here before this committee, and did he not give his estimates in 1883?

A. Yes, sir.

Q. And did he put them down where you put them now?

A. He simply had one year's record.

Q. Did he put them down where you do now?

A. He did not.

Q. How was the record of 1883 as compared with the record of 1881?

A. The record of 1883 is a little less than the record of 1881, — it is 1880, I should have said, 1880 and 1883.

Q. Is the record in the report of 1883?

A. It is the record for the year 1883.

Q. What did that record show?

A. It showed that in the year 1883 the average amount collected on the three sources of supply was only 10.15 inches.

Q. How much water did that give you?

A. It gave us, as I say, on the Sudbury river, about 19,000,000 gallons. We took 19,753,200 gallons per day from the Sudbury river supply, and that exhausted the source of supply. At Lake Cochituate, in order to keep the city supplied, we were obliged to erect temporary pumping machinery —

Q. I did not ask you about that. I want to get at the figures; you can tell about your difficulties some other time.

A. The simple statement is, we exhausted the supply.

Q. I want your figures, if you have them.

A. The total consumption from both supplies was 32,800,000 gallons.

Q. That is not what I asked you, — we will get at it by and by; the amount of water collected is what I want to get at?

A. The amount of water collected in the two sources of supply would be a great deal more than that, if that is what you want.

Q. That is what I want.

A. I do not carry the figures in my head. Of course, the amount of water collected includes the amount of water which passes over our dam; a large proportion of it passes into the river during the spring.

Q. Do you mean to say you are simply giving us the consumption in each year, 1883 and 1880?

A. No, sir.

Q. What are you giving us?

A. The 10.15 inches is the total amount which was collected.

Q. How much did it amount to per day?

A. I could not tell you without looking at the report.

Q. I thought you told us a moment ago that the experience of

1880 and 1883 led you to put a different estimate upon the capacity of these two sources of supply than Mr. Davis had heretofore done, and than Mr. Wightman did in the year 1883?

A. Yes, sir.

Q. He estimated, in 1883, that the capacity of these two sources of supply was 50,000,000 gallons?

A. He estimated the total at 50,000,000 gallons, when the Sudbury river source should have been developed.

Q. How many more basins did it take, and what was their capacity, to make the 50,000,000 gallons?

A. He expected there would be 50,000,000 gallons when two more basins were constructed; in other words, I figure 42,000,000 where he figured 50,000,000.

Q. What was the capacity of the two basins?

A. About 1,500,000,000 gallons.

Q. What would be the daily supply from them?

A. It would be about 7,000,000 gallons.

Q. Now, you also say that Mr. Crafts has not estimated correctly as to the cost of connecting the Cochituate and the Mystic systems?

A. By estimating that there are 50,000,000 per day at present, of course he did not estimate upon any cost of additional storage basins —

Q. Wait one moment. I am referring to the cost of running the pipe to connect these two sources of supply. You have given it at $500,000, and he has given it at $250,000, has he not?

A. Yes, sir.

Q. Your estimate is just twice as large as his?

A. Yes, sir.

Q. Now, will you tell us why you estimate it will cost twice as much to connect these two sources of supply as Mr. Crafts estimates?

A. Because, as I have said, in my opinion, it would be necessary to have a larger main than Mr. Crafts has estimated, and all the expenses of laying would be greater.

Q. His estimate calls for a 30-inch pipe?

A. Yes, sir.

Q. What capacity would you have?

A. Well, 36 inches.

Q. And do you want this committee to believe that to put in a 36-inch main between these two sources of supply would cost twice as much as it would to put in a 30-inch main?

A. I think that —

Q. This is a question which can be answered by yes or no. Do you think it would cost twice as much?

A. No, I do not think so.

Q. Why, then, did you tell this committee it would cost $500,000?

A. Because I think a 30-inch main and the laying of it would cost more than $250,000.

Q. Did you hear how Mr. Crafts made up his estimate?

A. Yes, sir.

Q. The reasons he gave for it?

A. Yes, sir.

Q. He has had a good deal of experience in this kind of work, has he not?

A. He has.

Q. Do you not think there is a little tendency in your mind to color your testimony here a trifle?

A. No, sir.

Q. No desire to favor your side of the case?

A. No, sir. These estimates have been made without any reference whatever to this case.

Q. When were they made?

A. Some of them were made five or six years ago. The estimates have been revised. I do not mean to say I have put in a figure to-day based on the old cost of work, and the old prices of materials.

Q. How do you get at your estimate?

A. From the cost of work as it has been done for the city of Boston.

Q. Under whose management?

A. Under the management of the Water Department and Engineer's Department.

Q. Does not the cost of laying pipe vary a good deal, according as to who happens to be managing the Water-Works in Boston?

A. I do not think so. The Water-Works, as far as the cost of laying of pipe is concerned, have been under the same management for some forty or fifty years.

Q. What percentage of cost more would it be to lay a 36-inch pipe than a 30-inch pipe?

A. I should think about twenty-five per cent.

Q. That is pretty liberal, isn't it?

A. No.

Q. Would the trench cost any more?

A. A little.

Q. Not much?

A. It would cost more.

Q. A little more?

A. Yes, sir.

Q. And the pipe would only cost a little more. Don't you really think ten per cent. would cover it?

A. No, sir.

Q. Fifteen?

A. I stated twenty.

Q. You said twenty-five.

A. I mean twenty-five.

Q. Which do you mean now, twenty or twenty-five?

A. I mean twenty-five. I should have to make an estimate to give you the exact figure.

Q. Then you have not made an estimate on this matter really, to give your original estimate to the committee, have you?

A. Yes, sir.

Q. Well, it is only approximate, is it not?

A. No, it is not an approximate estimate, except as anything of that nature must be an approximate estimate.

Q. Well, now, tell us why it is necessary to have twice the capacity of pipe that Mr. Crafts estimated upon? You say in order to carry an average of 13,000,000 a day you want a pipe that will carry 26,000,000 a day?

A. Because, there being no opportunities for storage of water at the Mystic pumping-station, your pipe would have to be large enough to supply the maximum demand.

Q. What is the capacity of the reservoir there?

A. The reservoir holds about 25,000,000 gallons.

Q. How many days during the winter is double the average supply drawn?

A. Perhaps half-a-dozen.

Q. Half-a-dozen days scattered through the winter?

A. Well, they will not be altogether scattered; they may come all at once; they are liable to.

Q. Is there a record of any time when they ever did?

A. Where there have been half-a-dozen consecutive days?.

Q. Yes, when for half-a-dozen consecutive days the draught on the supply has been twice what the average for the year shows?

A. I could not say; I do not think there has been.

Q. You do not believe there ever was, do you?

A. No, sir.

Q. Now, let us get at the truth about the facts, as near as we can. How many days do you think there have been continuously?

A. Oh, perhaps two or three.

Q. Perhaps two. Well, now, if there were not more than two or three days, with a supply of 25,000,000 gallons in the reservoir, you would be able to meet that call, would you not?

A. No, sir.

Q. Why not?

A. Because, if we lower the reservoir at all, we immediately deprive the people on the higher portions of the territory supplied of the water, and at the very time when the greatest demand is, it is necessary to have the reservoir full.

Q. You could very easily remedy that difficulty by a high service such as you have at Roxbury, could you not?

A. We could do a good many things, I suppose.

Q. The people ought to have it, ought they not?

A. I don't know but they ought.

Q. What is the object of having that reservoir out there, if it is not for some such purpose as that?

A. The object was, I suppose, originally, to store the water.

Q. To meet just such a contingency?

A. In case of absolute need it would furnish a supply for a portion of the territory at present; but it would not be considered good engineering to put in a pipe there which would necessitate drawing that reservoir down every cold snap.

Q. Is there a record in the experience of your water-works where they have ever drawn 13,000,000 gallons a day from the Mystic supply?

A. Yes, sir.

Q. When?

A. I am very certain there is.

Q. When?

A. I could not give you the exact date.

Q. Take the last year; what is the maximum for the last year?

A. I think it is nearly 13,000,000 last year. I do not carry these figures in my head exactly.

Q. You do not remember any time, do you, when it has been 13,000,000?

A. Yes, sir; I remember it has been.

Q. Was that not when East Boston was supplied from the Mystic?

A. It may have been. I am not certain that it has not been 13,000,000 this winter, but I am not positive about it.

Q. There would not be any difficulty, would there, in carrying the water into Mystic lake, and pumping it from there, as you do now?

A. Not if you continue the Mystic supply.

Q. Suppose you abandon it, what would be the trouble in using that as a reservoir?

A. You have got to do something with the Abbajona river.

Q. It would be very easy to take care of that, would it not?

A. I question whether it would be very easy or not.

Q. All you would have to do would be to run it around?

A. "All you would have to do would be to run it around," yes. If we could do it as easy as you say it, it would be very easily done.

Q. Can't you do it?

A. I suppose it is possible to do it.

Q. You are familiar with the country, and know about how far you would have to change the course of that stream to get it into the lower lake, I suppose? You have been around in the Mystic valley, have you not?

A. I have not with reference to that point.

Q. Are you not familiar enough with it to know about how far you would have to carry the waters of the river?

A. Yes; I think it would be some mile and a half, a mile or a mile and a half.

Q. Perhaps half a mile?

A. No, at least a mile.

Q. Did you make any inquiry as to the amount of water it takes to bleach yarns?

A. To bleach wool, that is all.

Q. Such as is manufactured at the Pacific mills; but as to the amount it takes to bleach yarns you do not know anything?

A. They manufacture woollen yarns before they make goods, I understand.

Q. Do you know anything about flax?

A. No, sir.

Q. That you do not know anything about?

A. No, sir.

Q. And you do not know anything about the wool that you have spoken of, as compared with the quality of the wool and the character of the goods manufactured by Mr. Bradlee?

A. Except as I have stated.

Q. And that is pretty near guess-work, is it not?

A. If you want to call it guess-work, it is founded upon information from a man who is posted in the manufacture of woollen goods.

Mr. Bruce..— Of a particular kind.

Mr. Bailey. — These were fine woollen products, and fine yarns, were they not?

A. That I cannot say.

Q. Do you not know that for three days of this last month the consumption of water from the Mystic was 11,000,000 one day, 12,000,000 the next day, and 13,000,000 the next day?

A. As I say, I do not carry these figures in my head; I thought it was in the vicinity of 13,000,000 a day.

Mr. Bailey. — I will state that to be the fact, upon the authority of Mr. Rockwell.

This closed the testimony.

Tuesday and Wednesday, April 20 and 21, were assigned for a view, and Thursday, April 22, for the arguments.

STATE HOUSE, April 29, 1886.

The Committee met at 10.30 A.M., Senator Scott presiding.

Mr. LOOMIS. — There are two gentlemen here this morning from the town of Burlington, and they desire to be heard in this matter. Not having been notified of the hearing early enough, it was impossible for them to be here before. They ask the courtesy of the committee for a few moments.

The CHAIRMAN. — I understood the hearing was closed ; but we will not shut anybody out who wants to be heard.

TESTIMONY OF SAMUEL SEWALL.

Mr. LOOMIS. — You are a resident of Burlington?

A. Yes, sir.

Q. Are you one of the Selectmen of the town?

A. I am.

Q. Vine brook, one of the tributaries of the Shawsheen, which the city proposes to take, runs through the town of Burlington, does it not?

A. Yes, sir, it does, almost, well, about the whole length.

Q. Will you please state as to the character of the land through which Vine brook flows, as to whether it is productive land or not?

A. Well, yes, it is meadow land ; of course, it is productive of meadow-hay, and is used a great deal by farmers there for feeding their stock ; large quantities of hay are cut upon it and fed.

Q. Is it land which fertilizes itself every year without manure?

A. It is.

Q. And whether it is owned in small parcels by farmers throughout the town?

A. Yes, sir, it is.

Q. The hay is used for keeping milk stock, is it, through the winter?

A. Yes, sir.

Q. Is the grass of good quality?

A. Yes, sir ; it is very good quality of meadow-grass. It is not English grass, but it is very good quality of meadow-grass, so considered.

Q. Whether the proposed reservoir will injure adjoining land, used for English grass, by soakage or flowage?

Mr. BAILEY. — Does he know anything about that?

Q. Have you examined the property?

A. I have looked at the map.

Mr. BAILEY. — Has he any experience on the effect of a water-basin? Has he ever examined into the question of water-basins and their effects?

Mr. SEWALL. — Well, we know if it covers the land it injures it.

Q. What is the effect on English grass if water flows over it part of the year, do you know that?

A. It destroys it.

Q. Now, whether there is any mill-privilege on Vine brook which would be taken ; Reed's mill, for instance?

A. I see by the map it would flow up to this mill ; and there is another place, above that a little, which I suppose would not be allowed to flow in, where it has been used for print-works and various other things, where they have a dam.

Q. Cumston's print-works?

A. Yes, sir ; it was originally his. It is used now by another man.

Q. Whether the Reed mill is the only saw-mill in town?

A. The Reed mill is the only saw-mill there is there now, and a grist-mill there.

Q. Whether, if the Reed mill should be taken, and the two mills in Bedford, the Staples and the Clark mill, there would be any mill about there where you could get your logs sawed and your corn ground? What would be the nearest mill to Arlington?

A. I don't know where the next one would be.

Q. Whether you, as representing the interests of the town, would be opposed to the taking by the city of a tract of land, say ten rods wide, or wider, which would be exempt from taxation?

A. Yes, sir, I should be opposed to it, if it was to be exempt from taxation. The town is small, only, I think, about 7,000 acres, and to take out a large portion of that would, of course, increase the taxes on the remainder. The town is small and the valuation is small anyway. To reduce it in this way, and especially if this water should flow on some of the adjoining land there, — some of our best land, not for meadow hay, but for English — it would diminish the value and increase the rate of taxation considerably.

Q. If the city should take land on each side of that stream, so it could not be manured in such a way as to pollute the waters, we will say for a distance of one hundred rods on each side of the stream, whether that would not take a very large proportion of the cultivated land in that part of Burlington?

A. I don't know how much; it would take considerable.

Mr. BAILEY presented the following bill : —

COMMONWEALTH OF MASSACHUSETTS.

IN THE YEAR ONE THOUSAND EIGHT HUNDRED AND EIGHTY-SIX.

AN ACT to Provide a Furthur Supply of Water for the City of Boston.

Be it enacted by the Senate and House of Representatives, in General Court assembled, and by the authority of the same, as follows : —

SECTION 1. The City of Boston, for the purpose of supplying said city and the inhabitants thereof with pure water, may, by the Boston Water Board, take and hold all the waters of the Shawsheen river, and of the tributaries thereof south and west of the tracks of the Boston & Lowell Railroad, in the towns of Wilmington and Billerica, and any water rights connected therewith; may prevent the pollution of said waters; may collect, store, and convey said waters into said city, and distribute and sell said waters to the inhabitants of said city; may construct and maintain dams, reservoirs, storage-basins, drains, conduits, and aqueducts, and erect buildings and machinery; may change the course of any streams within the water-shed of said portion of said river; may carry any pipes, conduits, or aqueducts over or under any river, water-course, railroad, highway, or other way; may enter upon and dig up such road or way for the purpose of laying down, maintaining, and repairing any pipe, conduit, or aqueduct, and may from time to time take, by purchase or otherwise, and hold any lands, rights, or easements that said board may deem necessary for carrying out the purpose aforesaid, and shall, within sixty days from such taking otherwise than by purchase, file and cause to be recorded in the registry of deeds for the county in which such lands, rights, or easements so taken are situate, a description of the same as certain as is required in a common conveyance of lands, with a statement of the purpose for which the same were taken; which description and statement shall be signed by the said Water Board.

SECT. 2. Said city shall at all times allow to run from the lowest dam constructed by it, for the purpose aforesaid, at least one and a half million gallons of water a day each and every day in the year; and shall permit the inhabitants of the towns of Billerica, Wilmington, Burlington, Bedford, and Lexington to take from the part of said river or its tributaries within their respective towns so much of the water hereby granted as shall be necessary for all ordinary domestic household purposes, for extinguishing fires, and for the generation of steam.

SECT. 3. Said city shall pay all damages that shall be sustained by any person in property by the taking of any waters, lands, rights, or easements under the authority of this act, and if any person sustaining such damages fails to agree with said city as to the amount of damages sustained, such damage shall be assessed and determined in the superior court for the county in which such property is situated, on the written application of either party therefor, to be filed with the clerk of said court within three years of such taking; but no such application shall be made after the expiration of said three years; and, upon such application, after such notice as said court shall order, the damages shall be determined by a jury in said court, in the same manner as damages for land taken for highways in the same city or town are determined; and costs shall be taxed for the prevailing party as in civil cases.

SECT. 4. No application shall be made to the court for the assessment of damages for the taking of any water or water-rights, or for any injury thereto, until the water is actually withdrawn or diverted by said city under the authority of this act; and any person or corporation whose water-rights may be thus taken or affected, may make his application aforesaid at any time within three years from the time when the waters shall be first actually withdrawn or diverted as aforesaid.

SECT. 5. If said city, for the purposes aforesaid, enters upon and digs up, or in any manner interferes with, any road, street, or way which is outside the limits of said city, it shall be subject to such reasonable regulations as may be prescribed by the selectmen of the town, or the aldermen of the city, in which such road, street, or way is located, and shall restore the same to as good order and condition as it was in when such digging or interference commenced; and the work shall be done and all repairs be made in such manner and with such care as not to render any road, street, or way unsafe or unnecessarily inconvenient to the public travel thereon.

SECT. 6. Said city shall at all times indemnify and save harmless any such city or town against all damages and costs which may be recovered against it on account of any defect or want of repair in such road, street, or way, caused by the placing, maintenance, repairing, or replacing of said pipes, or other work, or by reason of any injury to persons or property caused by any defect or want of repair in any of such pipes or other work, and shall reimburse to it all expense which it shall reasonably incur in the defence of suits therefor; *provided*, that said city has notice of any claim or suit for such damage or injury and an opportunity to assume the defence thereof.

Sect. 7. For the purpose of defraying all the costs and expenses of such lands, estates, waters, and water-rights as shall be taken, purchased, or held for the purposes mentioned in this act, and of constructing all aqueducts and works necessary and proper for the accomplishment of the said purposes, and all expenses incident thereto, the city council shall have authority to issue, from time to time, negotiable notes, scrip, or certificates of debt, to be denominated on the face thereof "Boston Water-Scrip," to an amount not exceeding in the whole the sum of four millions of dollars, bearing interest at a rate not exceeding the legal rate of interest in this Commonwealth, and said interest shall be payable semi-annually, and the principal shall be payable at periods not more than fifty years from the issuing of the said scrip, notes, or certificates respectively. And the said city council may sell the same, or any part thereof, from time to time, at public or private sale, or pledge the same to raise money for the purposes aforesaid, on such terms and conditions as the said city council shall judge proper.

Sect. 8. Whoever diverts the water, or any part thereof, taken or held by said city pursuant to the provisions of this act, or corrupts the same or renders it impure, or destroys or injures any dam, aqueduct, pipe, conduit, hydrant, machinery, or other work or property held, owned, or used by said city for the purposes of this act, shall forfeit and pay to said city three times the amount of the damages assessed therefor, to be recovered in an action of tort; and on indictment and conviction of either of the acts aforesaid shall be punished by a fine not exceeding three hundred dollars, or by imprisonment not exceeding one year in the house of correction in the county in which such offence is committed.

Sect. 9. Said city is hereby authorized, if it shall deem it expedient so to do, to supply the cities of Somerville and Chelsea and the town of Everett, or either of them, with water, in such quantities, under such conditions, and upon such terms, as may be agreed upon between said city of Boston and said cities of Somerville and Chelsea and said town of Everett, or either of them, respectively.

Sect. 10. If said city shall, for the purposes aforesaid, take any lands in the water-shed of said portion of said river, it shall not pay any taxes thereon, but it shall annually pay to the town in which the same is situated an amount of money equal to twelve dollars on every one thousand dollars of the average of the assessed valuations of said lands, without buildings for the three years previous to such taking, the valuation for each year being first reduced by the amount of all abatements allowed thereon; *provided*, however, that any lands within five rods of either bank of said river, or of any tributary thereof, or of any basin or reservoir, shall not be included in determining said valuation.

Sect. 11. If said city shall divert the water of Vine brook, in the town of Lexington, into Vine brook, in the town of Arlington, it shall do so on such route as the selectmen of said towns shall approve.

Sect. 12. This act shall take effect upon its passage.

CLOSING ARGUMENT OF ELIHU G. LOOMIS, ESQ., AGAINST
GRANTING THE PETITION OF THE CITY OF BOSTON TO
TAKE THE WATERS OF THE SHAWSHEEN RIVER, BEFORE
THE COMMITTEE ON WATER-SUPPLY.

Mr. Chairman and Gentlemen: — By agreement of counsel the
opening this morning has been assigned to me, and I will occupy
your time for only a few moments, as my learned and eloquent
Brother Bruce will bear the burden and heat of the argument.
The towns I represent in this matter, Billerica, Burlington,
and Bedford, come before the Legislature to oppose this petition,
feeling that, although they are weak in population, they are entitled to the same rights and consideration which the large and
powerful and wealthy city of Boston is also entitled to receive,
and that equal justice will be meted out to both parties at your
hands. The bill, which was prepared by the attorney of the city
of Boston, and presented to me yesterday afternoon for the first
time, has been handed to the members of the committee this
morning, and I shall make this bill the theme of what I have to
say.

For the first time in the course of this hearing we are now able
to get the city of Boston to a definite statement of exactly what
they desire to take, and of exactly what they do not desire to do.
I call the attention of the committee first to the omissions from
this bill.

There is no provision in the bill for the drainage of the villages
either of Lexington or of Bedford. This ought to be compulsory
upon the city of Boston. A bill which provides for the taking by
the city of Boston of the water-shed into which these villages
naturally drain, and which will bring the city of Boston under the
protection of the law which prohibits towns or cities from draining their sewage into streams whose waters are used for water
supply, ought to provide some equivalent to these municipalities
for the expense and labor which they will be at in making a diver-

sion of their drainage. The only section touching this vital matter is the final one, Sect. 11 (Reading) : —

> If said city shall divert the water of Vine brook, in the town of Lexington, into Vine brook, in the town of Arlington, it shall do so on such route as the selectmen of said towns shall approve.

It seems evident that a more perfect and full provision should be made for the drainage of the village of Lexington at the expense of Boston, and full provision should be made for the drainage of the village of Bedford, which, by the statement of the chairman of the selectmen of Bedford, as appears in evidence, is largely naturally drained into the valley of this stream, that is, into Elm brook, which flows directly into the Shawsheen river.

Second. The privileges of bathing and of fishing ought to be reserved by a special section to the inhabitants of the towns through which the streams flow. It is well known that the health of the people of the communities which are contiguous to streams of this kind is largely dependent upon the bathing facilities which are afforded to the youth. As a matter of fact, the Shawsheen stream has been for years the sole public bathing-place of the people of Bedford, and it has been continually used for that purpose. It is the only stream in which they could bathe. Bathing is one of the enjoyments of youth. The right to bathe in a clear and beautiful running stream ought not to be taken away from this community without some adequate recompense, or unless other provision is made for the wants of the community in that regard. The city of Boston provides for its youth free bathing-places. The youth of the town of Bedford also have always enjoyed a free bathing-place in this Shawsheen river, and, in case their privilege of bathing is taken away, some equivalent should be provided.

Third. We strenuously object to the limitations of the use of water by the inhabitants of these towns contained in this bill. The second section of the bill provides as follows (Reading) : —

> And shall permit the inhabitants of the towns of Billerica, Wilmington, Burlington, Bedford, and Lexington to take from the part of said river or its tributaries within their respective towns so much of the water hereby granted as shall be necessary for all ordinary domestic household purposes, for extinguishing fire, and for the generation of steam.

That section leaves us, the inhabitants of the above-named towns, without any right to use the water for ordinary manufacturing purposes. Aside from the generation of steam every class of manufacturing requires the use of water in greater or less quantities. And this bill practically shuts off the inhabitants of the whole area comprised within this water-shed from the use of water for anything except domestic purposes.

Now, it is well known that the city of Boston purposes to use this water if she gets it, at least 20 per cent. of it, for these very manufacturing purposes from which she proposes to prohibit the inhabitants of this region from using it. Boston uses water to run her water elevators; she uses it as a source of power for small engines; she uses it in her sugar refineries; she uses it in a thousand different mechanical ways, which, as the testimony at this hearing shows, are increasing every year. Since Boston uses water for many other purposes besides drinking purposes, certainly the towns within this area should also be permitted to use the water of their own river for manufacturing, and in connection with such establishments as may in the future be built among us; although if such use be permitted, it should be permitted in such a way, perhaps, that the water after use be purified again before returning it to the river.

Then, fourth, there is the question of taxation. Section 10 of this act is as follows: —

SECT. 10. If said city shall, for the purposes aforesaid, take any lands in the water-shed of said portion of said river, it shall not pay any taxes thereon, but it shall annually pay to the town in which the same is situated an amount of money equal to twelve dollars on every one thousand dollars of the average of the assessed valuations of said lands, without buildings, for the three years previous to such taking, the valuation for each year being first reduced by the amount of all abatements allowed thereon; *provided, however*, that any lands within five rods of either bank of said river, or of any tributary thereof, or of any basin or reservoir, shall not be included in determining said valuation.

Now, if it is reasonable that the city of Boston should go into this area and take the land, it is reasonable that they should pay the same rate of taxes which the other owners of land in the same area pay. That is a self-evident proposition, and does not need any demonstration. The average rate of taxation in this Commonwealth, I am informed, is $15 on $1,000. Why should the city of Boston be relieved from paying the same rate of taxes on $1,000 that the occupants of adjoining lands pay? And, furthermore, why should the value of the lands taken by her be fixed, for the purposes of taxation at the present time, so there can be no increment of it to correspond with the increment of the adjoining lands in value? It cannot equitably be done. And, in the third place, why should a strip of land ten rods wide, following the thread of the stream in every direction, be exempted from taxation? If it is right that the inhabitants of these towns should be taxed on this land, it is right that the city also should pay taxes on the land if she takes it; and if it is right that the city should pay taxes on any of the land taken by her, it is right the city should be taxed on all the lands taken by her for the purposes named in the act.

But the most important question, and the one which affects most vitally the interests of these towns, is that involved in the first section of the bill, and in the powers and privileges which are sought by the city in connection with it. The eighth line specifies "that the city may, by its Water Board, prevent the pollution of said waters;" and on the second page, in the first four lines, it is provided that the city "may from time to time take, by purchase or otherwise, and hold any lands, rights, or easements that said Board may deem necessary for carrying out the purpose aforesaid." In other words, having, in the first days of this hearing, set a one-hundred-rod limit, and having receded from it later to a ten-rod limit, the city comes in here now desirous of a bill providing no limit whatever within the water-shed to the amount of land she shall be able to condemn and acquire. The plain construction of the act is, that the only limitation to be imposed on the city of Boston in taking land within the Shawsheen basin shall be such limitation as the city shall choose to impose upon itself, in the discretion of the Water Board, in preventing the pollution of the water.

Now, upon all the testimony in the case, the evident intention of the city is to prevent the pollution of the waters by preventing any polluting substance from getting into or upon the water-shed anywhere, or at any time, in the future. In other words, they ask the Legislature to give them such rights to take lands as will enable them to take the entire area of the water-shed and hold the same through all time.

Now, to take the entire area of the water-shed and hold the same would, doubtless, as far as the interests of the city of Boston go, secure what it is desirous of — water untainted by any pollution. But, on the other hand, it would involve the ruin of the municipalities which are situated upon the area of this water-shed. This ring of towns and this area of country is situated in a belt of land between thirteen and seventeen miles from the City Hall in Boston. It is occupied by the ring of towns which surround the metropolis lying next beyond the already populous towns immediately contiguous to it. It is a part of the evidence in this case that the population of Boston in forty years from now will probably number a million souls. Where will these million souls find their homes? The experience of the past has shown that they will pour by thousands and tens of thousands out into the country around Boston, and the fact that the towns nearer the city are already densely populated, will naturally cause this ever-increasing population to spread out into the circle of towns within this area. Gentlemen, this land is worth more for homes than it is for an empty water-shed. It comprises thirty-four square miles right in the heart of Middlesex county, and contains some of the highest land and some of the most fertile and beautiful land in the whole country. It will be a wrong to coming generations of men to take this land and isolate it for the purposes of a water-shed, which confessedly must be totally insufficient for the wants of the city.

The land is needed more for homes than it is for water. Let the city of Boston go farther off, let it go out, away from the larger cities and from the habitations of men, into a country which will not be reached within thirty or forty or fifty years by the advancing tide of population, and there let it dig reservoirs, and take land. But do not let it take land which is already open for homes, which is every day being more densely populated, — land which is essential to the future prosperity of Middlesex county, and to all the municipalities within the limits of this area.

When William the Norman had conquered England he proceeded, by depopulating twenty-two villages, and by driving out all thei inhabitants, to make his " New Forest." He loved the tall stags, they say, as if he had been their father, and in this wasted country, depopulated of all inhabitants, the king found a spacious pleasure-ground. The city of Boston would thus also desolate our fertile lands. She would make practically a desert of them. She would keep human dejections, and all pollutions arising from the use and occupancy of men, away from this water-shed. That involves the desolation, so far as human beings go, of that area of our country. Gentlemen, the towns, the inhabitants of these towns, and all those interested in this land, most earnestly protest against this bill.

CLOSING ARGUMENT OF GEORGE A. BRUCE, ESQ., AGAINST GRANTING THE PETITION OF THE CITY OF BOSTON TO TAKE THE WATERS OF THE SHAWSHEEN RIVER, BEFORE THE COMMITTEE ON WATER-SUPPLY.

Mr. Chairman and Gentlemen of the Committee : —

I ask the careful attention of the committee to the question which I am going to discuss with you this morning. I know my argument will sound like a thrice-told tale. If I fail in my endeavor to interest you, I intend, in a way flattering to myself, to attribute it to the precedence of my associate, Brother Morse, who possesses a mind so comprehensive that the whole field of argument is completely covered with that nice sense of proportion that assigns to each part its true importance, and at the same time so microscopic that no detail escapes his mental vision.

BOSTON'S CONSIDERATION OF THE SHAWSHEEN SCHEME.

My Brother Bailey, in the third sentence of his presentation of this case before you, said that he should ask the committee to regard as part of his evidence " the fact that the City Council, after mature consideration, has asked the Legislature to authorize it to go to the expense of $2,000,000 or $3,000,000 for an additional water-supply for the city of Boston." It is quite true that the deliberate judgment of a legislative body is worthy of consideration on the part of another legislative body when considering the same subject; for this reason I have taken the trouble of looking over the official reports of the City Council of Boston, and I find that the order was passed without a word of debate or an explanation given upon it, in very much the same way that orders are passed in our Legislature for committees to consider and report upon different matters of legislation.

If such consideration of a subject as I have described is the " mature consideration " of a subject by the Boston City Council, it might be a matter of curiosity at least for us to learn what would be an immature consideration of a matter involving two or three millions of dollars by that learned body. I shall endeavor to show you before I close that nearly all of the evidence by the petitioners produced before you had been just about as maturely considered before it was offered as this question of taking the Shawsheen river had been by the City Council of 1885.

As against this judgment of the city of Boston, such as it is, I invoke the thrice-repeated judgment of the Legislature of Massachusetts, — that the city of Boston had shown no exigency that would justify them in taking the waters of this river; a judgment formed after exhaustive hearings and elaborate arguments, a judgment which with propriety I have the right to designate as "mature."

The questions before you are few and simple. It is not contended on the one hand that the Legislature should grant the power of taking one person's property and giving it to another except in case of a great necessity; and on our side we grant the right of the Legislature to confer this power whenever this great necessity is shown. The propriety, too, of granting this authority would, of course, be affected by the degree of the necessity and the extent of the injury that was likely to be inflicted.

The opening argument and the evidence offered by the petitioners were intended to show this necessity in two ways only : first, because the limit of the Mystic supply has been reached with a growing population ; second, that the Mystic supply ought to be abandoned, and, if so, a substitute therefor must first be secured.

BOSTON'S BENEVOLENCE TOWARDS SOMERVILLE, CHELSEA, AND EVERETT.

Before, however, I enter upon a discussion of these two propositions I want to call to your attention certain facts which have been disclosed by this hearing, that cannot be in dispute, which seem to me entitled to great weight in this discussion. This petition comes from the city of Boston. It is the duty of that city to look to the welfare of her own citizens, and if she is successful in that duty she will be doing quite as well as many of her own citizens think she is likely to do ; at least she need not be alarmed for the condition of her neighbors. The only inhabitants of the city of

Boston dependent upon the Mystic supply are those dwelling in Charlestown, a small district which is completely built upon, which is not likely to increase in the future, in the opinion of Mr. Rockwell, and which, in my opinion, is likely to decrease. At any rate, its population in 1873 was 33,556, and in 1880, 33,734, — an increase of only 178 in seven years. So far then as the city of Boston is concerned, excluding for the moment her trustee obligations, of which I shall speak hereafter, she has to provide for a population of the size just given, and which, on the admission of the chairman of the Water Board, is not likely to increase. For all future time a supply of 2,500,000 gallons daily would be ample, even upon the wasteful estimate of the Engineer's Department of the city of Boston. Therefore, on the question of *amount* of water, the inhabitants of Boston have just three times their present or future needs.

But these petitioners say that they are not satisfied with a simple performance of municipal obligations to their own citizens ; that they have a sacred trust to perform ; that, as trustees for the cities of Chelsea and Somerville and the town of Everett, they desire this legislation in order that we may not die from thirst, or our buildings be destroyed for want of water to put out the flames. Now, Mr. Chairman, has it not occurred to you as very singular that not one of the 66,000 inhabitants of Somerville, Everett, and Chelsea, all *cestuis que* trusts of the city of Boston, has been here to say a word in favor of having this authority granted to their trustee, which, so far as quantity of water is concerned, is sought solely in their interests? The reason is that not one person out of the whole 66,000 could be found, if the attempt should be made, who would be in favor of the granting of this petition at the present time.

Each of these cities and the town has its Water Board, who understand the wants of their respective municipalities at least as well as the Water Board of Boston. But I take pleasure in saying that the latter are honest and competent men, and that, after a longer study of the question, and the experience of this hearing, they will be able better to solve the problem than this premature attempt alone would lead us to believe.

Now why is it that these respective Water Boards are not here to give their advice and assistance? Why no one of the 66,000 people dependent on Mystic lake? Because they do not like the trusteeship of the city of Boston, and do not wish to see its power extended. And when I tell you just how these unfortunate *cestuis que* trusts are related to the city of Boston, their trustee, perhaps you will cease to wonder why they have not been here in aid of this petition. In 1868 Charlestown commenced to furnish water to Chelsea, in 1869, to Somerville, in 1872, to Everett, by contracts which allowed the Mystic Board to collect the full rates in those places, with a rebate amounting to about twenty-five per cent. to Somerville and Chelsea, and fifteen per cent. to Everett.

In other words, the city of Boston has pumped the water of Mystic lake into a common reservoir, and for that service she has received as compensation from the water-takers of Chelsea $682,518.27; from Somerville, $615,946.65; from Everett, $91,026.19; making a total of $1,388,491.11. These figures show that these contracts have resulted in profits so enormous that no water board of Boston has ever been able to justify them, and the utmost exertions of these city and town governments have not yet been able to modify them. I labored at this task of Hercules for three years while Mayor of the city of Somerville, and my successors have labored also with the same result.

Mr. Rockwell stated that these contracts were not profitable. This testimony must be excused, because of his newness in office and unfamiliarity with the subject. Let us test this statement of the Chairman of the Water Board on the basis of the last report signed by him and his associates. The city of Boston was paid for pumping water into the pipes of their *cestuis que* trusts $108,053.24, which cost the city just $14,567.02. But you can add to this any fair proportion of the cost of the works at Mystic lake, of the sewer, and of any and every part of the Mystic works outside of the street pipes in Charlestown, you may multiply that sum by three and add it to the cost of pumping, and you can't by any possibility figure it out that on these three contracts the city of Boston has been making, is making, and will continue to make, an annual net profit less than $50,000. Upon this showing, do you wonder that the *cestuis que* trusts are not here, and that the trustee is desirous of continuing its power?

There is a provision in these contracts, however, that when the
Mystic debt is paid these long-suffering towns shall be entitled
to a new contract, and in three years from this day that debt will
have been paid from the surplus revenues of the Mystic Department, and this statement above shows a conclusive reason why no
legislative permission should be givn for an increase of the Mystic
debt until the time comes, when by the terms of the contract,
Somerville, Chelsea, and Everett shall be entitled to a new contract, or until Boston shall voluntarily make a just concession.
Certainly this request can never be granted until all appearance of
speculation and profit is first removed.

Boston's Need of Additional Water-Supply in 1886 as Compared with 1881, 1882, 1883, when the Shawsheen was Refused her.

Now, passing over this insuperable objection to the granting of
this petition, let us fairly examine the other claims of these petitioners. To the exhaustive argument of my Brother Morse, and
the able pamphlet of Mr. Crafts, showing that the city of Boston
already has water enough if she will only use it with some degree
of economy, I will attempt to add but little, but, with your permission, will endeavor to point out some of the positions heretofore
taken by Boston and her representative men, which may, perhaps,
aid in convincing you that it will be safe for the Legislature to
allow the new Water Board to study the question of a water-supply
a little longer, and the Engineer's Department to make out a new
set of figures.

As has already been stated, Boston came before the Legislature
in the years 1881, 1882, and 1883, the last two years by her present
solicitor, and in 1881 by Mr. Stackpole, his predecessor, so that for
three times she has presented here her case, such as it was, and I
respectfully invite your attention to a cursory review of it. If for
three years the judgment of the Legislature has been adverse to this
request of Boston, and the event has proved the wisdom of that
judgment, let us see what greater exigency as to the amount of
water this evidence discloses over the evidence of those previous
years. The daily average consumption of water from the Cochit-

uate and Mystic Works in the year 1881 was 38,214,909 gallons; in 1882, 38,545,200; in 1883, 39,656,100 gallons; in 1885, 32,-444,550, showing a diminished consumption of 7,211,550 daily in two years, while the admitted increase of her supply by the completion of Basin No. 4 is 5,000,000 gallons.

In other words, by the undisputed facts, Boston is this year 12,211,550 gallons daily better situated as to quantity of water than she was in 1883, the last time she came here, as everybody understood, for the purpose of keeping Cambridge from the Shawsheen, rather than for the purpose of getting it herself.

Now is it not strange, almost unaccountable, that in the year 1886, when Boston is better situated by 12,211,550 gallons daily than she was in 1883, she should come here for the first time and seriously make the claim that there is an exigency for an additional water supply that would justify the Legislature in blotting out a river from the face of this earth, and at the same time bring sure and certain destruction to four flourishing manufacturing villages, which give a handsome support to 3,000 of our Massachusetts people?

For three years these hearings have gone on upon petitions to take the water of the Shawsheen, and I have carefully read them all, and have them here for speedy reference if my Brother Bailey questions my statement, when I say that heretofore Boston has admitted that she has a supply ample for many years upon the western side of the city for her own wants and for Chelsea, Somerville, and Everett, but has each year justified herself in not resorting to it on the ground that the Shawsheen was so much the cheaper.

Boston's Care in Making Estimates for Legislative Committees.

For three years the city engineers of Boston have come before the committee of which you are the successor and have given in their estimates of the cost of taking the Shawsheen at $700,000, but this year the Engineer's Department give us their first estimate of construction as $3,500,000, just five times the estimate of Mr. Wightman, who was held high in his profession as a man of ability and character. No word of explanation of this slight increase of $2,800,000 is given.

In 1881 that able and candid man, Mr. Wightman, came before this committee, and at once admitted that Boston had taken and paid for the waters of the Sudbury river, that there were 14,000,000 gallons daily going to waste which could be secured, but he thought as a business proposition it was not wise to do it, for the reason of the great expense it would oblige the city to incur, which, he told the committee, would be $400,000 for the basins and $400,000 for the connection ; in other words, the whole expense would amount to the large sum of $800,000, which he thought an injudicious expenditure.

In 1882 Mr. Wightman again restated his position and estimates substantially as he had done the year previous, and Brother Bailey made his two arguments before the committee against the two schemes of a Sudbury-river and a Mystic-basin supply, on the ground that it was not good business judgment to adopt either of those schemes because of the great expense, claiming that the Shawsheen was the cheaper of the two. It was never intimated that it was not feasible to supply the Mystic territory from the Sudbury river because of lack of water, but was put wholly on a business basis. Now I want to call the attention of our friend the City Solicitor to the position in which the Engineer's Department have placed him by their estimates of three and one-half millions as the cost of construction on the Shawsheen, and ask him to reconsider the estimates this year with those previously given, and whether he don't think the argument on the ground of economy so skilfully used before would be a little antiquated and out of place in the year 1886? I think this committee will feel that until this petitioner can come to the Legislature with evidence entitled at least to respect she shall continue to leave without any privileges granted to her.

So I say that it has been three times proved that Boston has an ample supply of water, if she will only use what she has, and this year she furnishes herself an answer to the previous arguments addressed to the committee, in her estimate of the cost, which is five times any previous estimate by well known and competent engineers. I will leave this part of the subject with a quotation from the pamphlet of Mr. Crafts, who, at the expense of my client, has pointed out the way to a water-supply for the city of Cambridge, and if the city of Boston also will give heed to his advice and superior judgment it will soon be discussing with her city sister what form of a testimonial they shall offer in recognition of his services.

"Now, in view of all the facts herein presented, it must be evident to any person of common intelligence that Boston needs no additional source of supply at the present time, and that by making a proper, prudent use of what she has the necessity for an increase of supply may be postponed for forty years. This is my deliberate judgment as a civil engineer who has had much to do with the water-supply of Boston."

The Mystic Supply and the Attack upon it by a Committee of the Medical Societies.

The argument already presented meets the position of Boston, that there is a necessity for additional supply even in case of a total abandonment of the Mystic supply. Upon that question, however, I desire to speak, both as an attorney for Mr. Bradlee and as a citizen of Somerville. I am one of the 66,000 *cestuis que* trust on behalf of whom Boston stands as a petitioner before you. I have wife and child, and as attorney for no man would I advocate a cause that involved the possibility of harm to them or any human being. I am satisfied that the city of Boston, in the position she has taken here, is not only wrong, but that she is wrong to the extent that there is no excuse for it.

Previous to 1876 there was danger to the Mystic water by reason of the large number of tanneries and other manufacturing establishments pouring their filth into the supporting streams. In 1879 the sewer was completed, and has since been in successful operation, with results such as were anticipated by those at whose instance it was built. From that time until the present the waters of the Mystic have been annually improving, as shown by the reports of the Boston Water Board. And that testimony is confirmed by the judgment of those who drink those waters. In the report for 1881 and 1882 it is stated that the quality of the water has been unusually good. In 1882–83 " the

quality of the Mystic water has been good throughout the year."
In 1883–84 the engineer says, " the quality of the water from all
the sources of supply has been better than for a few years past."
In 1884–85 the Board says, " the quality of the water during the
past year has been excellent." Prof. Wood, of Harvard Univer-
sity, analyzed the water regularly during the year, and the result
showed its quality to be as good as any large community in the
country. In 1885–86 Prof. Wood continued his analyses, which
show less impurities than the Sudbury, if I remember correctly the
testimony of Mr. Wilson, the engineer.

In 1882, only four years ago, my Brother Bailey, before this
same committee, in the course of his argument, in his enthusiasm
for the Mystic water, which he knows as well as any one, stated
that the building of the sewer had enabled them to remove pollutions from the streams. " And we have put it into the condition
in which it is to-day, — the purest water that comes into Boston."
As since then, on all hands, it is admitted that there has been no
change detrimental to this supply, I can imagine, but will not
attempt to express, the emotions of the learned solicitor as he sat
quietly by his table and brought before you the two doctors — very
reputable gentlemen no doubt, but whose names were not very
familiar to us — who made a holiday excursion one summer's day
for the first and only time to the banks of the Mystic, and after
devoting three or four whole hours to the subject, including the
time for travel, came home and wrote out those famous reports
condemning the Cochituate and Mystic supplies alike, which, to
characterize them mildly, are entitled to the same consideration
that sensible people would be likely to give to a colored advertise-
ment of Lydia Pinkham's medicines. These were the gentlemen
that the city of Boston brings here as experts, *scientific gentlemen*,
to instruct you upon questions of legislation. I want it understood
that this criticism is confined to Drs. Shattuck and Gerry, the
former of whom maintained well the reputation of the professional
expert in his constant endeavor to evade a fair answer to nearly
every question put to him. The world is fast getting to a just
understanding of the value of what passes under the general desig-
nation of expert testimony. A great part of it is not very unlike
the report made by these doctors, in which they off-hand condemn

as worthless several millions of property, creating alarm and distrust in the community, because the community at large have not the necessary information upon which to ground an opinion. And all this the result of a three-hours' holiday excursion in the summer of 1885. The evidence discloses that all of these doctors put their names to those reports, and only a small part of them had ever seen the waters which they condemn. Is this science? Is this learning? Is this judgment?

By such processes did Newton discover the law of gravitation, or Leverier point his telescope to the unseen planet?

My Brother Bailey will probably say that the doctors were right, and that the view they invited you to of a little brook that flows into the Mystic confirms them.

They did not take you to the lake which sparkles like a jewel in the spring sunshine, at the feet of its encircling hills. They did not take you to the river which fills its banks, but they showed you a little insignificant stream, so small that its impure waters have no perceptible effects upon the whole, but which, with the slightest effort on the part of the Water Board, could be entirely filtered before a gallon of it could reach the reservoir.

Mr. Chairman, there is not, there has not been, an intention on the part of Boston to abandon this source of supply, and it would not be abandoned if the Shawsheen was given to them. You will remember that these learned doctors told us that the Cochituate lake was equally bad with the Mystic, and I have myself seen pouring into it a far larger volume of impure water than ever flowed into the Mystic. And yet Mr. Wightman in 1883 was asked the question, which was the purest water, the Shawsheen, the Sudbury, or Cochituate, and he unhesitatingly answered that the Cochituate was the purest of the three. This opinion of his was not the result of a three-hours' holiday excursion, but a conclusion founded on ample knowledge and all the tests known to science. And I conclude this part of my argument with a quotation from the City Solicitor, expressed in 1881, while a member of the City Council, when the waters of the Mystic were by far less pure than they are to-day : " I say the Mystic water is as good as the Cochituate, and it is as good as I care to drink, and I defy the gentleman to bring up any reputable person who will say it is not." This challenge is still open.

The Manufacturers' Side, and the Threatened Destruction of the Town of Andover.

Now suppose for a moment that you grant the Mystic should be given up, grant that our position is not correct that Boston has sufficient water if she will only use it with an approach towards common prudence, — grant everything that is claimed thus far, and it does not follow at all that the Shawsheen river need be taken. For three years the city of Cambridge came here to get this river, and if you will take the trouble to read over those hearings you will find that no one ever questioned for a moment but that an exigency for a further or additional supply for that city was apparent. She came here with her eyes blinded to every other source of supply, and told the Legislature that her people must perish from a water-famine unless this stream was given to her, and for three years the Legislature refused her request because she had not shown but that there was relief for her elsewhere where the injury to other people would be less. The city of Cambridge went out of this State-House year after year for three times with the belief that she had been unjustly treated by the State; and yet to-day she would confess that the judgment of the Legislature was better than her own, and she now rejoices in the fact that her thrice-repeated request was not granted. Will you give to Boston, on this hastily gotten-up and ill-considered petition, where no necessity has been shown, what was three times refused to Cambridge, where an exigency was on all hands conceded?

It cannot escape the attention of the committee that when Boston went to the Sudbury river under the advice of Mr. Davis, than whom there is no abler engineer in America, she went there with the intention of finding a supply which would be ample for a hundred years. She has laid her pipes of a size sufficient to bring 115,000,000 gallons daily, and it was with the knowledge that the water was there to fill them. Mr. Wightman frankly admitted the fact to be as I have stated; but he said it would not be economy for Boston to take the Concord river, which would double or more than double her supply, for the reason that it would cost her $2,500,000, and he could not justify such an expenditure; and now, in face of this evidence, some one has been found to come up gayly before this committee and state that it is prudent and wise for Boston to spend $3,500,000 to stretch out to the Shawsheen to get a little supply that is to last only fifteen or twenty years after it is taken. Don't you think Boston, through her wise City Council, had better maturely consider this subject at least one year longer before she be allowed to embark upon a scheme of such magnitude?

It hardly seems necessary to go farther with this discussion, but as Brother Bailey will endeavor to make you believe he knows more about the manufacture of white flannels than the men do who have given their life to the subject, I will add a word or two, and then close. We say that Boston should not be permitted to take this stream because when you do it you inflict an injury that is of no slight magnitude, — an injury which is to blot out three or four as flourishing manufacturing villages as can be found anywhere. Brother Bailey will say this is not so, that he has sent his genial assistant, Mr. Brackett, to make inquiry of some manufacturers of coarse colored woollen goods, and found out how much water they use for scouring purposes, and will probably tell you that he has by that evidence shown you how much Capt. Bradlee and the other manufacturers ought to use. I am not going to split hairs upon this subject. I am going to assume that by this time this committee know who the managers of the Smith & Dove Manufacturing Company are. I am going to assume that this committee know who J. Putnam Bradlee is, and that when he, summoning to his aid his powerful will, came from his sick-bed as you saw him, and told you that when the waters of the Shawsheen river are taken from him he must close his mill, you are going to believe him. He can only manufacture his goods when the stream is full and the water is pure. Perhaps we would be willing to concede that three or four millions a day in quantity are sufficient; but those three or four millions must come from the upper surface of the full pond, which condition could not be fulfilled at all if this petition was granted. Mr. Torr says the same thing. Let it be understood then that there can be no joint ownership of the Shawsheen river.

If Boston takes it, the Ballardvale mills, the Smith & Dove Manufacturing Company, and the flourishing and happy villages which you have seen, will soon cease to be. They are as dependent upon those waters for life as a human being upon the blood that flows through his veins. And when you come to weigh and estimate the calamity which you are asked to allow to be inflicted upon Andover you should pause. The State looks with equal favor upon the great and the small. All alike are under her care. What is it that has made Massachusetts what she is? What is it that has made Boston, even, what she is? Have not the hundred little manufacturing communities scattered over her surface, like Ballardvale, been the means of the greatness of both? And are you going to strike out four of them at a single stroke, on the thoughtless petition before you?

My client is Capt. Bradlee. He is not an unknown man. For nearly half a century he has been connected with the Ballardvale mills. He owns them all to-day. If this petition should be granted, the law would, in theory at least, give him compensation. For half a century he has been collecting about his mills the families of those who labor for him. They all look upon Ballardvale as their home, and to those mills as their means of support. Strike out those mills, and what would be the result? I will not use the word desolation, but I express it mildly when I say that, for thousands of people, the associations of a lifetime must be broken in upon, new means of livelihood must be sought for and found, and the old homes abandoned, with a necessary loss to every owner of property in those villages, to whom no compensation will be given. Have you ever seen a laboring community that you would not sooner break up than those in Andover? Is there a place in Massachusetts where pleasanter relations exist between employer and employed than at Ballardvale, and with reason? The owner of those mills has passed the time when longer he is actuated by love of gain, and he stands here as protector of those who have faithfully served him.

I do not express his feelings too strongly when I say that those mills and the population about them, and the institutions which he has helped to plant and maintain there, the three churches, the library, the schools, the lecture-room, and the means of healthful and wholesome amusement which he has furnished, stand to him in place of wife and child, which he has not. And when the city which he has helped to build — a city which he has served for twenty-one years with a service to which, in these later years, she must be a stranger — attempts to destroy in this thoughtless and inconsiderate way what remains for him of charm in life, he feels the blow. And I know it will be your duty, and in that duty a pleasure, to throw the protection of the State over him and his property, his employés and their property, the town of Andover and her people.

CLOSING ARGUMENT OF ANDREW J. BAILEY, ESQ., CITY SOLICITOR, IN FAVOR OF GRANTING THE PETITION OF THE CITY OF BOSTON TO TAKE ,THE WATERS OF THE SHAWSHEEN RIVER, BEFORE THE COMMITTEE ON WATER-SUPPLY.

Mr. Chairman and Gentlemen of the Committee : —

After the full examination you have made of the case I have no fears that the threats of our opponents, to submit to no joint ownership in the waters of the Shawsheen river, will have the least effect upon you.

I have never known a committee of the Legislature to be deterred by threats from doing what their judgment, founded upon careful investigation, told them was the proper thing to do.

Nor, gentlemen, do I believe that the sneering manner in which my brother has seen fit to allude to the engineers of the city of Boston as " these young men" will influence you unfavorably to our cause. " These young men" have been the assistants and great aids of Mr. Wightman, himself but very few years the senior of the youngest of them, and a young man himself, being at the time he gave his first evidence in this case less than forty years of age ; and " these young men" can point to monuments of their ability which many an older man would be proud of. They can point to the bridges in the Back Bay park and throughout our city, built during the last ten years ; they can point to the system of improved sewerage just completed ; they can point to the magnificent works on the line of our water-works, the span over Charles river, the longest stone arch in the world, the Waban arches and the dams of our basins, as evidence of their ability in their profession.

But all this has no bearing upon the question ; and I only allude to it as showing how much our opponents must be in want of real argument to imagine a committee of the Legislature of Massachusetts will be influenced by arguments of such a nature.

Now, gentlemen, let us consider the situation.

The city of Charlestown, more than twenty years ago, obtained

authority to use the water flowing into the upper Mystic pond, in
Medford, as a water-supply; and by contract agreed to furnish
the inhabitants of Somerville, Chelsea, and Everett, with water
from the same source.

These communities, containing now over 100,000 inhabitants,
have been consuming water from this source ever since, and are
still using it, and it appears from the testimony before you that the
utmost capacity of the Mystic works in a dry season is 7,000,000
gallons per day. It also has been shown you that the past two
years these communities have used more than 7,000,000 gallons
per day, so that had either of these years been a very dry year
there would have been a great scarcity of water in those places.

Now, remember, Charlestown was annexed to Boston in
December, 1873, and Boston succeeding to the rights of the
city of Charlestown, and also its obligations, comes here to-day
and shows you the situation, and asks you to give her authority to
take more water from some other source to supply to these communities.

If these places constituted one community, as they did before
the annexation of Charlestown and Boston, and came before you
showing this state of things, would you not say it was high time
for them to be seeking for an increase of their water-supply? I
shall assume that you would, and that, if any community showed
such a situation, this Legislature would not hesitate to say that
such a community was entitled to a further supply at the earliest
possible moment, in order to get it ready for the increase of the
population that will inevitably come. All this, gentlemen, bear
in mind, without saying a word about the greatest reason of all,—
the dangerous condition of the Mystic water-shed.

Is there any doubt in your minds, gentlemen, that the Mystic
water-shed is becoming a dangerous source of supply?

You have made an extensive examination of the streams that
furnish this water; you have been over the same grounds that
these eminent physicians of the Norfolk and Suffolk medical
societies went in their examination which led them to condemn
this water-shed.

(*Evidence, pp.* 74 *to* 123.)

And, gentlemen, does it need more than that examination, with the testimony of these physicians, to convince you that that water-supply should be abandoned?

Does it require more than a two-hour examination of what you saw, to enable you to make up your minds whether this water is liable to great pollution?

My brother Bruce says it is a good water-shed, because chemical analysis shows that the water which comes from it is good, and because no danger has come from using. That is not a sufficient answer for me, nor, I respectfully submit, a sufficient answer for any thinking man in this Legislature. Why, gentlemen, how many a poor soul now in eternity, but a few short days ago was living in fancied security under the dam at East Lee. The dam had always been safe, and, arguing in the same line as my brother Bruce, must still be safe. Alas! for the argument, and for those who depended upon it. The time came when the weak spot was found, and without a warning those souls were ushered into the presence of their Maker.

My brother Bruce has introduced his personal relations into his argument, and tells you that he lives in Somerville, and his wife and children drink this water, and he is willing they should. I also, gentlemen, live in Charlestown, and my family are compelled to use this water; but I am not willing that they should continue to do so. I know the danger, and I have laid the proof of that danger before you, and I beg of you to remove it from us. It shall not be laid at my door when calamity comes, as surely it will, that I stood quietly by, knowing these dangers to my friends, and raised not a warning cry and an earnest word in their behalf.

That water to-day — and I repeat every statement I have ever made about it — appears to be as pure water, when you drink it, and when you analyze it, as you can find in any of the supplies of Boston. But what of it? Twenty-three thousand people, in an area of twenty-six square miles, are pouring their filth into the soil and making their discharges into the ground along the banks of the stream. You cannot prevent it. You cannot by any process of law restrain them from doing it. Privies are built along the banks of this brook, as you saw, within three feet of it, and uncemented vaults are there, and there is no law that can keep people from putting their discharges into the vaults.

Does it need any expert testimony to satisfy this committee that what goes into the soil must necessarily percolate through and come out into the water? Does it need I should introduce evidence here to satisfy this committee of that? I told you, when I began in this hearing, I depended more upon the view, to show you the Mystic water-shed was becoming an unfit source of domestic water-supply, than upon any evidence which I should otherwise present to you. And I depend upon it now. I took you along every stream, almost, upon the water-shed. I showed you a part of every branch and rivulet that makes the water-shed, and on every one of them is exactly the same state of affairs. Every brook runs immediately alongside these sources of pollution.

There is but one way to remedy it, and that is to exercise our powers under the law, and take land and buildings, five rods wide, on either side. That is, take all these tanneries and manufactories. What would be the result? Devastation in Bedford! Ruin in Andover! For heaven's sake, what would there be in Woburn and Winchester? Twenty thousand people have settled on the banks of that stream, who are dependent entirely upon these industries that pollute that water. You cannot take them out without damaging these people and the town in which they live, without speaking one word of the immense cost of it, a hundredfold more than any damage by the taking of the Shawsheen. The damage you would inflict is tenfold what it would be to go to any other source of supply in this Commonwealth. It cannot be done. It is an impossibility.

I depend upon your good judgment, from what you have seen and heard, to say whether that is a supply the city of Boston ought to content itself with, or to impose upon my brother Bruce and his family. I have not heard yet, and I do not believe it will ever happen, that any of these municipalities that depend upon Boston for their water-supply complain because the city is taking every means to protect them in · the enjoyment of a pure source of supply. They are not here to object to this. It remained for my brother Bruce to raise that spectre. The city of Boston will not sit quietly by and see these people obliged to use water from such a water-shed when it knows that almost within a stone's throw from its door there is one of the purest and most beautiful water-supplies on the face of the earth. You must be convinced that these communities should have another supply. Now let us consider where the city proposes to go.

We ask to go to the Shawsheen river. Our opponents come here and say we should move further. For heaven's sake where to? They have pointed out no place to which we can go. We say there is no other source of supply.

Mr. LOOMIS. — There are the lakes of New Hampshire, and we say go to them.

Mr. BAILEY. — I am glad to hear you say it; it is the first time it has been suggested.

Mr. BRUCE. — We thought we had discharged our full duty in showing to the city of Cambridge where they could get their supply; but if you are going to press this I presume we should be able to show you a supply.

Mr. BAILEY. — We have been trying to find a source of supply from 1846 up to the present time, and the efforts of the engineers of the city of Boston have been fruitless. We have been all over this Commonwealth, and we have made exhaustive reports containing a description of every source of supply, and when we are told to go further, it is proper for those who tell us to point the way. Is this insane cry, this insane suggestion about going to the lakes of New Hampshire, to be the ground on which we are to be told to go out of this Legislature? Do you know anything about the lakes of New Hampshire? Why, gentlemen, four years ago, when we had so much trouble with our basins, when *algæ* and other growths were fouling the water, and rendering it objectionable to the taste, and dangerous, we made an examination of Lake Winnipiseogee; and, gentlemen, I say to you we found the water of the lake more impure than that in any one of our basins. There was more vegetable growth in it and more impurities. Can it be presumed that the State of New Hampshire would allow a city of another State to take the waters of her lakes, damage her manufacturing interests by the withdrawal of the water, prevent settlements on the bank of the lake, and keep impurities from its waters, when the apprehension of damage to four mills in Andover is regarded as a convincing argument to prevent the utilizing of the best water-shed in Massachusetts, capable of supplying more than 20,000,000 gallons of water per day?

No, gentlemen, we have shown you the only water-supply available for these communities. You have seen it: and I ask you if it is not an ideal water-shed? You went the whole length of it, from the point where we propose to put our dam, away to the other end. You have seen that there is not a single manufactory there to pollute the water, and that there are but twenty-five slight sources of pollution on the stream. There are but half-a-dozen dwelling-houses within nearly a half a mile of the thread of the stream. Can you imagine a section of country that could be dedicated for all time as a source of water-supply where the injury done would be less than would be done there?

Now, what are the reasons and arguments brought against us?

The first reason is that Boston has, in the Sudbury system, a surplus of water; and if there is not pure water, or water enough in the Mystic, let it take this surplus for Charlestown, and let the other places look out for themselves.

It is true, gentlemen, the object of this petition is to obtain pure water for these neighboring towns; and, if Boston was looking only for itself, it would heed the selfish argument of my brother; but I feel proud that I can say that Boston to-day — as when, in 1861, it paid the interest on its bonds in gold, when not by law required to, and as it has always been — is ever ready to live up to the *spirit* of any contract it makes, rather than the strict letter. It is governed by the equity of its contracts, which should govern all in their action; and for that reason is here looking out for the interests of those depending upon it, and that it is so here should be an argument in favor of its petition rather than against.

Let me ask you, Mr. Chairman, can these towns assume an obligation of $3,500,000 as cheaply as the city of Boston, to procure this supply?

(*Evidence. p. 64.*)

How could they undertake such an obligation as the entering upon such a system of works as will be necessary? They could not do it. That is one reason why the city of Boston should be encouraged and aided, instead of being frowned upon, in asking for this supply. If there is any question as to whether these cities and towns want Boston's petition granted, their representatives in this Legislature can answer for them.

The second reason is, that Boston has, in the Sudbury system, a supply of water capable, by being developed, of furnishing 59,000,-000 gallons per day; that it has a population of only 356,000 outside of Charlestown, and that she can connect the Sudbury with the Mystic system and use the surplus for the towns using the Mystic.

The two systems, gentlemen, have been shown you, they are entirely distinct, not nearer in any place than eight miles, and it would cost to develop the supply, build additional basins, and connect the systems, at least $2,500,000, as our witnesses have shown you, — full as much as it would cost to supply the same amount of water from the Shawsheen.

(*Evidence, p.* 207.)

Now, gentlemen, if you owned two houses far apart, each occupied by you, and you had provided a supply of coal in the first house sufficient for three winters, and had no coal in the second house, would you consider it good judgment or an economical expenditure of money to take the coal from the first house where you would need it next winter, even if you did not this, and transfer it across the country to the second house and expend, in doing so, as much money as it would cost you to buy a new supply for the second house?

Yet that is what brother Bruce would have the city of Boston do, — take the water from the Sudbury, which we must have for Boston in a few years, and carry it over to the Mystic at a cost for which we could bring the Shawsheen to the Mystic.

This Legislature will not say that because we have water for our own citizens in another district, using an entirely different system, under entirely different circumstances, we should be obliged to spend the money for which we could furnish a new supply for these other communities to increase the Sudbury supply, and transfer it to these other places.

Mr. BRUCE. — Are you willing I should interrupt you to ask a question?

Mr. BAILEY. — Certainly, I am perfectly willing.

Mr. BRUCE. — I would like to have you answer this question, 'if you can : According to the estimate of Mr. Wightman it would cost $600,000 to build these basins where water is now running to waste at the rate of 14,000,000 gallons a day; it would cost $300,000 for the connection, which would be $1,000,000 in round numbers. It would probably be a little under that. The interest on what it would cost to take the water of the Shawsheen river would amount to $180,000 each year; the interest on the other would amount to $40,000. In ten years it would cost you $1,800,000 to secure the Shawsheen river, and the other would cost you $400,000. Then assume you throw away the $300,000 for the pipe, call it worthless, you would still be getting this waste water, which you do not use now, for $700,000, whereas the other would cost you for the same time $1,800,000. Now, I would like to have you answer that problem, whether it is not cheaper for the city of Boston to take that waste water for a certain time, and postpone for ten years or fifteen years the taking of the Shawsheen river?

Mr. BAILEY. — I will be very glad to answer it. You assume that it would cost $700,000 in ten years, if we took water from the Sudbury, and it would cost $1,800,000 if we took it from the Shawsheen.

Mr. BRUCE. — For interest on your investment for ten years.

Mr. BAILEY. — That is, there is $1,100,000 difference?

Mr. BRUCE. — There is simply $1,100,000 difference in the interest account.

Mr. BAILEY. — In ten years?

Mr. BRUCE. — Yes; that assumes that, at the end of ten years, throwing away the connecting pipe, which is to be put in at a cost of $300,000, as absolutely worthless, yet you will be $1,100,000 better off, on that proposition, by taking the waste water from the Sudbury.

Mr. BAILEY. — If we should do what you suggest, build basins to store more water on the Sudbury and transfer the water to the Mystic, in ten years the limit of our Sudbury will have been reached, and we should be at the limit of our supply, and should be obliged to get additional supply, and should ask for the Shawsheen.

(*Evidence, p. 36 to 38.*)

And here, Mr. Chairman and Gentlemen, is the very point of

this whole case! Ten years lying idle of the valley of the Shaw-sheen. What is it at the end of that time? Your $1,100,000 of interest is but a drop in the bucket compared with what you will have to pay for the factories that will then have established themselves on that stream, — for the buildings that will be on the land on the banks of that stream polluting it, which you will be obliged to buy up and remove in order to make the water-shed a fit source of a water-supply. Look at the history of Lake Cochitu-ate. When we took that for a water supply Pegan brook was as clear and as limpid a stream as flowed. The city of Boston, with a wise foresight, at that time could, by the expenditure of $100,000, have taken land and protected that stream forever, dedicated the land to the purposes of a water-shed and protected it forever. She did not do it, perhaps blindly, perhaps because she did not know what the results would be. What are the results to-day? On the banks of that stream 7,000 people are located and pouring into it their filth. It will cost the city of Boston, on the estimate which has been made by the drainage commission, some $300,000 to provide a sewer to take simply the sewage, and when that is done it has not taken the impurities that saturate the soil and will continue to pollute the water, and the brook itself must be taken from the Cochituate supply at a cost no one has estimated.

And that will be the condition of the Shawsheen river in ten years from now, and where will your $1,100,000 of interest stand then? Factories built, buildings for the operatives built, schools for the children built, — all to be destroyed to the great damage of the towns if the water-shed shall then be taken. If taken to-day, the communities on the water-shed will still have the same pros-perity they have to-day, and will continue in a line which is con-sistent with the preservation of the purity of that water-shed for a water supply. There is where even $1,100,000 would be a small loss compared to the benefit which the city of Boston would gain by taking this water now.

Is my brother answered?

Further, gentlemen, my brother's assumption is entirely wrong. I call your attention to the testimony of the city engineer, on p. 207, that it would cost $2,500,000, instead of $1,000,000, to furnish water from the Sudbury to the Mystic, and that the interest on this amount at the same rate as in his other, would be only $100,000, instead of $180,000, and in ten years the difference would be only $300,000 instead of $1,100,000.

These objections are puerile, they are objections only in name. There is one more, and, in my judgment, the only objection, and that is the damage which would be done to the mills in Andover on the river below our dam. I admit the force of this objection. Against Capt. Bradlee, the owner of the Ballardvale Mills, who is the principal opponent to this petition, not one word can ever pass my lips. No man in the city of Boston knows more than I do, and I doubt if there are many who know as well as I do, what Capt. Bradlee has done for Boston. No one appreciates that work more than I, and no one appreciates the deep love of his heart for his fellow-beings more than I do. I know him, and I have known him for years. I know him well, and I appreciate all the things he has done. But, gentlemen, as my brother Bruce has said to you, these mills are the apple of his eye, are wife and children to him, and he has made of them an idol. He has made here a beautiful and ideal mill, an ideal New England mill. You have seen it, and it is just what those who know Capt. Bradlee would expect from him, and he has so come to look upon it that if a man should go there and propose to take a cup of water out of this river Capt. Bradlee would almost believe it would be injuring his mill. And this is the same with all the people on the river.

But I firmly believe that no harm will be done to a single mill on that stream, that there is no danger of injury at all. When Boston took the water of the Sudbury river the opponents raised the same bugbear, just as they do here now, — we were going to blot out a river from the face of the earth, and destroy the town of Saxonville. Well, is it so much to blot out a river from the face of the earth for the good of mankind? This is not an unheard-of thing in this Commonwealth. The Legislature does it every year. It blotted out Stony brook from the face of the earth last year, in giving it to the cities of Waltham and Cambridge. It blotted out the upper Mystic river in giving it to Charlestown. It blotted out the Sudbury river in giving it to Boston. It blots out every river it gives to a town or city to be used as a water-supply. But, somehow or other,

Mr. Chairman and gentlemen, unfortunately for this argument of the remonstrants, the water still runs down the bed of these streams, and they refuse to be blotted out. When the Sudbury river, with its seventy miles of water-shed, was given to the city of Boston for a water-supply, it was provided that 1,500,000 gallons should be allowed to run over the lowest dam, and the river is there still. All the mills below that dam sent representatives here with the cry that it was going to destroy the industries along that river. But it was done and not a mill has stopped, and no injury has been done them. They have received fabulous damages from the city of Boston; but they go on with their business just the same.

(*Evidence, p. 205.*)

We let 1,500,000 gallons of water go over our dam, and between there and the village of Saxonville there is a distance of only two miles, and yet there is water enough to wash 13,000 pounds of wool per day and to carry manufactories beside which those on the Shawsheen dwindle into insignificance, and Saxonville is more flourishing than before.

Am I not right, then, when I say that the mills of Andover will suffer no harm if we take this water, when we allow them 1,500,000 gallons per day? You have heard Mr. Crafts' statement, — the engineer upon whom they rely, and an excellent engineer, whom we do not attempt to decry at all, — that there will be 4,500,000 gallons of water from the water-shed below our dam, which, added to the 1,500,000 we give them, make 6,000,000 of gallons, in the dryest day in the year, delivered at the mill.

(*Evidence, pp. 166 and 206.*)

Now, gentlemen, does it need experts, does it need the summoning of woollen manufacturers here to show to you that you need not fear any damage to the mills? Because the main purpose for which they want water is to wash their wool, and to wash the product of 2,200 pounds of wool.

(*Evidence, p. 192.*)

Six millions gallons of water to wash 2,200 pounds of wool and its product! Do you believe it? Is there any man on this committee who believes it? Let me call your attention here to what is said in the report of the Main Drainage Commissioners, on pages 225, 226, and 227 of their report.

" The Wanskuck Mills, Providence, R.I., are among the largest of those in the United States making woollen and worsted goods. Until 1881 the dirty water resulting from the different operations, amounting to about 400,000 gallons per day, flowed directly into West river. The yearly amount of refuse contained in this water included about 64,000 pounds of dyestuffs, 100,000 pounds of alkali, 4,000 pounds of acid, 53,000 pounds of fuller's earth, and 400,000 pounds of grease. A dyeing and bleaching company below brought a suit against the Wanskuck Company on account of the serious injury to its operations by the pollution of West river. After protracted litigation the Supreme Court granted a permanent injunction forbidding such pollution. In compliance with this injunction attempts have been made to purify the waste water before permitting it to enter the river.   .   .   .   .   .

Purification by precipitation was adopted, and has been continued since.   .   .   .   .

It is thought that of the whole liquid waste 50,000 gallons would comprise all of the water used in washing wool, and the greater part of the polluting refuse.

A method of wool-scouring is practised in the Lorraine Mills, Saylesville, R.I., by which the grease is preserved, and most of the other dirt is eliminated from the wash-water before permitting it to escape. The wool is washed in a machine having three bowls, — 600 pounds at a time, — with about 400 gallons of water which is very much less than is commonly used for the purpose, and probably is as little as will accomplish the work."

Now, if by improved processes 600 pounds of wool can be washed with 400 gallons of water, and when the water is allowed to run freely through the wool 400,000 gallons is the quantity used by the largest woollen mills in the United States, does the committee need any more evidence that 6,000,000 gallons is sufficient for a mill consuming 2,200 pounds of wool?

And remember that all we have to consider here is Mr. Bradlee's mill, because there is not a mill below Bradlee's on that stream that is not subject to him. He now holds the water until his dam is full, and if his dam fills and runs over, well and good ; the parties below can only take what comes from him. And you have heard Mr. Torr's testimony that his mill had all the water they wanted, and that they washed all the flax with that water.

(*Evidence, p.* 198.)

Now I ask, after what you have seen, and with this testimony before you, do you believe that when 6,000,000 gallons of water are delivered each dryest day in the year at Mr. Bradlee's dam, that any harm will happen to Mr. Bradlee, or to any other person on that stream? No, gentlemen, you cannot believe it. The city of Boston, in its desire to obtain pure water, does not desire or intend to harm anybody. It is not consistent with the history of Boston in these matters to advance the theory that they will injure any one of these industries. They always have guarded them.

As I have said to you, when they put into the Sudbury-river bill that 1,500,000 gallons should run over their dam for the benefit of the Saxonville Mills, it was after examination which satisfied every one that with that amount those mills would not be injured, and they were not. So, when we say we will allow 1,500,000 gallons of water to go down this river, added to the 4,500,000 gallons from the water-shed between our dam and the mills, we are guarding all these parties to the extent to which they need protection, and more. More than that: our engineers have said, and the other side have not denied, that these mills, with a sure daily supply of 1,500,000 gallons of good, clean water, drawn from a reserve basin of 4,000,000,000 gallons of water, is a better condition of affairs than what they have to-day.

Now, a word as to the effect of what we propose to do on this water-shed. Comparisons will show more clearly than a bare statement of figures the condition of things there, and what it will be. There is a water-shed of from 34 to 36 square miles, and by the building of a single dam we will get a basin which will hold 4,000,000,000 gallons of water. Can you realize how much 4,000,000,000 gallons of water is? Most of you have seen Lake Cochituate, and you know it is considered one of the best water supplies in the world. And why? Because we save up 1,500,-000,000 gallons of water on a water-shed of 18 miles.

Now, when I tell you we are going to build a lake that will be

nearly three times as large as Lake Cochituate, then you can begin
to realize what benefit it will be to the town in which it lies. We
shall build a lake nearly three times as large as Lake Cochituate,
and yet my friend Loomis, who will be right in sight of this lake,
and these people from Burlington and Bedford, tell you of the
injury that will be done these towns. Can you imagine any proposition that could come before this Legislature which could do any
town so much good as a proposition of the city of Boston to build
a lake three times as large as Lake Cochituate right in its midst?
Would it not add immensely to the value of its territory for residences? Will it do any injury to these towns? Why, when it
goes forth to the world that that water-shed is dedicated to purity,
as it will be if this act passes, — that it is dedicated to purity, so
that no person can plant any nuisance on that stream and pollute
that water, or do anything that will tend to pollute it or render it
unfit for drinking, — will not that section be deemed a most
desirable place for residences? What would not the citizens
of Winchester give, those who desire it as a place of residence, if
they could take away those tanneries and places of pollution?
The value of the property of this town for residences would be
worth much more than it is to-day if that could be done. But
here are these towns opposing this great improvement in their
midst. We say to them we will do you no injury. We take
away no manufactory. We say to the world that hereafter no
manufacture that would pollute the water shall be carried on
there. And this will do more for the welfare of those towns than
any other act this Legislature could possibly pass.

Now with that immense basin from which to draw, — and I beg
the committee's pardon if I dilate upon it more than some of you
think I ought, for I deem it very important, and if I could make
this committee see this subject as I see it, I would have no question about the result, — now having this supply, having this immense basin, how many years will it be before the city of Boston
will need all the water? The communities which would use this
water, now consume but 7,000,000 gallons per day, and for years
there will be from 5,000,000 to 10,000,000 gallons per day that
could be allowed to run down the river all the time. I do not
think anybody will believe the city of Boston will be such a dog

in the manger as to store that water up and say to the mills below, if there should happen to come a dry time, and they should be suffering, that they shall not have the water. I do not believe it, you do not believe it, and I do not believe anybody else believes it.

Consider it in any light you will, there is no individual, no corporation, no town, not a foot of land along the shore, or anybody having anything to do with the water-shed, but what will be benefited by the city of Boston building a dam on that river.

Gentlemen, I must close. I believe we have demonstrated the necessity for more water for the section supplied by the Mystic. We have shown you why we want it, and why we ought to have it. We have shown you what we have now, and we have shown you the place we want to go to, and I believe we have answered all the objections that have been raised against us. Remember the testimony which has been placed before you, that it will be years before we can actually avail ourselves of this water. Remember that the passage of this act does not give us water. The city of Boston, after the act is passed, has then to pass upon the question. It will have to go to these mill-owners and make arrangements with them for damages which they will be obliged to pay. The City Council will have to know just how much it will cost in dollars and cents before a foot of that land can be dug, or a cent's worth of material bought. Then it will take three years to build a dam and bring the water into use.

Considering all these things, are you not convinced that it must be five or six years before the water can be actually diverted for the purpose of being used? Do what you will, let what will occur short of actual water famine, or an epidemic in the Mystic section, it will be about six years before we can use this water, work as hard as we will. Take that into consideration with the testimony of Mr. Crafts, because I appeal to the testimony of their own witnesses on this matter, take Mr. Crafts and Mr. Wilson, the two experts they have brought. Mr. Wilson says, " Now is the accepted time," if you are going to take that water-shed ;

(*Evidence, p.* 175).

and Mr. Crafts says " For a population of 200,000 it is an admirable supply, and you cannot take it at any time better than you can take it now."   •

(*Evidence, p.* 163.)

Consider your own knowledge as to the effect of a large population on land used for a water-shed, consider your own knowledge as to the growth of places of pollution when they once get started, consider all the facts we have brought to your attention, and say whether the city of Boston ought not to be granted this act now, in order that it may fully and properly look after those who by contract she is bound to care for.

www.ingramcontent.com/pod-product-compliance
Lightning Source LLC
Chambersburg PA
CBHW030357270326
41926CB00009B/1155